Is There a Future for Heterodox Economics?

To all heterodox economists, especially those with a
long future ahead of them

Is There a Future for Heterodox Economics?

Institutions, Ideology and a Scientific Community

Geoffrey M. Hodgson

Institute for International Management, Loughborough University London, UK

 Edward Elgar
PUBLISHING

Cheltenham, UK • Northampton, MA, USA

Published by
Edward Elgar Publishing Limited
The Lypiatts
15 Lansdown Road
Cheltenham
Glos GL50 2JA
UK

Edward Elgar Publishing, Inc.
William Pratt House
9 Dewey Court
Northampton
Massachusetts 01060
USA

A catalogue record for this book
is available from the British Library

This book is available electronically in the
Economics subject collection
DOI 10.4337/9781789901597

ISBN 978 1 78990 158 0 (cased)
ISBN 978 1 78990 160 3 (paperback)
ISBN 978 1 78990 159 7 (eBook)

Typeset by Columns Design XML Ltd, Reading
Printed and bound in Great Britain by TJ International Ltd, Padstow, Cornwall

Contents

Preface

I have long been, and I remain, a strong critic of much of contemporary orthodox economics. I first got involved in heterodox networks in the 1970s. But I began to perceive problems within heterodoxy as well as orthodoxy.

In the 1970s, heterodox economics was dominated by Marxist and post-Keynesian approaches. Some heterodox economists quoted and defended Marx uncritically. Others seemed unable to move beyond Keynes. Over the decades that followed, these two names endlessly reappeared, overshadowing all rivals. They are two of the greatest economists of all time, but surely others have made a major contribution too?

Heterodox scholarship seemed insufficiently cumulative. It sometimes appeared to go around in circles. New ideas were raised and then forgotten. There was applause, but little sustained scrutiny. There was insufficient interrogation, testing and consolidation of new insights.

Heterodox economics was largely macro-oriented. Although macro issues interested me, I became more fascinated by alternatives to neo-classical microeconomics. I sensed then, and I still believe now, that the theoretical core of mainstream economics is in micro, and it is on that terrain that its core assumptions should be critically examined.

Over the years I have met many heterodox economists who held the flawed view that mainstream economics is largely and necessarily an apologia for a market economy. (I shall later explain why this view is mistaken.) I concluded that a major (but often covert) driving force behind much heterodox dissent in economics was ideological. Main-stream economics was often disliked because it was seen to support capitalism.

Yet heterodox economists held a variety of opposing theoretical views. Although not all heterodox economists are leftists, anti-market and pro-planning sentiments have helped to bind the majority of them together. Of course, mainstream economists are also ideological. But the neoclassical core of mainstream economics has been used to support socialism as well as capitalism. Neoclassical theory is not ideologically neutral, but it is extremely adaptable. By contrast, heterodox economists do not agree on their common theoretical core. In its stead, a left ideology has prevailed throughout: despite major theoretical disagreements, ideology unifies the majority of its adherents.

By the late 1970s my growing knowledge of economics, including my interest in debates on the feasibility of socialism, led me to the view that markets could not and should not be completely abolished in modern, large-scale, complex economies. This made me a critic of traditional socialism, which has typically meant central planning with public ownership of the means of production.[1]

I was struck by the failure of most of my heterodox colleagues to discuss the great economic debates about the viability of socialism, central planning and the role of markets. I refer mainly to the so-called socialist calculation debate of the 1920s and 1930s. Many heterodox economists promoted socialist ideas without mentioning these disputes. Some socialist economists have even argued that markets should be entirely abolished (Albert, 2004; Hahnel, 2005, 2007; Ollman, 2004). If serious economists are to promote socialism, then they need to answer well-established questions concerning its viability and detailed workability. This has rarely been done.[2]

While an ideology-free economics is neither desirable nor possible, economics should not be dominated by two impossible utopias – markets for everything versus state planning of everything. Many mainstream economists promote markets with insufficient attention to the moral, cultural and institutional prerequisites of commercial exchange (Schultz, 2001; Satz, 2010; Sandel, 2012; Hodgson, 2015b). Obversely, heterodox economists should not promote socialism without addressing the key debates concerning its feasibility, and without adequate consideration of

---

[1]   See Hodgson (2019c, ch. 1) for a historical review of definitions of socialism. The word first appeared in English in 1827 among the followers of Robert Owen to mean 'the abolition of private property'. Similarly, Karl Marx and Frederick Engels saw the shared goal of communist and socialist movements as an economy under full common ownership, without markets. This definition of socialism prevailed until attempts were made to revise it in the latter half of the twentieth century. These attempts have not nullified the original definition.

[2]   One of the few attempts to outline a feasible socialism is by Devine (1988). In their efforts to rebut those who questioned the feasibility of socialism, Adaman and Devine (1996) mistakenly proposed that all tacit knowledge can be converted into codified knowledge and thereby used by the planners. This rather misses the key point made by Michael Polanyi (1967) that much knowledge is always irredeemably tacit. See my responses to Adaman and Devine in Hodgson (1998b, 1999a, 2005).

how their proposed socialism could work in practical detail (Hodgson, 2018, 2019c).[3]

I believe that economics must rely much more on (historical and geographical) comparative analyses of real-world institutions and policies. At the policy level it should engage in cautious experimentation. It should be driven much less by the unrealistic utopias of full-blooded socialists or ultra-individualistic marketeers. Such a pragmatic vision of economics is not free of ideology – far from it – but it is a much more pragmatic and empirically-oriented science than many practitioners currently exemplify.

Since 1970, heterodox economics has grown and diversified. There is now much more on offer and the networks have multiplied. But if anything, the global influence of heterodoxy within leading journals and departments of economics has decreased rather than increased. It is more difficult for a heterodox economist to get a job in a good department of economics or to publish in a leading economics journal than it was 50 years ago. This paradox of heterodox growth alongside increasing exclusion is one of the motivations for writing this book.

My early interest in the philosophy of science widened to include the sociology of science, social epistemology and the study of sciences as social systems. I realized that this body of knowledge could help us understand why heterodox economics found sustained advance difficult and why it failed to enter the citadels of influence and power. This book is in part an attempt to explain and apply these insights.

The author wishes to thank Tanweer Ali, Philip Arestis, Sebastian Berger, Fernando Carvallo, Lynne Chester, David Colander, Samuel Coldicutt, Ricardo Crespo, Hulya Dagdeviren, John Davis, David Dequech, Wilfred Dolfsma, Denise Dollimore, Sheila Dow, Gary Dymski, Peter Earl, Francesca Gagliardi, Nils Gilman, David Gindis, Wade Hands, Geoffrey Harcourt, Mark Hayes, Joonas Järvinen, Thorbjørn

---

[3]   There is something important in common between the present book and the Hodgson (2019c) volume on the feasibility of socialism. By necessity, both science and modern economies are decentralized coordination systems operating by devolved mutual adjustment among individual agents. These systems are both highly complex and rely on dispersed tacit and fragmented knowledge. Consequently, they cannot be adequately planned from the centre. But they differ in other crucial respects. In particular, science is not a market (Hodgson, 2019d) and it relies more on reputational over pecuniary motives. A major contributor to the study of both kinds of decentralized coordination system was Michael Polanyi (1940, 1941, 1945, 1951, 1958, 1962, 1967, 1997). He is cited frequently in both volumes.

Knudsen, János Kornai, Juha-Antti Lamberg, Mark Lavoie, Tony Lawson, Vinny Logan, Deirdre McCloskey, Robert McMaster, Andrew Mearman, Edward Nell, Jochen Runde, Gerry Silverberg, Engelbert Stockhammer, Jan-Willem Stoelhorst, Wolfgang Theil, Matt Vidal, Bart Verspagen, Ulrich Witt, anonymous referees and others for conversations, comments and other help.

Chapter 4 draws from a bibliometric analysis in a joint article published with Juha-Antti Lamberg (Hodgson and Lamberg, 2018). I am very grateful for the agreement of my co-author to re-use this material here.

Introduction

> The Theory of Economics does not furnish a body of settled conclusions immediately applicable to policy. It is a method rather than a doctrine, an apparatus of the mind, a technique of thinking, which helps its possessor to draw correct conclusions.
>
> John Maynard Keynes (1922)

The Great Financial Crash of 2008 had several effects, not only on the global economy, but also on global politics and economic policy. Post-crash austerity policies in several countries widened economic inequality and undermined welfare provision. Subsequent disillusionment with established politicians and parties fuelled populist movements of the right and left – all promoting relatively simple solutions to complex problems. In several countries the established political framework was challenged or even overturned.

But few prominent economists budged in their opinions as a result of the Crash. A typical response was to defend the abstract model-building of mainstream economics but to explain the failure to predict the Crash in terms of losing 'sight of the bigger picture' and 'a failure of the collective imagination of many bright people' (Besley and Hennessy, 2009). The self-questioning rarely went any deeper than that. The preoccupation with technique over substance persisted. The consequences of this fixation include the overly-narrow and unrounded training of economists.[1]

Yet despite the inertia of their teachers, students objected in their thousands to the formalistic unreality of much teaching in mainstream economics. They formed organizations, mounted demonstrations, pushed for alternative curricula and published books (Moran et al., 2017; Fischer

---

[1]   The letter by Besley and Hennessy (2009) was a response to a question posed by Queen Elizabeth when she visited the London School of Economics in November 2008. She asked why no economist had predicted the Great Crash. The present author and nine other prominent economists sent a second letter to the Queen. It argued that the response by Besley and Hennessy had failed to note that economists are now largely trained in techniques and model building, and often lack the broader skills to deal with real world problems. 'What has been scarce is a professional wisdom informed by a rich knowledge of psychology, institutional structures and historical precedents' (Dow et al., 2009; Earl, 2010).

et al., 2018; Tielman et al., 2018). There were previous student revolts against mainstream economics (Fullbrook, 2003), but this one was bigger, globally-networked and more sustained.

The dissident students turned to heterodox economics. Much heterodox thinking seems considerably more relevant than dry mathematics: it often engages with real-world problems. Networks of ageing heterodox economists had survived since the 1970s, but they were fragmented and had been increasingly excluded from positions of influence. Frederic Lee, who was one of the foremost organizers of heterodoxy and its leading chronicler and historian, had shown that the heterodox movement had been in sustained retreat (Lee and Harley, 1997, 1998; Lee, 2009).[2]

The post-crash influx of students brought extra numbers and energy to heterodox economics. But there is no sign that its influence over economics as a whole, or its power within the academic discipline, have increased. Heterodoxy lacks a clear identity. Among the few things on which the heterodox community agree is the need for more pluralism in economics. It is widely argued that perspectives in addition to the reigning neoclassical approach should be taught on economics degrees.

APPRAISING HETERODOX ECONOMICS AS A SCIENTIFIC COMMUNITY

This book considers the future of heterodox economics. But it is not principally a dissection of ideas. This book is an appraisal of neither Cambridge economics, post-Keynesian economics nor heterodox economics as bodies of thought. These streams of enquiry have made major contributions in several areas of the discipline, and often they have received too little recognition. For example, there are major insights in the areas of money and finance, in the methodology of economics, and in evolutionary economics. Yet these achievements have been insufficiently acknowledged by the mainstream.

This shortfall cannot be explained by simply focusing on any theoretical or empirical flaws. The sources of limited success in these cases are to do with the social structures of science, as well as any ideological resistance. It is an often-repeated but inadequately-appreciated mantra

---

2   See Heise and Thieme (2016) for the decline of heterodox economics in Germany since the 1980s. For broader reflections see Backhouse (2000) and Coats (2001). Mearman et al. (2018) argued that the reform of the economics curriculum has made little progress after the 2008 Crash and it remains narrow and lacking in pluralism.

that science is a social process. It consists of habits and practices that are structured within, and facilitated by, institutions (Dequech, 2017). It creates habits of thought and relations of power that help to determine its course of development.

This book is about the institutions, culture and habits of thought that can enable or disable the forces of change within economics. It addresses the institutional contexts and drivers of scientific development in economics as an organized discipline. This book is about academic power and powerlessness.

To understand academic power and inertia, philosophy and social science has been applied to the scientific study of science itself. There is the famous work by Thomas Kuhn (1970) and the massive sociological study by Randall Collins (1998). Some have argued that pluralism is insufficient for progress in science and it can even be pushed to excess (Polanyi, 1962; Kitcher, 1993). While some pluralism is vital, a degree of consensus is also required, to enable cumulative advance and to avoid endless, repeated discussion of everything. Such an accord, based on positions of authority and power within academia, is also necessary (while insufficient) for quality control – to limit the permeation of low-quality research. Despite major achievements in some areas, inadequate quality control has created severe reputational problems for heterodox scholarship.

Poor quality control has cumulative effects. As well as lowering the bar for additional entrants, it diminishes reputation-based incentives to cite work or to take it seriously. In turn, this weakens mechanisms for cumulative advance on previous scholarship. Good publications are swamped by others of inferior quality. Bad quality demeans and drives out the good.

Quality is also worsened by over-politicization of economics research. For example, if authors or referees are chosen or excluded because of their ideological alignments, rather than on the grounds of their expertise and scientific quality, then the calibre of published output suffers. In academic conversation, political tolerance and ideological pluralism are just as important as theoretical pluralism. A viewpoint diversity that engages varied political standpoints and promotes constructive dialogue is essential for the social sciences.[3]

---

[3] The Heterodox Academy has been set up to promote viewpoint diversity (Heterodox Academy, 2019).

This book addresses the failure of the heterodox community to establish sufficient consensus over core issues and to develop alternative positions of power within academia, especially after the loss of heterodox control of the Faculty of Economics and Politics in the University of Cambridge in the 1980s. The reasons for this failure are varied, and they involve external factors as well as intrinsic limitations. Whatever the reasons, Cambridge was a global high point of influence from which heterodoxy has never recovered, despite its increased number of adherents worldwide.

Because of current global economic problems and the manifest limitations of mainstream economics, young scholars are attracted to heterodoxy. But what reputational or other incentives are there for young economists to study heterodox economics, or for established economists to address and build upon heterodox insights?

If we start asking such questions, then we set off on a track of enquiry that is different from the typical debates about the virtues and limitations of particular theories. Heterodox achievements have received insufficient attention and constructive development, largely because there are inadequate incentives to engage with them. Mainstream economics selects the issues that it deems worthwhile and creates opportunities for those who participate in its community.

Of course, some people are devoted to scientific truth and might contribute to a heterodox discussion anyway. But even honourable altruists can have mortgages to pay and kids to feed. Eventually, moral philanthropists need remuneration. Pecuniary as well as moral incentives for researchers are important. The mainstream perpetuates itself through its access to power and resources, and with its chosen metrics of evaluation.

Aware of this problem, some heterodox economists have attempted to establish alternative ranking schemes for heterodox research (Lee, 2009; Lee and Elsner, 2010). This does not resolve the difficulty: it simply kicks the can down the road. It adds the problem of trying to get alternative research *rankings* recognized and accepted by academic authorities, to the previous unresolved problem of trying to get alternative *research* recognized and accepted by academic authorities. Alternative research rankings will be noticed and used in academic institutions, but only if heterodoxy builds centres of academic power and influence.

We may dislike journal rankings, especially when they are dominated by mainstream criteria. But even if formal rankings did not exist, an informal pecking order would emerge anyway. We may dislike the ever-growing academic propensity to rank, appraise and audit research. But these things are part of the reality of modern, large-scale scientific communities, divided into a multitude of specialisms, with all subject to limited public and private funds and to budgetary controls. Their operation affects the fortunes of any scientific project.

These mechanisms are not peculiar to capitalism either: the system of research prioritization and ranking in the USSR was more intrusive than it has ever been in the West (Polanyi, 1940; Blinov, 2016). As Max Weber (1968) noted, bureaucracy is an inevitable outcome of large-scale organizations that process huge amounts of complex information. Organized judgemental rankings are intrinsic to the inevitably bureaucratic process of academic organization.

Despite growth in numbers, the heterodox community has lost access to many of the levers of academic power. It has been caught in vicious circles of cumulative decline. Exclusion from high-ranking journals reduces the chances of promotion, lowers influence, confines academics to lesser-ranking universities, awards less time for research, reduces research grant possibilities, and leads to further exclusion from power. The fate of heterodoxy is about the extent of its institutional power and esteem, as well as about its ideas.

INSTITUTIONS OF ACADEMIC POWER AND AUTHORITY

We need to address the systems of power and authority within the organizations of science and academia. We also need to consider the ways in which that power is created and enforced, including the habits and conventions of scientific communities.[4] To do this we need to break from individualistic views of how scientists operate. Much research and writing may be performed alone, but it never develops in separation from others. This was even true in the eighteenth and nineteenth centuries, before modern research universities had been established.

Crucial for the development of science in Britain were the creation of learned societies and networks. The Royal Society of London for Improving Natural Knowledge was founded in 1660. The Society for the Encouragement of Arts, Manufactures and Commerce was founded in 1754. The Lunar Society of Birmingham (it held its meetings when the moon was full) met regularly from the 1760s and its attendees included Matthew Boulton, Erasmus Darwin, Richard Lovell Edgeworth, Samuel

---

[4] See Dequech (2017) for a discussion of the conventions of mainstream economics, and the difficulties faced by heterodoxy in challenging them.

Galton, Joseph Priestley, James Watt and Josiah Wedgwood.[5] Other scientific groups were less formal and met in the London coffee houses. These institutions and meetings created networks of scientists and inventors and built up interactive communities of researchers. Edgeworth described in his *Memoirs* how they operated:

> [The] first hints of discoveries, the current observations, and the mutual collision of ideas, are of important utility. The knowledge of each member of such a society becomes in time disseminated among the whole body, and a certain *esprit de corps*, uncontaminated with jealousy, in some degree combines the talents of numbers to forward the ideas of a single person. (Edgeworth and Edgeworth, 1844, p. 118)

Edgeworth also explained how, in one London coffee-house group, the admission bar for new candidates was kept high: '[We] practised every means in our power, except personal insult, to try the temper and understanding of each candidate for admission. Every prejudice, which his profession or situation in life might have led him to cherish, was attacked, exposed to argument and ridicule.' (Edgeworth and Edgeworth, 1844, p. 119).

It was not only important to organize scientific associations and networks, but also vital to establish routines for the scrutiny of new candidates and for the maintenance of quality control.

Charles Darwin was descended from scientists and innovative entrepreneurs. Working in apparent isolation in Down House in rural Kent, he awaited the daily postal deliveries with enthusiasm. Although not a member of a university, he was the commanding nexus in a network of esteemed scientists. As the philosopher of science Philip Kitcher (1993, p. 11) explained:

> We should not be beguiled by the picture of the unworldly invalid of Down, whose quiet walks in his beloved garden were the occasions only for lofty musings on points of natural philosophy. Darwin's study was the headquarters of a brilliant campaign (which he sometimes saw in explicitly military terms), directed with energy and insight.

---

[5]   Matthew Boulton and James Watt formed a partnership that developed, produced and marketed steam engines. Erasmus Darwin was a physician and scientist, and a grandfather of Charles Darwin and Francis Galton. Richard Lovell Edgeworth was a politician and inventor, and a grandfather of the economist Francis Y. Edgeworth. Samuel Galton was an arms manufacturer and the other grandfather of Francis Galton. Joseph Priestley is one of those credited with the isolation and discovery of oxygen. Josiah Wedgwood was a pottery entrepreneur and the other grandfather of Charles Darwin. Clearly, family connections were important too.

Darwin used his voluminous correspondence – notably with Thomas Henry Huxley, Joseph Hooker, Charles Lyell, Alfred Russell Wallace and Asa Gray – to obtain feedback on his ideas, to obtain supportive evidence, to consider ways of testing his theories, to hone them to perfection, and to help broadcast them more widely, in turn to obtain more critical responses and useful information from a wider community.

As Kitcher (1993, p. 31) explained, 'the diversity of different practices' in biological science were 'each affected in different ways by reading the *Origin*'. Yet, despite this diversity, Darwin established 'a *consensus practice*, something that represents the common elements of the individual practices and that becomes part of the cross-generational system of transmission of scientific ideas.' Darwin's heterodox ideas eventually, and after a long struggle, became orthodox, despite resistance from religious authority (Bowler, 1997).

Success or failure depends on the strategic manipulation of the institutions of science. Instead of merely promoting pluralism – which can amount to a cornucopia of theories of varied quality – attention must also be directed towards screening out low-quality research and ultimately changing the consensus discourse. This must entail a strategy to establish positions of power within academia. Heterodox economists have given far too little attention to these issues, upon which their future depends.

THEORETICAL AND IDEOLOGICAL ROUTES TO HETERODOXY

Consider two possible reasons to become a strong critic of mainstream economics. They are not mutually exclusive: many heterodox economists may have been impelled by both.

We may move toward heterodoxy because of a concern about core axioms or modes of analysis, such as the assumption of rational agents, the predisposition toward equilibrium analysis or the requirement that almost everything must be expressed in mathematics. This first route is charted, for example, by Thorstein Veblen's (1909), Herbert Simon's (1957) or Amartya Sen's (1977) critiques of the rationality assumption, or the Austrian critique of mainstream assumptions (Hayek, 1945), or Tony Lawson's (1997) claims concerning the ontologically inappropriate use of mathematics.

Many heterodox economists refer to Veblen or Lawson, but it is shown in Chapter 2 below that Veblen's attention to microeconomic issues of psychological motivation is replicated infrequently, and Lawson's argument is followed less often by heterodox scholars than it is cited. It is also shown that the arguments of Simon and Sen are infrequently quoted by prominent heterodox economists. Also, the heterodox community has an uneasy relationship with the Austrian School.

The second route to heterodoxy derives from a concern about mainstream policy conclusions, such as an allegedly excessive reliance on markets rather than state intervention. But mainstream economists themselves occupy a wide variety of political and policy positions, including some Nobel Laureates who criticize what is sometimes called 'market fundamentalism' (Krugman, 2012; Stiglitz, 2010, 2012). Consequently, discontent with even prominent mainstream policy positions is an inadequate reason to become a heterodox economist. Without further justification than policy discontent, it would be better to emulate Paul Krugman and Joseph Stiglitz and remain in the mainstream, use mainstream techniques, publish in top mainstream journals, and even win Nobel prizes for your efforts.

Concern about mainstream policy conclusions would be a justifiable route to become heterodox if it could be demonstrated that there is a close mapping between theory and policy, to the extent that prominent policy conclusions rested on prominent mainstream theories and assumptions. On close inspection, such a mapping is far from obvious.

It is undermined in particular by the earlier use of mainstream general equilibrium by Oskar Lange and others to defend the viability of a socialist planned economy in the so-called 'socialist calculation debate' in the 1930s (Dickinson, 1933, 1939; Lange, 1936–37; Lange and Taylor, 1938; Lerner, 1934, 1937, 1938). It is also challenged by the use of mainstream economics – including rational choice, game theory and general equilibrium analysis – by 'analytical Marxists' such as Jon Elster (1982, 1985, 1986), John Roemer (1986a, 1986b, 1988) and Erik Olin Wright (1994). Although these days many mainstream economists favour the extensive use of markets and minimal state regulation, this may be a result more of their ideology than their theory: instead the theory may itself point to a much more cautious use of markets, if it were to give any substantive guidance at all (Hahn, 1975, 1984). Too often there is a false presumption that mainstream economic theory is basically a legitimation for free markets.

Obversely, much of heterodox theory does not automatically lead to a critique of capitalism or markets. For example, the approach of Piero Sraffa (1960) was inspired by the free-trader David Ricardo as well as by Karl Marx. There is nothing in Sraffa's analysis to show that markets are inferior to planning, or vice versa. Joseph Schumpeter was strongly influenced by Marx's economics yet politically he was a conservative. And, of course, John Maynard Keynes was a liberal: he opposed socialism and defended a regulated form of capitalism.

Of course, theory and policy interact. But their relationship is subtler than widely assumed. Neoclassical theory is not ideologically neutral. Neoclassical theory resonates with some core ideological assumptions concerning the individual. Relations between individuals or social structures are not ignored, but are typically under-theorized, because of the supreme focus on the individual and her preferences. These biases can affect ideology. The widely adopted Pareto criterion is inherently conservative (Hodgson, 2013a). The utilitarian assumptions at the core of neoclassical economics neglect the kind of moral motivation explored by Adam Smith (1759) among others. But to a substantial degree, the neoclassical core is ideologically *adaptable*. The ideological mutability of utilitarian assumptions is illustrated by their resonance with Marxism.[6]

In sum, the idea that mainstream economic theory is basically a legitimation for free markets is falsified on several accounts. These include the use of mainstream theory to support socialism, Marxism or state intervention. But these elements of mainstream economics are often omitted in leading accounts by heterodox economists. The over-conflation of theory with ideology relies on a neglect of important parts of the theory. All this suggests that ideology is doing much more work in making heterodox choices and keeping heterodox communities together than is often admitted.[7]

IDEOLOGY AND HETERODOX ECONOMICS

Ideology inevitably guides the vision of economists, it frames their choice of topics for research, and it often motivates enquiry (Myrdal,

---

[6] On the links between Marxism, socialism and utilitarianism see Veblen (1906, p. 583; 1909, p. 623), Keynes (1931, p. 291), Parsons (1937, p. 110), Allen (1998, p. 141) and the penultimate section of Chapter 2 below.

[7] I do not deny the role of ideology in my own recruitment (in the late 1960s) to heterodoxy and beyond. But from the beginning, of even greater importance for me were the apparent weaknesses of mainstream theory. In the 1970s I became interested in the Austrian School (while rejecting their market-fundamentalist ideology) and I recoiled from the mainstream theoretical assumptions of analytical Marxism (Hodgson, 1989). Consequently, for me, the first (theory-oriented) route was more important than the second. I believe that I am in a minority, and the majority come to heterodoxy via the second (policy-oriented) route. To put my political cards on the table, for 30 years or more I have not seen myself as a socialist, instead as a social democrat or a left liberal (Hodgson, 1999a, 2018).

1953). Economics is inevitably permeated by ideology. But unavoidable as it is, ideology should not be used as a criterion to distinguish good science from bad science. The criteria of appraisal should be intrinsic to science itself.

But sometimes ideology overpowers theory. Cases of excessive ideological bias are found among pro-market economists and among their critics. Many mainstream economists use economics to justify the status quo. Theory and ideology are sometimes conflated: mainstream theory is wrongly presumed, by both supporters and critics, to always lead to pro-market conclusions. The task of heterodox theory is wrongly designated as a critique of pro-market economics. These one-to-one mappings of ideology upon theory are mistaken and destructive, for reasons noted in this book.

This protrusion of ideology has led to another post-crash outcome. Some dissent within the academy concerning the state of economics has joined with the renewed politics of the left. Many heterodox economists are socialists, playing their part in renewing the kind of full-blooded socialist ideology that had been prematurely declared dead in the 1990s.

Heterodox economics was strongly associated with left politics in Cambridge in the 1960s and 1970s. This ideological affiliation persists. Andrew Mearman et al. (2019, pp. 3–4) noted the 'unsurprising' fact that many heterodox economists 'define heterodox economics in terms of an opposition to prevailing social structures and power relations within economics and within capitalism. Further, they define heterodox in terms of pro-social movements designed to achieve real change.' Heterodox economics is thus seen as part of a political mobilization to reform radically or to supersede capitalism.[8]

The fact that some prominent analysts of heterodoxy find the link 'unsurprising' tells us something about the nature of the heterodox community. On the contrary, it should be rather *surprising* that heterodox economics, in all its theoretical diversity, should lead logically and inexorably to a critique of capitalism. There is no such logical connection. Heterodox Karl Marx was of course a critic of capitalism, but heterodox John Maynard Keynes was not. The presumed connection between economic theory and political leftism is more to do with the ideological culture within the heterodox community: it draws its members together, despite their varied views on economics.

---

[8] The quoted claim was supported by a reference to contributors to the *Heterodox Economics Directory* (Kapeller and Springholz, 2016).

David Colander and Craig Freedman (2019) argued that economics 'went wrong' when the Chicago school of Milton Friedman and others conjoined their theory with their strident political views, and then gained influence within the profession. The history of Cambridge economics shows that the conflation of theory with policy was not unique to Chicago or to pro-market economists. From the 1960s, positive feedback between Chicago-style rightists and Cambridge-style leftists helped the over-politicization of economics as a whole. Economics has suffered as a result.

The core assumptions of mainstream economics do not lead logically to the promotion of markets. Assumptions such as scarcity and rationality do not imply a pro-market stance. Numerous socialist economists have adopted these assumptions and promoted planning. While the welfare assumption of Pareto optimality disallows strong redistributive measures, it too does not logically imply a market system. Markets entail other assumptions, including the institutional preconditions of contracts and private property.

Just as orthodox economics does not logically lead to support for capitalism or markets, criticism of orthodoxy does not automatically lead to their rejection. Yet much (but not all) of heterodoxy has aligned itself with leftist or anti-market politics. The practicality and superiority of a socialist alternative is too often taken for granted.

The most important economic debate in the twentieth century was between proponents of socialism and capitalism. But the debate within economics over the feasibility of socialism has often been dismissed or disregarded. It is largely ignored by heterodox economists (with the very important exception of the Austrian School) and it is rarely taught on orthodox or heterodox curricula.

THE CONTENTS OF THIS BOOK

Mearman et al. (2019, p. 291) noted a severe risk within heterodoxy. 'A great danger then is that heterodox economics becomes an increasingly self-ghettoised sect of people who are stuck in a double-bind of resentments.' This present book suggests that this entrapment has become real and it is difficult for heterodoxy to escape. But on a constructive note, this book ends with a chapter on eight possible strategies for heterodox economics. They are not all mutually exclusive, and experimentation is required. But 'carrying on as before', especially while ignoring how institutions of academic power operate, is not a viable option.

To reach the point where these strategies may be assessed, the preceding five chapters consider different aspects of heterodoxy and orthodoxy in economics. Insights are used from social epistemology and the philosophy and sociology of science.

Except for evolutionary economics, which is considered in a separate chapter, modern heterodox economics was very much influenced by the non-neoclassical economics developed in Cambridge from the 1940s to the 1970s, under the leadership of Joan Robinson, Piero Sraffa, Nicholas Kaldor and others. This is the subject of Chapter 1. Its focus is not primarily on their contributions, important as they are, but on the institutions that affected their development, and the leftist ideologies that motivated the protagonists and infused their presentations.

Prevailing attributes of current heterodox economics can be traced back to pre-1980 Cambridge heterodoxy. They persist, despite the internal diversity and the failure to agree on a theoretical core. For example, there is a recurrent use of political ideology, particularly in the description of heterodox economics as *left* and orthodox economics as *right.* Orthodox economics is sometimes seen as pro-market and heterodox economics as anti-market.

Consider another persistent post-Cambridge feature. Despite lack of agreement on the nature of heterodox economics, there is much more enduring, tacit agreement on what it excludes. Hence, just as Cambridge ignored some important heterodox critiques – such as Herbert Simon's original behavioural approach – this omission has been replicated by much of current heterodoxy.[9]

Chapter 2 addresses different attempts to define what *heterodox economics* means, the most important of which are by Tony Lawson and Frederic Lee. A neglected possible criterion to distinguish orthodoxy from heterodoxy is suggested, centring on the use or non-use of utility maximization. Possible reasons for the neglect of this Max U demarcation criterion are outlined.

Chapter 3 appraises claims by David Colander, John Davis and others that mainstream economics is moving away from the central assumption of utility maximization. By contrast, it is argued that current behavioural economics has reconciled itself to utility maximization as a norm, from which behaviour is said to sometimes deviate. The argument that Max U still prevails has major consequences for the definitions of orthodoxy and

---

[9]   But note that evolutionary economics in the genre of Nelson and Winter (1982) makes much of Simon's work – see Chapter 4 below. Chapter 3 below underlines the fact that Simon's more radical version of behavioural economics is very different from the 'new behavioural economics' found in the mainstream today.

heterodoxy. It also suggests that, despite numerous important developments in recent decades, mainstream economics may prove much more difficult to budge from its enduring core assumptions.

Chapter 4 – which uses material from joint research with Juha-Antti Lamberg – considers the 'separate heterodoxy' of evolutionary economics. It is separate in a double sense. First it did not stem from the heterodox crucible of Cambridge. Second, it is largely ignored by Cambridge-inspired heterodoxy, perhaps partly for ideological reasons. Because of its prominent use of the terms *evolution* and *evolutionary* – whatever they are taken to mean – these key words provide an opening for a bibliometric analysis and its connected fields. This analysis exposes several features of the kind of evolutionary economics related to the enduringly prominent work of Richard Nelson and Sidney Winter (1982). Evolutionary economics has largely moved out of departments of economics. Exiled from its former homeland, it has become fragmented and divided, by multiple specialisms and disciplinary boundaries.

Chapter 5 brings together insights from the philosophy and sociology of science and from social epistemology, to analyse heterodox economics as a scientific community. In line with the work of Michael Polanyi (1962), Thomas Kuhn (1970), Philip Kitcher (1993) and others, it is argued that, while pluralism is necessary for innovation, a degree of consensus over core issues is also necessary for sustained progress in science. Such a degree of agreement is absent in current heterodox economics. This leads to the final chapter, which considers possible strategies for heterodox economics in the future.

APPENDIX: SOME TERMINOLOGICAL CONVENTIONS

I end this introduction with some remarks on the choice of terminology. For mainstream economists today, theory means mathematics. But that was not the case before about 1960. When I use the word *theory* it does not necessarily imply mathematics. Neither Adam Smith, Karl Marx, John Maynard Keynes, Joseph Schumpeter nor Friedrich Hayek used mathematics. Many ground-breaking theories elsewhere have been expressed without the use of mathematics, including the theory of evolution developed by Charles Darwin.

Although the meaning and value of the word *neoclassical* have been contested (Hodgson, 1999b, ch. 2; Colander, 2000a; Lee, 2009; Lawson, 2013; Morgan, 2016), it was widely used in Cambridge heterodox circles and it remains globally prevalent today. Generally, I retain the association of the term *neoclassical* with utility maximization, equilibrium-oriented theorizing, marginalist price theory, and (perhaps) theories of distribution based on aggregate production functions. In later parts of the book there is sometimes a narrower focus on utility maximization per se, and there I adopt Deirdre McCloskey's (2008, 2016) poignant and satirical term *Max U.*

It is important to emphasize that *neoclassical* does not necessarily mean pro-market. This is a widespread misconception, based on an unwarranted conflation of theory with ideology.[10] It is refuted by the fact that some prominent neoclassical economists (who assumed utility maximization, equilibrium-oriented theorizing and marginalist price theory) including Léon Walras (1874), Abba Lerner (1934, 1937, 1938, 1944), Oskar Lange (1936–37) and Kenneth Arrow (1978), were Marxists, socialists or other leftists. This ideological misconception concerning *neoclassical economics* is so pervasive that I hope that the reader will forgive me for repeating the refutation more than once in the text.

I use the term *mainstream* to refer to the global community of economists who de facto dominate economics within the academy, who publish in journals most highly ranked by that group, and who populate its most esteemed departments. As David Dequech (2007, p. 281) put it: 'mainstream economics is that which is taught in the most prestigious universities and colleges, gets published in the most prestigious journals, receives funds from the most important research foundations, and wins the most prestigious awards.'

As Dequech (2007), Davis (2008) and others indicated, *orthodox* and *mainstream* may not be identical. *Mainstream* is defined in terms of its power and popularity: *orthodox* is defined in terms of a set of core beliefs and practices. Approaches that may be considered *mainstream* but not *orthodox* (by some criterion) are considered below. One possible example is evolutionary game theory, for reasons considered later.

For brevity and flow, I sometimes abbreviate *orthodox economics* to *orthodoxy* and *heterodox economics* to *heterodoxy.* No other meanings or insinuations are intended by these abbreviations. I use the term

---

[10]   For example, the prominent Marxist academic David Harvey (2005, p. 20) conflated *neoclassical* economics with *neoliberal* politics. In fact, many neoclassical economists (including Nobel Laureates Paul Krugman, Paul Samuelson and Joseph Stiglitz) disagree with so-called *neoliberals* such as Friedman and Hayek. And some neoliberals – such as Hayek – were not neoclassical economists because they rejected the assumption of utility maximization and equilibrium approaches.

Cantabrigian heterodoxy to refer not simply to heterodoxy from Cambridge, but also to all streams of heterodox that were strongly influenced by Keynes, Robinson, Kaldor or Sraffa.

The word *institution* is used in an inclusive sense, to refer to any system of embedded social rules (Hodgson, 2006a). Hence organizations (such as universities) are institutions. Languages, shared routines and customary rule-systems are also institutions.

When Joan Robinson, Paul Davidson and others established their inter-continental heterodox network they settled on the term *Post Keynesian*. Yet we still find variants such as *post-Keynesian* in widespread use, perhaps often due to the insistence of copy-editors. Partly to keep the latter happy, and with a preference for the standard stylistic rules, I mostly adopt *post-Keynesian* here.

Another name that can be contested in the copy-editing process is Ludwig von Mises. Some copy-editors (particularly in the US) insist that the 'von' should always immediately precede the 'Mises', ignoring the fact that *von* was later acquired to indicate nobility, and is not otherwise part of the family name. Hence, 'von Mises' would wrongly appear under 'v' and not 'M' in the index. My suggestion henceforth is that Ludwig Mises becomes the norm. Friedrich Hayek dropped his *von*, so why shouldn't his mentor too?

1. Space exists to stop everything happening in Cambridge

> It has been said that time is a device to stop everything happening at once –
> to which Dr Dharma Kumar quipped that space was a device to stop
> everything happening in Cambridge.
>
> Geoffrey C. Harcourt (1969)

Cambridge is one of the most prestigious universities in the world. Its Faculty of Economics embraced Alfred Marshall, Arthur Pigou and John Maynard Keynes. Until the 1980s it was a remarkable outpost for innovative heterodox economics, with leading figures including Nicholas Kaldor, Joan Robinson and Piero Sraffa. Subsequently it became a mainstream department. This chapter considers the intellectual and cultural environment of the Cambridge Economics Faculty, particularly from the 1930s to the 1980s. Post-Keynesian economics and modern heterodox economics sprang largely from this milieu, and they still bear signs of their Cambridge legacy.[1]

I do not believe that the inadequate global headway made by heterodoxy in Cambridge or elsewhere in the last fifty years can be pinned on the insufficiency of its highest achievements. Many setbacks are due to hostility from orthodoxy. But heterodoxy must bear some responsibility. Its fate is partly to do with its practices and its ideological sub-texts, and its persistent avoidance of some major questions.

Science is a dynamic social system that is embedded in shared habits and institutions. We should consider the institutional contexts in which

---

[1]   By contrast, the evolutionary economics of Nelson and Winter (1982) emerged in the US. This 'separate heterodoxy' is considered in Chapter 4 below. In addition, a radical economics – composed of Marxists and other socialists – took off in the US in the 1960s (Canterbery, 2010, ch. 5). The French *régulation* school emerged in the 1970s as an important heterodox stream (Boyer and Mistral, 1978; Aglietta, 1979; Orléan, 1994; Jessop, 1997a, 1997b, 2001). For more on the Cambridge institutional environment see Winch (1969), Johnson and Johnson (1978), Robinson (1978), Tribe (2000) and Neild (2012). Thirlwall (1987, 2015), Marcuzzo et al. (1996), Pasinetti (2007), Harcourt and Kerr (2009), King (2009), Martins (2014) and others provide accounts of the ideas of leading Cambridge economists.

science is fostered and passed on. This chapter is more a history of institutions and practices than it is a history of economic thought. It addresses the institutional settings in which post-Keynesian and hetero-dox economics were nurtured in Cambridge, before heterodoxy lost control of that citadel in the 1980s. Ideas are vital, but institutions are their vehicles and their enablers.

Influence within a scientific discipline depends on engagement with others, especially with those who hold sway within academic systems of authority and prestige. Cold logic is important, but not enough. The success or failure of a school of thought is governed by more than the persuasiveness or weaknesses of its ideas. Groups of researchers make headway through conversations with prestigious communities with shared concerns. It is important to address the prevailing agenda in those communities, especially if it is hoped to change it. Avoidance of pressing issues can be damaging. Shortcomings are often errors of omission, and not merely errors of commission. It is shown in this chapter that there were some characteristic lacunae in the Cambridge heterodox agenda.

Science advances through critical scrutiny and dialogue with experts in the same field. Hence science requires concentrations of specialists who intensively interact with one another, to correct errors, to pose alternative hypotheses, to check results, and to draw attention to related work in the area. If someone was to design the institutional structure of a modern university that maximized such interactions, then it would look very different from the rambling, byzantine structures of Cambridge or Oxford. Yet despite their arcane and time-consuming organization, these ancient universities prospered because of their prestige and their ability to attract great talent.

Before 1960, university education in Britain was the privilege of a male-dominated group of less than 4 per cent of the adult population. In 1945, Britain emerged victorious, but battered and impoverished, from a devastating world war. Resources for research and university appoint-ments were highly limited. All located in London or within its commuter belt, three elite universities dominated research in economics. As the historian of economics Roger Backhouse (1996, p. 35) wrote:

> In 1945, British economics was dominated by three institutions: Oxford, Cambridge, and the London School of Economics (LSE). There were other institutions, but they were small in size and provincial in more than the geographical sense. Of these LSE was perhaps the most open to international influences ... contrasting strongly with the Cambridge habit of focusing mainly on work by other Cambridge economists.

Of the three, economics at Cambridge was globally the most prestigious, largely because of the enduring influence of Marshall, Pigou and Keynes. By 1945, the global stature of Keynes was enough to make Cambridge pre-eminent.

The Canadian economist Harry Johnson read economics at Cambridge from 1945 to 1946. He was a lecturer there from 1949 to 1956. He noted a prevailing attitude where 'only a small number of ... economists, almost exclusively in Cambridge, Oxford, and London, [were] considered as worthy of attention or criticism' (Johnson and Johnson, 1978, p. 98).

But the number of economists in Cambridge before and immediately after the Second World War was tiny, consisting of about seven active university lecturers and 'half a dozen fellows scattered around the various colleges' (Robinson, 1978; Durbin, 1985, p. 104).

The modern research university was much more developed in the US than in the UK. At least until the 1970s, relatively few lecturers or professors in economics in the UK had PhDs (Simpson, 1983, 2009). Even at Oxford and Cambridge, college-based institutional structures ensured that priority was often given to undergraduate teaching, rather than to postgraduate studies and research.

After a brief further discussion of the Cambridge context, this chapter touches on the Cambridge debates on capital theory, the relative neglect of individual motivation and microeconomics by Cambridge heterodoxy, some ramifications of Joan Robinson's socialism, and the general Cambridge neglect of the socialist calculation debate. The chapter finishes on the battles between 'left' and 'right' in the Faculty of Economics and Politics and on the active promotion of Cambridge heterodox ideas in North America and elsewhere.[2]

The avoidance of some key microeconomic issues, the neglect of the socialist calculation debate and the tendency to assume that neoclassical theory is generally pro-market are all unfortunate features that persist to this day in the global networks of post-Keynesian and heterodox economics that were largely spawned by Cambridge from the 1960s onwards. The global evolution of heterodox economics has been highly path dependent.

---

[2]   When I was at Cambridge in 1992–98, the term 'left-wing economics' was often used by its proponents. It was also used in radical circles of economists in the US (Canterbery, 2010, ch. 5).

THE CAMBRIDGE CRUCIBLE

The importance of a scientific community, combining a degree of competition with norms of cooperation, was underlined by the sociologist Robert Merton (1942), and by philosophers of science Michael Polanyi (1962), Thomas Kuhn (1970), David Hull (1988) and Philip Kitcher (1993). Johnson regarded Cambridge as inadequate in these respects, and he explained this weakness largely in terms of the pre-eminence of the colleges (Johnson and Johnson, 1978).

The Oxbridge universities and their associated colleges are all separate legal entities, although they are tied together by numerous customs and contractual obligations. Their legal separability means that it is possible (at least in principle) to be employed by the university and not by a college, by the college and not by the university, or by a college and the university. (There are some differences between Oxford and Cambridge in this area, but they need not concern us here.) Keynes, for example, was primarily a fellow of King's College. He never became a professor at the university. Furthermore, while the universities have been under-financed, some of the older Oxbridge colleges were, and still are, among the richest property owners in the UK.

Dominated historically by teaching and accommodation requirements for residential undergraduates, the legally autonomous Oxbridge colleges were less well suited for research and for postgraduate education.[3] Oxbridge college fellows were given 'heavy burdens of elementary teaching in which they had to cover the entire range of economics' but 'were under little pressure to publish' (Backhouse, 1996, pp. 34–5). As Robert Locke (1988, p. 99) pointed out: 'isolating ... students and tutors in colleges ... denied them the specialised instruction taught by acknowledged experts in specific fields of economics, which is the hallmark of American undergraduate and graduate education.'

Yet there were compensating mechanisms. Oxford and Cambridge recruited from the upper echelons. Although the ancient college system was ill-suited to the formation of dense networks of specialist university researchers, Oxbridge provided links with elites outside the university, including opportunities for some to advise business or government.

In this manner, Keynes was able to use his connections and engage with a wider community of intellectuals and policymakers. His father was an accomplished economist and administrator at Cambridge. Like

---

[3] In the 1960s, two colleges (Clare Hall and Darwin) were set up exclusively for postgraduates. The remaining 29 Cambridge colleges have a large undergraduate intake.

several prime ministers, and numerous members of the British Establishment, John Maynard attended Eton Public School. As a student at Cambridge he was taught by Marshall. From 1913 onwards, he advised governments and participated in Royal Commissions. In 1915 he took a position at the UK Treasury, representing it at the 1919 Versailles Peace Conference. In 1931 he visited the US, at the invitation of the University of Chicago. Visits to the US followed in 1934 and several times in the 1940s. His economics benefited from rich practical experience and his prestigious Anglo-American connections.

Academic networks were then almost entirely male. Born twenty years after Keynes, Joan Robinson was from an upper-middle-class background. She studied economics at Girton College in Cambridge, and came under the influence of Maurice Dobb, who was a member of the Communist Party and a gifted Marxist academic. She graduated in 1925. In the 1930s she was engaged in intensive debates surrounding Keynes's research. In 1933 she published her milestone work on *The Economics of Imperfect Competition.* But it was not until 1937 that she obtained a university lectureship at Cambridge. Despite her influence and prodigious output, it was not until 1965 that she obtained a full professorship at her university.

As Geoffrey Harcourt and Prue Kerr (2009, pp. 8–9) have noted, Robinson suffered from prejudice against her gender, including from at least one leading economist who believed that women were incapable of abstract economic theory. But Robinson declared in later life that if she had suffered discrimination it was because of her ideas, not because she was a woman (Golden, 1976). She had a dogged personal determination and a sincere concern about the injustices of the world.

Keynes's connections with political life were mainly through Establishment networks. He was a supporter of the Liberal Party. By contrast, Robinson was a fervent socialist, closely connected with Marxist economists such as Dobb at Cambridge, and with the Polish Marxist Michał Kalecki, whom she befriended in 1936. Kalecki became a major influence on Robinson's thinking and he was placed alongside Keynes as a pioneer of the Keynesian Revolution. 'Many of her writings in the 1930s and 1940s were directed towards the formation of Labour Party policies in the light of Keynes's and Kalecki's findings' (Harcourt and Kerr, 2009, p. 10). But while she was influenced by Marxism, she did not swallow Marx whole. She rejected Marx's labour theory of value and his theory of the tendency of the rate of profit to fall (Robinson, 1942). She criticized those who parroted Marx uncritically.

Piero Sraffa was another major figure in Cambridge economics. Born in Turin in Italy, he had been active there in socialist politics, and thereby he had become a close friend of the famous Marxist Antonio Gramsci. In a seminal article, Sraffa (1926) exposed serious problems in Marshallian analysis. Sraffa came to Cambridge as a lecturer in 1927 and was elected to a fellowship at Trinity College in 1939. Although it is less than 100 pages, his most famous work entitled *Production of Commodities by Means of Commodities* (Sraffa, 1960) took decades to complete. Sraffa built on the classical approaches of David Ricardo and Karl Marx, particularly from the reproduction schemes in the second volume of *Capital* (Marx, 1978).

Its logic is brilliant, but the work is idiosyncratic in its notation and style. A modicum of cooperation by its author with someone versed in matrix algebra could have sorted out the notational oddities and aided further mathematical development.[4] His work has been interpreted not only as a 'prelude' to a critique of mainstream theory, but also as an opening fanfare for a modernized revival of Marxist economics (Meek, 1961; Dobb, 1970; Eatwell and Panico, 1987; Hollander, 2000; Sinha, 2016).

SRAFFIAN ANALYSIS AND DEBATES OVER CAPITAL THEORY

Robinson (1953) triggered the famous Cambridge controversy in capital theory by asking how capital was measured. By *capital* she generally meant *capital goods*. The latter are clearly heterogeneous, and any single scalar measure of an aggregation required a set of weights or values to quantify them as an aggregate. Sraffa (1960) showed that relevant economic measures of such aggregates of physically heterogeneous items were not independent of prices or of the distribution of income between wages and profits.

Sraffa's arguments developed into a concerted attack on the neo-classical aggregate production function. Production functions serve several purposes in mainstream economics. In neoclassical theory, wages and profits are related to the marginal revenue products of labour and capital respectively. Going further, John Bates Clark (1899) and others suggested that the aggregate production function upheld a normative justification of the appropriation of profits by capitalists. These distributive shares of labour and capital were controlled by a 'natural law'.

---

4   See Steedman (1977) and Schefold (1989), for example.

Hence production functions were used in attempts to explain or justify the distribution of income between rival social classes under capitalism.

This pro-capitalist political conclusion energized the Cambridge economists to attack the aggregate production function. But they treated it largely as a technical problem. In 1961, Robinson visited the Massachusetts Institute of Technology (located in Cambridge in the US) with Pierangelo Garegnani from Italy. They argued with Samuelson over the aggregate production function. Their debate focused on the possibilities of *capital reversing* and of *capital reswitching*. Capital reversing means that, contrary to many neoclassical textbooks, a less capital-intensive production technique may be associated with a lower value of the rate of profits. Reswitching means that the same technique, having been the most profitable for a range of profit rates and wage rates, could also be the most profitable at another range of profit rates and wage rates, even though different techniques were the most profitable at intermediate values. If such things could happen, then the standard, 'well-behaved' aggregate production function would be undermined.

In response, Samuelson (1962) tried to rescue orthodoxy with the 'surrogate production function'. But within four years, Samuelson (1966) admitted that capital reversing and capital reswitching were possible. In a powerful technical paper, Garegnani (1970) triumphantly demonstrated that with heterogeneous capital goods, aggregate production functions could take a variety of exotic and 'badly-behaved' forms. Samuelson (1962) had been decisively refuted.

The Cambridge UK side of the debate were triumphant. They believed that they had struck a major blow against neoclassical economics and its use to bolster the ideology of capitalism. Incidentally, the timing of the final theoretical battle, from 1962 to 1970, coincided with a huge global upsurge of popular protest, particularly against the Vietnam War but also against capitalism. In his definitive account of the capital controversy, Harcourt (1972, p. 13) saw a correlation between analytic views on economic theory and normative stances on capitalism and the Vietnam War:

> [If] one were to be told whether an economist was fundamentally sympathetic or hostile to basic capitalist institutions, especially private property and the related rights to income streams, or whether he were a hawk or a dove in his views of the Vietnam War, one could predict with a considerable degree of accuracy both his general approach to economic theory and which side he would be on in the present [capital theory] controversies.

But Harcourt failed to identify any causal mechanism that might explain this apparent correlation. Why did two sides in an argument over capital theory correlate with different ideological positions on capitalism or the Vietnam War? There is no logical connection between these stances.

But there is a possible causal explanation for the correlation. Critics of neoclassical capital theory saw their arguments as an assault on a theoretical justification for a capitalist economy based on wages and profits. Their critique drew support from their anti-capitalist ideology. Ideological opposition to capitalism also fuelled opposition to its wars against Communist regimes. Leftist ideology thus explains the adoption of the Sraffian critique plus the rejection of capitalism and its wars against Communism. On the other side, status quo attitudes to politics are often linked to status quo attitudes to economics. Hence the correlation between stances on the Vietnam War and positions on the capital controversy are explained by political ideology, rather than by economic analysis. Ideology motivated the different positions.

Cambridge heterodoxy neglected other criticisms of the neoclassical theory of distribution. As an exception, sometime after 1970, Robinson (1979, pp. 37–40, 94–5, 116) acknowledged Thorstein Veblen's (1908) criticism of Clark (Cohen, 2014). Robinson was especially impressed by Veblen's observation that economists had habitually conflated the notions of capital-as-finance and capital goods. Veblen had also emphasized the relative economic importance of knowledge, held within a community. He pointed out that if physical capital was destroyed, then possession of appropriate knowledge could restore the production technology. But if the necessary knowledge and skills were lost, then any surviving capital goods would be unusable. He also stressed the financial and credit-related aspects of capital, and their dependence on historically-specific social institutions. But while praising Veblen, Robinson made little of these insights in her own analysis. She carried on treating capital as physical stuff.

Robinson and her co-workers overlooked other important, non-mathematical criticisms of Clark's position, including by the liberal economist John Atkinson Hobson. Hobson (1900) noted that with production functions, all (positive) factor inputs help to determine the output. In marginal analysis, other factors are held constant as one factor varies. But with positive values throughout, the variable factor still acts in combination with flows of the other factors. Contrary to Hobson's critics, this did not amount to a confusion of total with marginal productivity. Hobson simply pointed out that a marginal output is not produced by the varying factor alone. Identifying the marginal effect of a variation in the services of one factor cannot suppress the causal impact of the other factors on output, even though their rate of flow is held constant. All the inputs act causally at every point: they are interdependent. Consequently, one cannot conclude that shares of output are attributable to separate factors.

Yet leading economists make this mistake. For example, in a text on price theory, Milton Friedman (1962, p. 198) relayed the idea that 'marginal productivity theory shows that each man gets what he produces' (as long as there is sufficient market competition). He did not consider that the notion of one factor 'getting what it produces' is problematic. Production functions involve a combination of capital goods and labour as joint and interdependent inputs. Hence the very notion on one factor 'getting what it produces' is mistaken, even within the assumed terms of a standard production function. Furthermore, because of this interdependence of factors, justifications in Lockean terms of property rights over outputs fail: all input facts are 'mixed' with the output. Clark's normative theory thus collapses, even if his production function survives.[5]

But defeating an important argument that was used to defend capitalism does not mean that capitalism is indefensible. To attack capitalism effectively one must critique the core notion of a market system driven by profit and propose a feasible and superior alternative. To his credit, Harcourt (1972, p. 91) also argued that economists ought to be asking whether profits are justified, and not simply how profits are determined. But few among the Cambridge left economists pursued this philosophical question. It was as if the objections to a system based on profits were obvious, and socialism was an unassailable solution to replace capitalism and its defects. They lived and worked in a prestigious leftist bubble where such 'obvious' claims often went unchallenged.

While Marx's *Capital* and Keynes's *General Theory* explicitly engage with empirical reality, Sraffa's book does not, despite its Marxist allusions. As Mark Blaug (1974, p. 28) put it: 'there is hardly a sentence in the book which refers to the real world and it is perfectly obvious that Sraffa is only too keen to exchange practical relevance for logical rigour.' Blaug (1990, pp. 225–6) later commented: 'it is time to ask whether it is something about the very nature of Sraffa's approach that has so far made it totally irrelevant to practical issues.'

---

[5]　See Pullen (2010) for an excellent discussion. Note also that, for the sum of marginal productivity allocations to correspond to total output, the production function must be assumed to be linearly homogeneous, which Edgeworth (1904) among others doubted were true in reality.

Blaug (1974, 1990) compared Sraffian economics with neoclassical general equilibrium theory. Although the Sraffian system is static, it does not mention equilibria or equilibration mechanisms, and it may thus plead that it is not an equilibrium theory (Sinha, 2016). But both are fact-lite approaches, suspended in mid-air from inflated abstract assumptions, generating internal puzzles rather than engaging with empirical reality.

The neoclassical citadels were largely unshaken by the Cambridge theoretical assault (Cohen and Harcourt, 2003). Sraffa's *Production of Commodities* received a flurry of citations in the literature but afterwards its impact declined (Hodgson, 1997). The Sraffian results rest on the assumption of heterogeneous capital goods and point to the problem of valuing them in the aggregate. Disaggregated versions of neoclassical theory – particularly of general equilibrium theory – did not face this problem. As Blaug (1974, p. 9) pointed out: 'so long as we stay firmly within the microeconomic tradition of Walrasian general equilibrium theory, we avoid every one of the endlessly reiterated dilemmas of the Cambridge critics'. Similarly, Frank Hahn (1975, p. 362) argued that 'there is not a single formal proposition in Sraffa's book which is not also true in a General Equilibrium model constructed on his assumptions.' Furthermore, against 'the followers of Sraffa', Hahn (1982, p. 353) concluded that 'there is no correct neo-Ricardian proposition which is not contained in the set of propositions which can be generated by orthodoxy' in a disaggregated general equilibrium analysis. Hence 'the neo-Ricardian attack *via* logic is easily beaten off.' Hahn's 1982 article was published in the heterodox *Cambridge Journal of Economics*, with the aim of reviving a debate that orthodoxy had mostly ignored. But no defence of the Sraffian approach appeared in response to Hahn in the journal.[6]

This does not imply that general equilibrium theory is a viable way forward. Blaug (1992, 1997, 1999) repeatedly emphasized that the development of general equilibrium theory after the Second World War, which displaced the previous Marshallian dominance, had driven economics in an unhelpful direction, leading to an obsession with formalized, technical problems and a disengagement from empirical reality. Although Hahn had been a major contributor to the development of general equilibrium theory (Arrow and Hahn, 1971), he fully understood that its research programme had been derailed in the 1970s. Theoretical results showed that 'well-behaved' aggregate demand functions could not

---

[6]   Much later, Sinha (2016) claimed to rebut Hahn (1982).

be guaranteed in a disaggregated general equilibrium framework. The supreme quest for secure micro-foundations had failed (Hahn, 1975; Kirman, 1989; Rizvi, 1994a).

Hahn was a university lecturer at Cambridge from 1960 to 1967. He returned in 1972 to take up a full professorship. His criticism of Sraffian economics was enough for him to be labelled on the 'right' of the Cambridge Faculty. This was an absurd political appellation. Hahn was a social democrat. He opposed unlimited markets and campaigned against the policies of Prime Minister Margaret Thatcher. Kenneth Arrow, who was Hahn's co-author of their 1971 text on general equilibrium theory, was a strong socialist. Once again, Hahn's 'left' opponents at Cambridge seemed enduringly unaware that general equilibrium theory had been used in the 1930s in attempts to show, against Hayek and Mises, that socialism was possible. Hahn himself used general equilibrium theory to argue that the necessary conditions for a competitive general market equilibrium were so difficult to satisfy in reality that consequently there is an important economic role for the state.

While the Sraffian critique on the aggregate production function was important and logically robust, much of the remaining neoclassical apparatus was untouched by the Cambridge attack. In fact, Sraffian analysis had much in common with orthodoxy. Blaug (1974, p. 3) put it forcefully: 'If there is something wrong with neo-classical economics – as there may well be – the Cambridge theories share all of its weaknesses and practically none of its strengths.' Both types of analysis are largely static. Key problems of information, knowledge and uncertainty are underestimated in both Sraffian and neoclassical models.

The foundational use of purely physical inputs and outputs in the Sraffa system neglects questions of learning and knowledge which had been given inadequate attention by orthodoxy and heterodoxy alike. This was the nub of Veblen's (1908) astute attack on the neoclassical concept of capital. Knowledge and learning are dynamic and relate uneasily to the fixed physical coefficients and other static assumptions of the Sraffa system. Knowledge and learning are difficult to reconcile with maximizing agents, unless learning is treated unrealistically as asymptotic to some final equilibrium outcome.

The Sraffian critique leaves the maximizing, equilibrium-oriented core of neoclassical theory intact. It does not entail an alternative theory of human agency and interaction. It assumes that the long-period positions will somehow reflect and affect the expectations and actions of agents, without explaining how the average rate of profits and prices are attained. Whether conceived as an internal critique of neoclassical theory, or the foundation of an alternative paradigm for economics, Sraffian economics has no theory of individual human action and no account of the actions of agents, their interactions and their consequences.

These lacunae weakened the Sraffian approach in a crucial theoretical area. Neoclassical economics always emphasized individual incentives. But it took a questionable view of what those incentives mean and how they could be modelled: it assumed self-interest and utility maximization. Any successful assault on the neoclassical citadel would have to criticize these assumptions carefully, and not simply dismiss them with vague labels such as 'marginalism' or 'methodological individualism'. A superior theory of human motivation and interaction was required. Sraffian economics did not provide one.[7]

Unlike some other aspects of Cambridge economics – particularly the empirically oriented work of Kaldor (1966, 1972, 1975a, 1975b) – Sraffa's economics makes few testable claims. It does not challenge neoclassical economics by proposing a novel and superior explanation of accepted facts. Like neoclassical general equilibrium theory, it does not engage with the real world. Both are self-contained logical exercises, generating their own internal technical challenges to keep their adherents intellectually occupied.[8]

---

[7] In the following chapter and in Hodgson (2007) I show that methodological individualism is an ambiguous term. There is no consensus on its meaning. See also Arrow (1994).

[8] I add a personal recollection here. Enthralled by Cambridge ideas in the 1970s, I noticed that money was central to the analyses of Marx and Keynes – albeit in different ways – but it was entirely missing from Sraffa's *Production of Commodities*. If there were to be any synthesis between Sraffa and Keynes – as Robinson, Eatwell and others proposed – it seemed vital to span this gap. I sent a draft paper on 'Money and the Sraffa System' to Robinson in 1974. She generously responded, and we corresponded for a while. The crux for her was expressed in a letter to me of December that year: 'Money is a social convention not a physical product' but by contrast 'Sraffa's model is for industrial *production*' (Robinson 1974, her emphasis). She was of course right about money, especially when it is not a produced commodity of intrinsic value, such as gold. But production too involves social conventions and institutions, and not merely physical stuff. Sraffa's model also involves prices, wages and profits, which in the real world are also related to money. It seemed to me that Robinson was adopting a version of the pre-Keynesian classical dichotomy, where physical assets were placed on one side of an analytical divide, with money on the other. In any case, it still perplexed me how Sraffa, Marx and Keynes could be reconciled. I tried to press the point, but eventually she passed our correspondence to Eatwell, which came to nothing. Some years later I published a revised version of the paper, and this work became part of a wider book on the topic (Hodgson, 1981, 1982). But soon afterwards I realized that a coherent synthesis between Keynes and Sraffa is impossible because of their fundamentally different ontological and other assumptions. Capitalist production is about institutions, albeit played out in a material world. So I turned to American institutionalism – particularly Veblen – instead (Hodgson, 1988).

INDIVIDUAL MOTIVATION AND MICROECONOMICS

Cambridge economics as a whole lacked an alternative theory of motivation and interaction. Little work was done on an alternative, psychologically grounded theory. Critiques of utility maximization were often brief. For example, in her *Economic Philosophy* Robinson (1964a, p. 48) attacked the core neoclassical concept of utility: '*Utility* is a metaphysical concept of impregnable circularity; *utility* is the quality in commodities that makes individuals want to buy them, and the fact that individuals want to buy them shows that they have *utility.*'

A good point, nicely phrased. But Robinson seemed to think that finished the matter. Although circularity and unfalsifiability are important and consequential limitations, effective critique of utility maximization cannot rely on these alone.[9] Beyond occasional remarks such as this, Robinson devoted little attention to the critique and replacement of the assumption of utility maximization. In her high-profile attempt to outline the priorities for economic theory in her article on 'What are the questions?' in the prestigious *Journal of Economic Literature*, the topic of utility maximization and its possible replacement does not appear (Robinson, 1977b).

If utility is to be rejected, then an alternative theory of individual motivation is needed. One possible port of call would have been the instinct-habit psychology adopted by Veblen (1914). But the influence of American institutionalism on Cambridge economics was minimal.[10]

An obvious place to look for insights on human cognition and motivation would have been the behavioural economics of Herbert Simon (1947, 1955, 1956, 1957, 1979). Simon drew from psychology and he researched cognitive processes and organizational behaviour. He was

---

[9] Note how Robinson used 'metaphysical' as a negative word, in accord with Comtean positivism. Similarly, Robinson and Eatwell (1973, pp. 3, 9–10, 29, 36, 42, 149, 171) repeatedly dismissed 'metaphysical' propositions in their textbook. But Willard van Orman Quine (1953) had already showed that even positivism and empiricism depended on metaphysical assumptions. Since then it has become generally accepted in the philosophy of science – as Veblen understood long ago (Veblen, 1900; Camic and Hodgson, 2011, pp. 12–13; Hodgson, 2004a, pp. 147–8, 215) – that some unfalsifiable and unprovable 'metaphysical' propositions are essential for science to operate. These include the assumption of causality and the principle of the uniformity of nature.

[10] Another problem was that the psychological aspects of Veblen's thinking had been largely abandoned by later American institutionalists (Hodgson, 2004a). Nevertheless, American institutionalism had some influence on the Keynesian revolution and Keynes briefly corresponded with Commons. In addition, Robinson (1964a, pp. 103–10) cited Clarence Ayres (1944), and there was an indirect link through Allyn Young and Gunnar Myrdal to Kaldor (Hodgson, 2004a, pp. 152–3, 285, 309–315).

influenced by the American institutional economist John R. Commons, among others (Simon, 1979, p. 499). But Simon's work was generally ignored by leading Cambridge economists. I have found no mention of Simon in the published works of Kaldor, Robinson or Sraffa.

Or the Cambridge critics could have looked closer to home. They could have taken their cue from Marshall. He had a notion of human motivation that was superior to the mechanical 'pleasure machines' of much neoclassical theory. Marshall (1920, p. vi) insisted in his *Principles* that 'ethical forces are among those of which the economist has to take account.' He was sceptical of attempts 'to construct an abstract science with regard to the actions of an "economic man," who is under no ethical influences and who pursues pecuniary gain warily and energetically, but mechanically and selfishly.' Cantabrigian heterodoxy made little attempt to build on this Marshallian legacy.

Robinson briefly mentioned morality in a few places (for example Robinson, 1969a, pp. 33–4; Robinson and Eatwell, 1973, p. 271). But she never articulated a theory of moral motivation. She wrote nothing about moral sentiments and their emotional grounding. She treated morality as a normative yardstick of behaviour, to be fulfilled when capitalism has been replaced by socialism. Hence Robinson (1973, pp. 4, 13, 37; 1977a) disliked markets because she believed they promoted a selfish morality. She also rejected 'market socialism', partly because of 'the erosion of socialist morality that monetary incentives bring about'. Robinson saw morality as vital for a planned socialist economy, where hard work and loyalty would be energized through moral propaganda.

There was inadequate recognition that capitalism too relies on moral values (Schumpeter, 1942). Indeed, no society is possible without moral bonds and widespread sympathy for others (Smith, 1759). And contrary to what Robinson suggested, markets do not always lead to selfishness. Markets enable wider interpersonal interactions and can help to promote mutual understanding and trust. Consideration of morality does not necessarily mean the abolition of capitalism.[11]

Although she paid notable attention to prices and imperfect competition, other vital microeconomic issues were neglected in Robinson's work. For example, Marshall (1920, pp. 138–9) had insisted on the importance of knowledge and organization: 'Knowledge is our most powerful engine of production ... Organization aids knowledge; it has many forms ... it seems best sometimes to reckon organization apart as a

---

[11] See Hirschman's (1982) brilliantly nuanced analysis of markets, and the evidence in Henrich et al. (2001, 2004) that involvement in markets does not generally increase selfish behaviour.

distinct agent of production.' Redolent of Veblen and consonant with Simon, this Marshallian emphasis on knowledge and organization had surprisingly little impact on Cantabrigian heterodoxy.

Even Kaldor treated knowledge too casually. For example, Kaldor (1966, p. 13) proposed that different plants in a multinational corporation 'must have had the same access to improvements in knowledge and know-how'. This ignored the importance and ubiquity of 'unteachable' (Penrose, 1959) or 'tacit' knowledge (Polanyi, 1958, 1967), which we know but cannot readily explain. For example, we follow the rules of our native language, while being unable to make many of them explicit. Tacit knowledge cannot easily be transferred from individual to individual, or from production plant to production plant, even if copyright or other legal impediments are lacking.

Research opportunities in key areas were missed. The young Sen wished to research social choice and welfare theory for his PhD. He attempted to find a supervisor in Cambridge. He could not find anyone at Trinity – his own college – or in the university as a whole. Sen (1999) wrote: 'I had to choose quite a different subject for my research thesis ... The thesis was on "the choice of techniques," which interested Joan Robinson as well as Maurice Dobb'.

Sen received his PhD in 1959. But he was soon to make major contributions to his preferred topic of social choice theory (Sen, 1970). Sen (1973, 1977) then published some of the best-ever critiques of the rational, utility-maximizing individual. Sen (1979, 1981, 1985a, 1987a, 1987b) went on to make a number of additional major contributions in the areas of welfare economics, human motivation and identity, as well as to develop his analysis of famines, which earned him the Nobel Prize in 1998. Sen's earlier work from Cambridge on the choice of techniques has received much less attention.

Peter Earl studied at Cambridge from 1974 to 1979. He became interested in Simon's behavioural economics. He was advised that his prospects for a position in Cambridge 'were not very good since [his] enthusiasm for behavioural economics would mean that [he] would be rejected by both the neoclassical economists and those on the left' (Earl, 2018). Earl also became interested in the work of George L.S. Shackle (1955, 1972, 1974). Shackle gave even more prominence to Keynes's concept of uncertainty than several other post-Keynesians and he empha-sized the role of imagination and 'potential surprise'.

More complex theories of human motivation do not necessarily lead to socialist policy conclusions. Much of the emphasis on morality and duty, for example, is found in conservative as well as radical strands of thought. Generally, understanding humans as more complex creatures, with finite cognitive and computational capacities, may help us understand some limitations of the market mechanism, but it does not necessarily steer us toward socialism. Perhaps the politically ambivalent or uncertain outcomes of these ideas were part of the reason for neglect by leftist heterodox economists?

Largely, with some exceptions, the Cambridge left economists gave precedence to macroeconomic over microeconomic theory. Excursions into micro were often concerned with price theory or imperfect competition, and only rarely with the psychological or other grounding of human motivation.[12] From 1968 to 1970, Jan Kregel was a research student at Cambridge, under the supervision of Robinson and Kaldor. Subsequently, Kregel (1973, p. 203) wrote: 'The micro-analysis of the macro theory remains one of the least refined areas of post-Keynesian theory.' This precedence toward macro- over micro- was also obvious in the long-awaited but short-lived Cambridge textbook authored by Robinson and John Eatwell (1973). Blaug (1974, pp. 69, 71–2) commented:

> Joan Robinson's much-awaited textbook in 'modern economics' perfectly exemplifies the typical attitude of Cambridge economists to micro-economics. The whole of traditional price theory is covered in one chapter ... [some] prices are formed by conventional mark-ups on prime costs, the level of the mark-up itself being left unexplained. Apart from this chapter, the book is doggedly macro-economic in treatment ... A striking omission from the book is any mention of the closely related concepts of externalities and public goods, which most economists would nowadays regard as the basic ingredients of 'market failure' that has come to be fruitfully applied ... to problems of pollution and congestion.

The neglected concepts of externality, market failure and social cost were used by Pigou (1920) and others to identify the limits to the general use of the market mechanism. Pigou's analysis was traditionally part of the theory of a mixed economy, to which Samuelson (1954) and Galbraith (1958) added the concept of public goods. Were these areas of analysis neglected in the textbook because they suggested a mixed economy involving markets, rather than wholesale socialist planning?[13]

---

[12] An exception is Steedman's (1980) powerful but neglected paper on non-autonomous preferences. Steedman studied at Cambridge. Hollis and Nell (1975) also criticized core neoclassical assumptions.

[13] Robinson and Eatwell (1973, pp. 309–310) briefly dismissed Pigou's analysis, without explicit mention of the concepts of externality or market failure. Robinson and Eatwell (1973, p. 47) caricatured his position as one where 'Pigou described a number of cases in which *laissez-faire* is not necessarily beneficial, but he treated them as exceptions to a rule which, in general, could not be questioned.' In fact, Pigou took a pragmatic and

Not only were Pigou and Samuelson given short shrift in the Robinson–Eatwell textbook, but also their critics were ignored. Approaches to externalities and public goods came under attack from the Chicago school, following Ronald Coase's (1960) classic article. But the textbook gives its student readers no guidance on how to deal with the rising pro-market reaction to the 'market failure' analyses of Pigou, Samuelson and others. Robinson and Eatwell even neglected the alternative theory of social cost developed by K. William Kapp (1950), which was influenced by Pigou and reached conclusions that were more aligned with their left politics.[14]

From the 1950s to the 1980s the Cambridge department was relatively pluralistic, with a variety of different viewpoints. But there was more pluralism in some areas than others. We have noted the lack of opportunities for scholars like Sen and Earl to research on particular microeconomic issues. Pluralism without an adequate consensus on core issues is dysfunctional. There was insufficient agreement on some basic theoretical issues and this absence made dissident economics in Cambridge vulnerable. When their final defeat came, it was relatively swift.

THE POLITICS AND ECONOMICS OF JOAN ROBINSON

Cambridge was a hotbed of leftist political radicalism and Robinson was the most influential figure within Cambridge heterodox economics. From the 1960s she was to play a central role in the development of post-Keynesian and heterodox economics in the US as well as in Britain.

---

experimental approach toward the question of socialism versus capitalism. While accepting capitalism 'for the time being', he stressed the importance of 'graduated death duties and graduated income tax ... with the deliberate purpose of diminishing our glaring inequalities of fortune and opportunity which deface our present civilisation.' He also favoured substantial government-promoted investment in 'the health, intelligence and character of the people' (Pigou, 1937, pp. 137–8). Robinson and Eatwell (1973, p. 243 n.) mentioned Samuelson momentarily, in one footnote in the entire textbook, in regard to international trade, but not to his seminal work on public goods. Galbraith gets three mentions, but none is to his classic *Affluent Society* (Galbraith, 1958) with its famous popularization of Samuelson's (1954) concept.

[14]   Kapp (2016) focused on the failure of market prices to reflect social costs and individual needs. He seemed to assume, but did not show, that any meaningful calculation of costs or prices was possible in a planned economy. He appraised the limits of markets, but not those of planning. During their correspondence in 1941, the leading American institutional economist J.M. Clark noted this lack of 'balance' in Kapp's analysis (Berger, 2017, pp. 100 ff.). Like Commons, Clark promoted a reformed capitalism.

Her political standpoint, as well as her economics, influenced these movements. Some consideration of her political views is essential for this narrative.

Political attitudes help to determine what an economist thinks are important for further study, what can be taken as given, and what is ignored. Robinson's political views affected the agenda in terms of economic theory, framed political opinion and recruitment in these dissenting communities, and guided views on the relationship between economic theory and political practice. But one omission stands out as of enduring importance. Robinson simply took the viability of socialism for granted and she failed to discuss the twentieth-century theoretical debate on the economic feasibility of socialism. This omission persisted among the rising post-Keynesian and heterodox movements.

Before and during the Second World War, Robinson produced pamphlets, short pieces, newspaper articles and radio talks on socialist planning (Robinson, 1937, 1943a, 1943b, 1943c, 1943d, 1943e). This material was largely designed for a wider audience. In one place she advocated complete nationalization of the productive sector, because 'a patch of national control here and there cannot make a great improvement on the design' (Robinson, 1943a, p. 19). In her planned economy, as Harcourt and Kerr (2009, p. 66) pointed out: 'She would leave some fringe consumer items in the hands of private production just to provide some choice.' Robinson believed that an entire modern complex economy could be planned from the top.

As Harcourt and Kerr (2009, p. 66) elaborated, she looked, 'uncritically and idealistically, to Russia as an example of successful, rational planning. The Soviet example was an inspiration to the socialists and Joan Robinson defended Stalin into the 1950s and 1960s.' In her review of Dobb's (1949) *Soviet Economic Development since 1917*, Robinson (1949) was impressed with the 30 years of Soviet progress and saw it as a 'grand moral' for under-developed nations.

Robinson (1965, p. 28) supported the North Korean regime and extolled its 'economic miracle ... All the economic miracles of the post-war world are put in the shade by these achievements.' But the North Korean Seven-Year Plan launched in 1961 turned out to be a massive failure by its own targets: growth slowed dramatically, with relatively little increase in living standards (Chung, 1972). Meanwhile the South Korean economy was beginning to forge ahead. These were serious misjudgements by a prominent economist.

After the Chinese Revolution of 1949, Robinson visited China several times and was a supporter of Mao's policies until his death in 1976. Robinson (1965, p. 193) once wrote that 'no one starved' in the Great

Leap Forward of 1958–61. In fact, it had led to a catastrophic famine and about 40 million deaths (Dikötter, 2010).

Robinson (1969b, p. 19) also supported Mao's Cultural Revolution and praised Mao's 'moderate and humane' intentions. But after Mao's death 'she discovered, to her horror, that the Chinese had not told the truth even to trusting analysts ... she admitted to having been starry-eyed about the decade of the "Cultural Revolution"' (Harcourt and Kerr, 2009, p. 145). The Cultural Revolution created anarchy for years and led to between half a million and several million deaths – estimates vary widely – due to famine and Red Guard violence (Dikötter, 2016). Robinson had been naïve and deluded by ideology: she had believed the official pronouncements of totalitarian regimes.[15]

The severity of her economic and political misjudgements is rarely noted by her followers. By contrast, links between Chicago economics and the murderous Chilean regime of Augusto Pinochet are often rightly criticized (Valdés, 1995). Pinochet's government killed over 3000 and tortured about 40 000 people (BBC News, 2011). But the scale of Robinson's mistake in backing Mao is rarely recognized. Mao's regime led to about 65 million deaths, some millions of which resulted from beatings or torture. This death toll is about 2000 times greater than Pinochet's appalling score. Why is Robinson so rarely criticized for her naïve and irresponsible credulity concerning Mao's monstrous crimes? Perhaps this silence tells us something about the political dispositions of Cantabrigian heterodoxy?

Harcourt and Kerr (2009, p. 58) confirmed that Robinson 'was a Fabian socialist but not a Marxist'. Harcourt and Kerr (2009, p. 74) also admitted that her socialism was 'idealistic and not well-informed by contemporary debates over planning and over the Soviet case.' Blaug (1974, p. 77) was more disparaging: 'A careful perusal of Joan Robinson's voluminous writings ... contributes little of substance to the famous question of capitalism *versus* socialism.' But the issue of capitalism versus socialism was always prominent in her thinking.

For Robinson, 'Capital accumulation was the key; to overcome "backwardness"' (Harcourt and Kerr, 2009, p. 146) where capital was regarded as physical means of production, and socialism was believed to be the

---

[15] But to be fair, the full scale of suffering under Stalin, Mao and other Communist regimes was not revealed until the 1990s. Courtois et al. (1999) estimated that Stalin's regime in the Soviet Union was responsible for 20 million premature deaths and that Mao's rule in China lead to 65 million premature deaths. Some other estimates are even higher (Rummel, 1994). Tahir et al. (2002) stated that Robinson changed her position in the 1970s, to favour the introduction of market reforms in China. But they gave no clear evidence of this shift in her opinion.

best arrangement to ensure the rapid accumulation and distribution of this physical stuff. There was little consideration of the institutions, knowledge and incentives that were required to make any system work effectively.[16]

By focusing on the accumulation of capital as physical stuff, Robinson and others neglected the problem of meaningfully evaluating inputs, outputs and processes – otherwise known as the problem for planners of economic calculation. Adequate responses emphasize the price mechanism and an understanding of capital as the money value of investments. This monetary view of capital aligns with what is commonplace in business and accounting, but not in economics. In the monetary view, capital is both the expression, and the instrument for the creation, of money-values, in the historically specific type of economic system known as capitalism. Robinson's largely ahistorical and physicalist view of capital and her failure to appreciate the socialist calculation debate were thus linked.

Other heterodox thinkers exhibited similar limitations. Robinson was not alone. Yet the influence of founders on movements is often greater than that of followers, because organizations and networks congeal and become self-reinforcing as they mature, and it becomes more difficult to change their basic assumptions and their direction.

THE CAMBRIDGE NEGLECT OF THE SOCIALIST CALCULATION DEBATE

In the 1930s and 1940s most academic economists were at least vaguely aware of the 'socialist calculation debate', which occurred between, on the one hand, the Austrians Friedrich Hayek and Ludwig Mises, and on the other hand, the socialist economists Oskar Lange, Henry Dickinson, Abba Lerner and others.[17] Because the London School of Economics was

---

[16] Robinson's *Accumulation of Capital* (1969a) is said by some to be her most important work – an attempt to extend Keynes's analysis to the long-run. Capital is never clearly defined in the book, but it is treated as physical stuff throughout. This physicalist conception of capital is commonplace in orthodox economics as well, and criticism is expressed by a tiny minority (Menger, 1888; Mitchell Innes, 1914; Fetter, 1927, 1930; Schumpeter, 1954, pp. 322–3; De Soto, 2000; Piketty, 2014; Hodgson, 2014b, 2015b; Braun, 2015). Physicalist notions of capital are even less-well suited to a modern, knowledge-intensive economy where much production takes the form of services and where information-based, intangible assets are paramount (Pagano, 2014).

[17] Hayek (1935), Mises (1920, 1935), Lange (1936–37), Lange and Taylor (1938), Dickinson (1933, 1939), Lerner (1934, 1937, 1938). It was called the *socialist calculation debate* because at its centre was the problem of calculating meaningful prices in a planned

temporarily moved to Cambridge in the war years, Hayek was no stranger to this ancient university and he interacted with Keynes.

Within his voluminous writings on socialism, Dobb quickly dismissed the arguments of Mises and Hayek against planning (Dobb, 1929, 1937, 1949, 1955, 1960, 1969). Johnson reported that Dobb gave lectures on the 'Economics of Socialism, which was a fairly hot topic in 1945–46 ... they were mostly about the 1930s arguments about socialism, which started with von Mises's assertion that socialism, simply "could not work"' (Johnson and Johnson, 1978, p. 129). Dobb attempted to show that Mises was wrong. According to Johnson, Dobb would lecture by reading from his notes in a 'flat monotone'. He would start off with 40 or 50 students and end up with a hard core of Communist Party members and few others. Dobb was active in recruiting students to the Communist Party. Among them was Kim Philby, who became a Soviet spy.

Dobb was not unusual in dismissing the Austrian analysis. The overwhelming verdict among economists by 1945 was that Lange and others had won the socialist calculation debate with sound economic arguments.[18] It was widely believed that the arguments of Mises and Hayek concerning the unfeasibility of socialism had been answered and refuted by Lange, Dickinson, Lerner and others.

Thus Joseph Schumpeter (1942, pp. 167, 172–3) asked: 'Can socialism work?' Although he did not favour such a system, he echoed contemporary and widespread opinion with his immediate answer: 'Of course it can'. He further insisted that: 'There is nothing wrong with the pure theory of socialism.' Like others, Schumpeter accepted the Lange–Taylor model as a convincing demonstration of the feasibility of a socialist system. For him, Mises and Hayek were 'definitely wrong' (Schumpeter, 1954, p. 989 n.). Schumpeter influenced his student Paul Samuelson, who promulgated a similar assessment of the debate in his famous textbook (Samuelson, 1948).

---

economy. But the debate also addressed other problems with socialism, such as the lack of incentives and the totalitarian dangers in the concentration of economic power in the hands of the state. Often neglected were earlier economic arguments against socialism by Albert Schäffle (going back to the 1870s) and later ones by Michael Polanyi. The *calculation debate* label concentrates on one aspect of one argument, where in fact there were more issues, more debaters and more debates (Hodgson, 2019c).

[18]   It is a mistake to describe the models of Lange, Dickinson and others as 'market socialism'. Their proposals involved simulated market arrangements where the state ended up fixing final prices. They did not involve devolved property rights that were meaningfully established and contractually exchanged.

Any scientific community relies on trust in authority. It is impossible for every researcher to scrutinize every argument or debate. Consequently, when renowned figures such as Schumpeter and Samuelson claimed that Lange was right, most did not question the verdict. Dissenters to this opinion were dismissed or ignored.

D. Mario Nuti obtained a PhD from Cambridge and was a Fellow of King's College, Cambridge from 1965 to 1979. In 1972, Alec Nove – an expert on the Soviet economy – and Nuti published a reader on socialist economics. It included classic articles by Mises and Lange that were part of the debate. Yet the editors assumed in their introduction that Lange had 'found an answer' to Mises and other critics of socialism (Nove and Nuti, 1972, p. 12).[19]

Years later, Elizabeth Durbin (1985, p. 233) – the daughter of one of the participants in the debate – still believed that Lange's work was 'the authoritative answer' to Mises and Hayek, and that practical socialism was possible with central planners using Lange's simulated market mechanism. Even later, the influential US economists Andrei Shleifer and Robert Vishny (1994, p. 166) – who themselves were not socialists – wrote in a prestigious American Economic Association journal that the objections of Mises and Hayek to socialism 'were effectively rebutted by Lange'.

The notion that Lange and others had triumphed in the socialist calculation debate did not meet an effective challenge until the 1980s. Then the tide of interpretative opinion over the debate began to turn. The swell was increased by the growing political influence of Chicago-style, free-market ideas and by the rising academic stature of Hayek and other Austrian economists. All this destroyed the former authoritative consensus in favour of Lange.

But the questionable political context does not invalidate the content of the argument. Among others, Karen Vaughn (1980), Peter Murrell (1983) and Donald Lavoie (1985) produced scholarly re-evaluations of the socialist calculation debate.[20] The overwhelming and persuasive conclusions of these studies were that Lange and others had failed to answer adequately the criticisms of Mises and Hayek. Lange and others had not provided a satisfactory outline of a workable and dynamic socialist

---

[19]   Nove later expounded the view that extensive markets were necessary in any feasible socialism (Nove, 1980, 1983).

[20]   See also Steele (1992), Boettke (2000, 2001) and Hodgson (1999a, 2018, 2019c). The broad validity of the Austrian critique of central planning is accepted by some authors who are sympathetic to socialism (Burczak, 2006).

system and they had not appreciated the chronic inadequacies of the Walrasian general equilibrium approach.

But these developments were too late to change Cantabrigian heterodoxy. Dobb and Robinson did not question the feasibility of socialism any further, because like others they wrongly believed that Lange and others had demolished the Austrian case.

Robinson (1964b, p. 410) once approved a remark by Robert Solow that 'the notion of factor allocation in conditions of perfect competition makes sense in a normative theory of a planned economy rather than a descriptive theory of a capitalist economy, and that the notion of the marginal productivity of investment makes sense in the context of socialist planning.' This remark questionably assumes that marginal products are meaningful and measurable in a socialist planned economy, and can serve as guidelines for socialist managers, as Lange and others had presumed. Blaug (1993, p. 1571) wrote with appropriate derision:

> The Lange idea of managers following marginal cost-pricing rules because they are instructed to do so, while the central planning board continually alters the prices of both producer and consumer goods so as to reduce their excess demands to zero, is so administratively naive as to be positively laughable. Only those drunk on perfectly competitive, static equilibrium theory could have swallowed such nonsense.

The omission of the socialist calculation debate endured in key Cambridge texts. The long-awaited but ill-fated textbook by Robinson and John Eatwell (1973) has chapters on socialist states and socialist planning, but there is no mention on its pages of the socialist calculation debate. Related epistemic problems of knowledge and uncertainty are given no more than brief attention, despite the declared devotion to the legacy of Keynes.[21]

The New Palgrave Dictionary of Economics, edited by Eatwell with Murray Milgate and Peter Newman, was published in 1987. It has 4100 pages and four volumes. Blaug (1990, p. 236) commented:

> Despite entries on socialism, socialist economics and market socialism, and biographical entries on Oskar Lange and Ludwig von Mises, the Socialist Calculation Debate, so crucial in the revival of general equilibrium theory and

---

[21]   On the fate of the Robinson–Eatwell textbook see King and Millmow (2003) and Harcourt and Kerr (2009, ch. 10).

the rise of modern welfare economics in the 1930s, is nowhere discussed at length in the *New Palgrave*.[22]

The socialist calculation debate was important not simply because it questioned the viability of socialist planning. Lange and others had used Walrasian general equilibrium theory to defend socialism. In this context, Hayek (1948) developed a major critique of general equilibrium theory, which highlighted the nature and role of knowledge. Robinson and Eatwell were also strong critics of general equilibrium theory, but they did not mention the use of that theory in defending the viability of socialism. On the contrary, they wrote: 'For the neoclassicals *laissez-faire* became a dogma, and the benefits of free trade an article of faith.' They saw 'equilibrium theory' as 'an exposition of the presumption in favour of *laissez-faire*' (Robinson and Eatwell, 1973, pp. 47, 336).[23]

Even today, the socialist calculation debate is seldom taught on undergraduate or postgraduate courses in economics. It does not readily fit into formal models. When students – now alas rarely – get taught some history of economic thought, it is often excluded from there too.[24]

Yet it is arguably the most important debate in economics in the twentieth century. Furthermore, for Cambridge left economists, the battle between socialism and capitalism was among their foremost considerations. Yet they quickly passed over this vital controversy on the feasibility of their socialist goals. The Austrian critique was unanswered and generally assumed to be wrong.

The core analytic concerns of this debate are extremely important. These include the roles of information and knowledge in the economy, and the importance and nature of incentives. Orthodoxy gives much

---

[22]   In his forensic review of the *New Palgrave*, Blaug (1990, pp. 211–12, 231) wrote that 'there is a large number of extremely sympathetic and even adulatory expositions of Marxian economics but not one single critical account of Marx's ideas (with one possible exception …). Similarly, there are some 50 expositions of Sraffian economics under various headings but only two entries … which even begin to entertain the possibility that Sraffa's words may not represent the alpha and omega of economics. … Marx and Sraffa are quoted … much more frequently than Adam Smith, Alfred Marshall, Leon Walras, Maynard Keynes, Kenneth Arrow, Milton Friedman, Paul Samuelson or whoever you care to name.'

[23]   Similar claims that 'orthodox economics is a *de facto* defense of capitalism' (Canterbery, 2010, p. 99) were promoted by US radical economists Edwards et al. (1972) and others.

[24]   Alessandro Roncaglia researched in Cambridge in 1971–73 under the supervision of Sraffa. Roncaglia's (2005, p. 318 n.) prize-winning *History of Economic Thought* mentions the debate between Mises, Hayek and Lange over socialism in one footnote, where it is written that Lange 'answered' the arguments of Mises and Hayek. No credence is given to the possibility that his answers were inadequate.

attention to incentives, even if its answers can be faulted. By contrast, Cambridge heterodoxy, and the heterodox economics it has inspired, have given less attention to the role of incentives and to their psychological grounding. Problems of dispersed information and tacit knowledge are often overlooked. Cambridge heterodoxy was forged in these terms.

Lange and others had used neoclassical general equilibrium models and assumed away key information problems including dispersed and tacit knowledge. This should have alerted vigilant Cambridge critics of neoclassical economics that something might be wrong in the defence of socialism by Lange and others. Cantabrigian heterodoxy failed to pick up this scent, partly because their socialist ideology prevailed over any spirit of critical investigation into this discrepancy.

Cantabrigian heterodoxy made much of the claim that they were socialists, yet the socialist calculation debate raised questions of the feasibility of comprehensive central planning under socialism. Furthermore, attention to the debate would have overturned the frequent – but false – heterodox claim that neoclassical economics necessarily supports a market economy. The neglect of the debate betrayed major problems within Cantabrigian heterodoxy itself.

Of course, markets have their problems. As heterodox economists are aware, there are problems with externalities, social costs and the social and ecological limits to growth (Pigou, 1920; Kapp, 1950; Hirsch, 1977). But planning has problems as well. Saying (rightly) that markets have problems does not remove the difficulties from planning.

FACULTY BATTLES

The Faculty of Economics and Politics at the University of Cambridge was a battleground, where matters of institutional control, economic doctrine and political affiliation were fiercely contested. Johnson reported that to get elected to the Faculty Board required, among other things, 'strong attachment to the left or the right wing of the Department. The Faculty Board was a strongly political body, in the sense of both academic and party politics.' He also noted 'the bitterness of the controversies' (Johnson and Johnson, 1978, pp. 91, 134). This polarization discouraged the occupation of moderate or centre-ground positions. Political affiliation sometimes overshadowed academic merit.

Robert Neild obtained an economics degree at Cambridge in 1947. He returned to Cambridge in 1956 as a Teaching Fellow at Trinity College. In addition to lectures, he had to do twelve hours of college supervising (tutoring) of individual students each week, one or two at a time. 'The other dark aspect of life was the political goings-on in the economics faculty' (Neild, 2012, p. 73). Neild reported later in an interview: 'I found the faculty awful, it was so political and savage and full of prima donnas' (Hodgson et al., 2018, p. 769). Richard Kahn once expressed disappointment when Neild voted in the Faculty elections for a mixed ticket, rather than wholly for the left list. Neild (2012, pp. 73–4) felt he 'was caught by a mafia and had been subjected to bullying by its capo. My distaste for the ways of the faculty was one reason why I left Cambridge after two years. ... I was interested in doing research into how the economy worked, for which I had little time while committed to so much teaching'.[25]

Amartya Sen came to Cambridge as a student of economics in 1953. In 1958 he received a four-year Prize Fellowship from Trinity College. Sen (1999) recollected 'intense fights between different schools of thought' where 'the political lines were, in general, very firmly – and rather bizarrely – drawn. In an obvious sense, the Keynesians were to the "left" of the neo-classicists, but this was very much in the spirit of "this far but no further".' Sen recalled an incident where Dobb had defeated Kaldor in an election to the Faculty Board, which suggests that Kaldor was not on the left ticket at that time. Sen (1999) continued:

> Kaldor was, in fact, much the most tolerant of the neo-Keynesians at Cambridge. If Richard Kahn was in general the most bellicose, the stern reproach that I received often for not being quite true to the new orthodoxy of neo-Keynesianism came mostly from my thesis supervisor – the totally brilliant but vigorously intolerant Joan Robinson.

In the early 1930s, as a research student at the London School of Economics, Kaldor had been influenced by Hayek. But he became disenchanted with Hayek's monetary theory and became a Keynesian. Kaldor was appointed a Fellow of King's College and a university lecturer in economics in 1949. He was a practical social-democrat rather than a supporter of full-blooded socialism. He was also a friend of Hugh Gaitskell, who was leader of the Labour Party from 1955 to 1963, and the champion of its 'right' or 'revisionist' wing. Kaldor became an

---

[25] Neild returned to Cambridge as a full professor of economics in 1971. He took advantage of a relatively generous retirement package in 1984. In retirement he worked on institutional and evolutionary economics (Neild, 1995, 2002). Hitherto, institutional and evolutionary economics had been largely neglected in Cambridge. But Neild's work in this area was developed largely in the isolation of Trinity College, and it failed to cite many related or complementary publications elsewhere. Consequently, it passed relatively unnoticed within the rising global communities of institutional and evolutionary economists (Hodgson et al., 2018).

advisor to the newly-elected Labour Government under Harold Wilson in 1964 (Targetti, 1992; Thirlwall, 1987). Although Kaldor had published some major theoretical papers in his early years, his economics developed in a practical and empirical direction to an extent greater than the norm for Cambridge left economics. Kaldor 'cared little about the measurement of capital and its aggregation, or about the production function, obsessions for Joan Robinson' (Bliss, 2010, p. 635).[26]

Luigi Pasinetti (1974, 1981) was at Cambridge from 1960 to 1976, and he tried to combine Kaldorian and Sraffian approaches. Pasinetti was denied a chair in Cambridge and returned to his native Italy in 1976.

Christopher Bliss was a lecturer at Cambridge from 1966 to 1971, and he reflected on the faculty fights: 'Kahn had an outstanding mind, much of it eventually wasted when he devoted his energies to devious academic politicking. ... Robinson had a bad habit of bullying anyone who did not accept her opinions' (Bliss, 2010, p. 633). But, if true, she had no monopoly on such behaviour: it also came from the other side of the Cambridge battle-lines.

Bliss (2010, p. 632) attributed the culture of animosity in Cambridge economics to the 'tradition of self-righteous intolerance that flowed from Keynes'. But it is difficult to believe that Keynes was largely responsible for more than half a century of vicious antagonism. Other factors were the politicization of its economics from the 1930s onwards, heightened by the Cold War, and later by the revolutionary 1960s. Some Cambridge economists saw themselves as fighting a war against the West. Such heightened ends encouraged belligerent means.

Cambridge economists were divided on matters of both analytical approach and political standpoint. It was not a simple division between political left and right, but it was made simpler by (quite wrongly) the frequent assumption that proponents of neoclassical economics must necessarily be right-wing apologists for a market economy.

Cambridge left economics was developed when the world was divided between capitalism and socialism. In the 1930s, politics had been pulled apart by communism on the left and fascism on the right: less credence had been given to the centre ground. Liberals like Keynes were the exceptions. Socialism dominated progressive thought in this era. As Michael Polanyi (1945, p. 142) put it: 'as the century advanced the socialist movement came near to absorbing all that was progressive,

---

[26] Some major empirical contributions were partly stimulated by Kaldor's (1966, 1975b, 1978) attempts to establish 'stylized facts' about capitalist dynamics (Rowthorn, 1975a, 1975b, 1979; Rowthorn and Wells, 1987). The empirical work of Singh (1975) should also be recognized, among others.

humane and intelligent in the mind of the age.' The development of the middle ground was stunted. Apart from Kaldor and a few others, Cambridge heterodoxy offered little defence for any economy involving markets or a private sector. A pragmatic economics for a social-democratic mixed economy was slow to develop. It was overshadowed by abstract theory of little empirical relevance and an impractical and ill-informed socialist idealism.

CAMBRIDGE COLONIES WITHOUT THE CAMBRIDGE CITADEL

The victory of the Cambridge UK side in the capital theory debates in the late 1960s boosted the confidence of Cantabrigian heterodoxy. Robinson visited the US several times in the 1960s. Cantabrigian 'left-wing economics' (as some have described it) became international.

The Cambridge-inspired network involved prominent American post-Keynesians including Paul Davidson, Alfred Eichner, Jan Kregel, Edward Nell and Sidney Weintraub. Nell was introduced to Cambridge criticisms of neoclassical economics while at Oxford in the 1950s. Davidson corresponded with Robinson in the 1960s and he took study leave in Cambridge from 1970 to 1971. Influenced by Davidson, Kregel went to Cambridge for the 1968–69 academic year. Eichner worked on the theory and empirics of oligopoly and mark-up pricing. He contacted Robinson in 1969. Weintraub also engaged with Cambridge ideas (Lee, 2009, ch. 5).

In 1971 Robinson met Eichner and Luigi Pasinetti at Columbia University in New York. They agreed on further initiatives, including a meeting within the large forum of the Allied Social Science Association (which houses the American Economic Association and several other economics societies) in New Orleans in December 1971. Among the 17 attendees were Davidson, Eichner, Kregel, Nell and Hyman Minsky. These efforts, at which Robinson was at the centre, launched post-Keynesian economics in North America (Lee, 2009, ch. 5).

The *Journal of Post Keynesian Economics* was established in 1978, under the joint editorship of Davidson and Weintraub. They made links with other US-based heterodox groups, principally the (original) institutionalist Association for Evolutionary Economics and their *Journal of Economic Issues*, the Marxist-inspired Union for Radical Political Economics and their *Review of Radical Political Economics*, and with the

Association for Social Economics and their *Review of Social Economy.*
All these were pluralist, left-leaning heterodox networks (Lee, 2009,
ch. 5).

But the days of ascendant heterodoxy in Cambridge were numbered.
Its defeat resulted from external and internal forces. By 1975, Kaldor,
Robinson and Sraffa had all retired from their positions at Cambridge.
Their departure weakened an already-fragmented Cambridge heterodoxy.

The expansion of the UK university system was another factor. An
increase in the number of UK universities followed the Robbins Report
of 1963. A second wave of expansion began in the late 1980s. Overall
participation in higher education in the relevant age group more than
doubled from 3.4 per cent in 1950, to 8.4 per cent in 1970, and more
than doubled again to 19.3 per cent in 1990 (National Committee of
Inquiry into Higher Education, 1997). It has more than doubled again, to
over 40 per cent, in subsequent years. The expansion of the UK
university sector put pressure on the ancient Oxbridge universities. They
could no longer automatically assume pre-eminence.

This substantial expansion came too late to prevent a decisive shift of
intellectual dominance in economics from Britain to the US. The increase
in the number of UK universities, plus the conclusive shift of international leadership in economics to the US, put Cambridge economics
under pressure to adapt.

The Economic Journal was the most prestigious journal in this
discipline in the UK. It had been located at Cambridge since its
foundation in 1891. From 1912 to 1944 it was edited by Keynes. But
with its membership swelled by economists from the expanding UK
university sector, the Royal Economic Society decided to move the
journal away from Cambridge. This was accomplished in 1976. This
move was a major stimulus behind the launch in 1977 of the heterodox
and left-leaning *Cambridge Journal of Economics.*

While he was an undergraduate at Cambridge, Samuel Coldicutt
(2010) conducted interviews with several of the key participants in the
climactic Faculty battles of the 1980s. The Cambridge left were generally
better organized. To mobilize their potential support on the Faculty
Board, they would organize telephone canvasses of voters. By contrast,
the orthodox faculty members often did not agree on a single candidate
and hence their vote was split. Consequently, the left candidates for key
elections – most importantly for the Appointments Committee – were
often successful.

Robin Matthews was regarded as one of the more orthodox economists
in Cambridge. At the time he was on the University Council of the
Senate with influence over the General Board of the Faculties. He

proposed that the single transferable vote system (STV) be used in all elections throughout the university. Under STV, candidates are ranked in order of preference, and those with weaker support are eliminated one by one, each time transferring subsequent preferences to the remaining candidates. So even if the orthodox or 'right' vote were split between multiple candidates, STV meant that preferences could transfer to the remaining 'right' contenders. Matthews admitted in his interview with Coldicutt (2010, pp. 30–31) that while the introduction of STV was a rule that applied to the university as a whole, for him the undermining of heterodox control in the Faculty of Economics and Politics 'was the whole point' of the change. Although according to Harcourt (2017), Matthews expressed some regrets about the outcome in the Faculty.

As a result of this university-wide change of rules, the heterodox majority on the Faculty Board dwindled in 1987 and had disappeared for good by 1988. Another factor was the introduction of a national system for assessing university research, then known as the Research Assessment Exercise (RAE). The first nationwide RAE was held in 1986. With the second, held in 1989, the RAE became the primary means for determining public allocations of research funds to UK universities. The nationwide RAE panels charged with assessing university research in economics were dominated by orthodox economists from the beginning. Even if heterodoxy had held onto power in Cambridge, it would have faced the severe problem of orthodox dominance of the nationwide RAE.[27]

Under orthodox control, the Faculty made changes to the curricula and swelled their ranks with new orthodox appointments. While previously the MPhil exams at Cambridge were disposed towards questions on the economics of Sraffa, Robinson and other heterodox dissenters, these 'traces of heterodoxy were absent from MPhil examinations after 1998' (Coldicutt, 2010, p. 16). But of course, Keynesian approaches were still discussed in the macroeconomics curriculum.

Once orthodoxy became a serious challenge to the heterodox economists in Cambridge, they were forced to debate on some issues that were prominent elsewhere but had been relatively neglected in their previous teaching or research. As Harcourt pointed out in an interview: 'it's hard to be a heterodox economist because not only do you have to develop heterodoxy but you have to keep up to date with orthodoxy – you have double the work to do and this has worked against the left' (Coldicutt, 2010, p. 47).

---

[27]   The RAE has since been re-named the Research Excellence Framework (REF).

If it were not located in a prestigious faculty of a leading world university, it is doubtful that heterodox economics would have survived in Cambridge until the 1980s. Status and prestige made it possible to choose its own agenda and overlook some important ideas from elsewhere. Heterodox economists in other universities were less fortunate. But as the academic world moved on, research in economics became more global, and Cambridge was forced more and more to compete with leading universities elsewhere and abroad. This too was a factor in the termination of heterodox control.

CONCLUSION: THE EFFECTS OF ISOLATION AND EXCESSIVE POLITICIZATION

As academia expanded and globalized, it was perhaps inevitable that American-style orthodox economics would triumph in Cambridge. A relevant question is whether it would have been possible for Cambridge heterodoxy to adopt a strategy that could have led to a more pluralist outcome, where a significant heterodox contingent endured alongside a substantial orthodox block. Among other things, this would have allowed Cambridge economics to recruit students who were attracted by its heterodox tradition of thought, while giving them a fuller exposure to what was happening within orthodoxy as well.

A number of factors worked against a pluralist settlement of this kind. Some of the orthodox economists were intolerant of heterodox dissent, and this was a serious problem. But taking such intolerance as given, what could heterodoxy have done to improve the chances and extent of its survival?

Greater attention to microeconomics would have helped. But the leading Cambridge heterodox economists did little work on market mechanisms (except their major contributions in imperfect competition and pricing theory), or on public goods and externalities, or on alternatives to the utility-maximizing model of individual behaviour. This large microeconomic territory was mostly conceded to orthodoxy from the outset.

The heavy politicization of economic rhetoric by Cambridge heterodoxy did not help either. There was little if any justification for labelling heterodoxy as *left* and orthodoxy as *right*. It needlessly antagonized the orthodox wing. In an interview, Matthews complained that he had been labelled as *right*: 'I always objected to that designation because I never regarded myself as particularly right-wing – quite the contrary, I was a man of the left' (Coldicutt, 2010, p. 21). The false description of social democrat Hahn as *right* has already been noted above.

As another example, James Meade was a professor at Cambridge from 1957 to 1967. He then became a senior research fellow of Christ's College – a post he held until 1974. He became a Nobel Laureate in 1977. He was a Keynesian in macroeconomics while embracing neo-classical microeconomics. He was a strong exponent of worker cooperatives and an advocate of a mixed, market economy. Embracing neoclassical theory and a mixed economy did not go down well with many on the Cambridge left.

Johnson observed how economics theory had been overly embroiled with political ideology in Cambridge: 'Keynesian economics was not a theoretical advance to be built on for scientific progress and improved social policy. It was only a tool for furthering left-wing politics at the level of intellectual debate.' (Johnson and Johnson, 1978, p. 150).

Heightened political polarization pushed people to the extremes. Those with nuanced or intermediate positions became casualties. Johnson witnessed in Cambridge 'the suppression of the free spirit of scientific enquiry by the use or threat of a witch-hunt'. He continued:

> An economics profession in which people have to think 'before I dare to say what I think, I have to be sure that what I say will not damn me as hopelessly orthodox' is not one likely to discover new and important scientific truths. This baneful influence of concern about orthodoxy or heterodoxy as the hallmark of 'bad' or 'good' economics is vastly reinforced by the identification of Keynesian economics in Britain with left-wing or at least Labour party politics, and the politicization of economics that it has entailed. (Johnson and Johnson, 1978, p. 215).

Each side in the Cambridge battles bathed in the confirmation biases of like-minded thinkers. Groupthink encouraged searches for evidence to confirm a view, rather than to challenge it. Whole areas of research, which might have questioned each side's orthodoxy, were neglected. The value of political viewpoint diversity in the academy was under-unappreciated.

Any movement bears hallmarks from the context in which it was forged. As post-Keynesian and heterodox economics spread from Cambridge, some of their formative marks remained visible. Many of the Cambridge heterodox traits are found in its colonial outposts. We may summarize some of the important features of the strand of Cantabrigian thinking that spread from Cambridge from the 1970s, particularly under the leadership of Robinson:

1. Keynes and Marx were the main icons of Cantabrigian heterodoxy. Kalecki was a crucial additional figure who bridged the two, and Sraffa was important in his own right. Adopted versions of Keynesianism stressed state intervention, but had less to do with his liberalism and his defence of capitalism.

2. Generally, there was greater attention to macroeconomics than microeconomics. Among the few microeconomic topics that were explored were alternatives to marginalist pricing theory, particularly administered or mark-up pricing.

3. Among the neglected microeconomic issues were psychological theories of motivation that do not entail utility-maximization (such as Simon's version of behaviouralism). Also overlooked were the nature and role of property rights and other key institutions, in framing activity and providing incentives. The importance of knowledge in production and markets (as stressed in different ways by Marshall, Veblen and Hayek) was inadequately appreciated. Instead there was a widespread focus on physical coefficients in production processes.

4. Neoclassical theory was sometimes identified as being intrinsically pro-market, despite the strong socialist views of pioneering neoclassical theorists such as Arrow, Lange and Lerner.

5. The economic and political feasibility of democratic socialism was often taken for granted. Debates within economics about the viability of socialism were either ignored, or theoretical arguments questioning the feasibility of socialism were briefly dismissed. Despite heterodox opposition to neoclassical theory, the use of neoclassical general equilibrium models by defenders of socialism was overlooked.

6. Just as Marshall and Keynes were sceptical of the value of formal models (Hodgson, 2012, 2013d), Cambridge heterodoxy made less use of mathematical models than orthodox economists. But before the work of Tony Lawson (1997), the Cambridge arguments for the limitation of mathematics were unclear.

These six features were also prominent, albeit with exceptions and variations, in the outposts of heterodoxy that were established in North America, Europe and elsewhere, under the influence of Robinson, Sraffa and other leading Cambridge scholars. As demonstrated in the following chapter, and despite its internal heterogeneity and its failure to define itself clearly, heterodoxy still bears the marks of its Cambridge origins. But thrust into the world beyond Cambridge, it had magnified problems in maintaining its status and identity.

2. What is heterodox economics?

> Furthermore, although we can delineate very easily *homo sapiens* from, say, *panthera leo* (lion) because they do not breed, it is harder to delineate *economicus orthodoxus* from *economicus heterodoxus*
>
> Andrew Mearman (2012)

The aim of this chapter is not to appraise particular heterodox theories, but to address the meaning of *heterodox economics* and its current viability (or otherwise) as an organizing label. As several prominent exponents of heterodoxy have noted, there is little consensus on the meaning of the term. Obversely, the nature of *orthodox economics* has been construed in different ways, depending on ideological, theoretical, ontological or other considerations. This creates a problem in using *heterodox economics* as a label to organize critics of orthodoxy. Heterodox economics can legitimately and beneficially be diverse. But it is unlikely to make substantial progress unless the criteria of inclusion and the *raison d'être* are agreed, at least in some rough outline. Unfortunately, after several decades, such minimal agreement does not yet exist.

One might attempt to establish the nature of *orthodox economics* and define *heterodox economics* in opposition to a list of prominent orthodox claims or features. Alternatively, one may start with an attempted description of heterodoxy, and establish the nature of orthodoxy by comparison. Or the researcher may combine both moves. In any case, the meaning of *heterodox economics* implies a conception of *orthodox economics* and vice versa.[1]

Frederic Lee was one of the leaders and organizers of the heterodox movement. Lee (2009) charted the history of heterodox economics, addressing both its assumed substance and the past use of the label. The term *heterodox economics* became prominent as an organizing banner in the final quarter of the twentieth century, alongside other labels, particularly *post-Keynesian*. There is an Association for Heterodox Economics

---

[1] Dequech (2007) pointed out that if *mainstream* is not identical to *orthodox*, then it is possible to define heterodox economics as *non-mainstream*, with a different result.

(in Europe) and a Society for Heterodox Economics (in Australia). Prominent publishers such as Edward Elgar and Routledge use the label *heterodox economics* to market publications that are critical of the mainstream. The American Economic Association's *Journal of Economic Literature* has a classification system for research in economics, including category B5 – 'Current Heterodox Approaches'.[2]

But what does the *heterodox* label mean? Tony Lawson (2006, p. 484, emphasis in original) wrote that 'very few ... have questioned the nature of heterodox economics' and when queried 'it is recognised ... as an umbrella term to cover ... *separate* heterodox projects or traditions.' Andrew Mearman (2011, p. 480) analysed a survey of members of the Association for Heterodox Economics and found 'little agreement on any core concepts or principles' and 'that there is little structure to heterodox economics beyond that provided by pre-existing (or constituent) schools of thought' (which are, most importantly, post-Keynesianism and Marxism). Clive Spash and Anthony Ryan (2012) conducted a different survey that confirmed a similar result. The editors of *The Routledge Handbook of Heterodox Economics* concur that the question of the nature of heterodoxy 'has been the subject of a long-standing debate by heterodox economists although no consensus has been reached' (Jo et al., 2017, p. 8).

Given this lack of accord, one wonders what keeps the self-described 'heterodox' community together. It cannot be simply opposition to orthodoxy, as the heterodox are not themselves agreed on the nature of their adversary. Beyond a demand for greater pluralism in economics, and an opposition to whatever is described as orthodoxy, it is unclear upon what else heterodox economists agree.[3]

The *post-Keynesian* label has similar problems of definition and the two groups have a sizeable overlap in doctrine and membership (Lee, 2009). When the *post-Keynesian* label emerged in the 1970s it was understood to include a number of dissenting economists, including Marxists, institutionalists and (in some but not all accounts) Austrians (Davidson, 1980; King, 2002). Again, there was disagreement about its meaning and identity. Christopher Bliss (2010, p. 632) studied economics

   [2]   The American Economic Association's *Journal of Economic Literature* category B5 on 'Current Heterodox Approaches' includes the following subcategories: Socialist, Marxian, Sraffian, Historical, Institutional, Evolutionary, Austrian, Feminist Economics, Social Economics, and Other.
   [3]   There is now a large collection of literature on pluralism in economics, but Salanti and Screpanti (1997) remains an important and sometimes neglected early landmark.

in Cambridge in the 1960s and wrote: 'I did not recognize a post-Keynesian school in the Cambridge that taught me my economics. The reason could be that there was no such school.'

Lawson (2006, p. 484) argued that 'post-Keynesianism' is internally divided and inadequately defined. Attempts by post-Keynesians 'to produce substantive theories, policies or methodological stances have usually led to such a degree of variation or competition that post Keynesians, and their observers, have tended to conclude that the only definitive point of agreement among post Keynesians is that they stand opposed to mainstream or "neoclassical" contributions.' Lawson cited evidence in support of this claim, which suggests that both 'heterodox' and 'post-Keynesian' economics define themselves principally by their opposition to what are perceived as mainstream views. But some conceive post-Keynesianism more narrowly, as one heterodox approach among several, in contrast to 'heterodox economics' which has always embraced multiple perspectives.

Similar problems of definition and identity apply to some other heterodox approaches, including *evolutionary economics* as discussed in Chapter 4 below. But this present chapter gives more attention to the kind of *heterodox economics* that spread globally from Cambridge in the 1970s. It includes a discussion of the influence of ideology.

HETERODOX ECONOMICS – THE PROBLEM OF POLITICAL IDEOLOGY

In social science, if there were a one-to-one mapping of theoretical explanations on policy outcomes, and vice versa, where a particular theoretical approach sustained one unique type of policy stance, and a particular policy outcome pointed to a particular theoretical approach, then the establishment of the theoretical core of *heterodox economics* would imply a designated set of policy positions. These might cover prominent issues such as the roles or limitations of markets, different attitudes to macroeconomic austerity, and so on.

The outcome of this one-to-one mapping would provide both theoretical and policy grounds for distinguishing heterodoxy from orthodoxy. One could identify heterodoxy or orthodoxy by simply identifying policy stances. The contest between heterodoxy and orthodoxy would prominently be a battle between ideological positions. Each ideological standpoint would signal a corresponding theoretical position. Heterodoxy and orthodoxy would neatly divide in both theoretical and policy terms.

But things are not that simple. I join with Lawson (2006) in rejecting policy-driven demarcations of orthodoxy from heterodoxy. A one-to-one mapping is untenable. Many prominent theories can serve multiple policy outcomes, and particular policy outcomes can be defended from multiple, contrasting theoretical positions. The relationships between economic theory and policy are patterned by multiple links of many-to-one, one-to-many, and several-to-several.

Other attempts to link theory with policy start from the claim that 'facts are inseparable from values'. Of course, they are bound together. Scientists unavoidably make value-infused judgements over priorities, methods, assumptions and so on. But this does not mean that particular values imply particular theories, or that it is impossible to distinguish judgements (mostly) about facts from judgements (mostly) about values. If they were indistinguishable, then science would dissolve into ideology, and facts would be disempowered.

Of course, mainstream (that is, dominant) theory nowadays is often used to sustain free market policies. But numerous mainstream economists have not been free-marketeers. Many of the pioneers of mainstream economic theory were sympathetic to left ideas. Léon Walras called himself a 'scientific socialist' and advocated price regulation, worker cooperatives and the public ownership of natural monopolies, including of land. In the 1930s, a group of mainstream economists led by Oskar Lange used general equilibrium theory in attempts to demonstrate the viability of socialism.[4] Mainstream general equilibrium theory was the weapon of these socialists *against* the pro-market critics of planning in the Austrian School, including Ludwig Mises (1920, 1935) and Friedrich Hayek (1935, 1944, 1945).

As noted in the preceding chapter, leading general equilibrium theorists Kenneth Arrow and Frank Hahn declared their sympathies for various socialist and social-democratic economic policies. Indeed, Hahn and others have justified the whole mainstream general equilibrium theoretical project as an attempt to demonstrate the *limits* of the market mechanism. Some 'analytical Marxists' such as Jon Elster (1982, 1985, 1986), John Roemer (1986a, 1986b, 1988) and Erik Olin Wright (1994) have explicitly embraced mainstream tools of economic analysis, including rational choice, general equilibrium analysis and game theory. Hence mainstream economic theory has been used by several prominent *opponents* of free-market policies.

---

[4]   Lange (1936–37), Lange and Taylor (1938), Dickinson (1933, 1939), Lerner (1934, 1937, 1938).

Even today, mainstream theorists span the conventional political spectrum – from the pro-planning left to the pro-market right – and the mainstream, despite its biases, is not definable in terms of the policy stances of its adherents. While many mainstream economists advocate free-market policies, Nobel Laureates including Kenneth Arrow, Paul Krugman, Paul Samuelson and Joseph Stiglitz – all from mainstream positions – have favoured a mixed economy and supported Keynesian rather than austerity measures. Consequently, the evidence is stacked against the idea that there is a simple one-to-one mapping of theoretical positions onto policy outcomes.

Yet identifiable political currents within theoretically fragmented heterodoxy remain strong. Despite significant political diversity within heterodoxy, it is difficult to avoid the impression that there is a prominent political as well as a diverse theoretical agenda at work, which affects many heterodox economists. This will be considered below.

FREDERIC LEE ON THE NATURE OF HETERODOX ECONOMICS

The two most important attempts to define the nature of 'heterodox economics' are arguably by Lawson and Lee. While they overlap on some points, there are also major divergences between them.[5]

Lee (2009) did more than anyone else to document the *heterodox* tradition, to attempt to define its nature, and to organize it into a viable international movement. In his entry on this topic in the second edition of the *New Palgrave Dictionary of Economics*, Lee (2008) described heterodox economics as a tendency standing 'in some form of dissent relative to mainstream economics'.

In turn, for Lee (2008), 'mainstream theory is comprised of a core set of propositions – such as scarcity, equilibrium, rationality, preferences, and methodological individualism'. For Lee (2009, p. 7) mainstream economics assumes 'asocial, ahistorical individuals ... fictitious concepts ... a deductivist, closed-system methodology ... methodological individualism', a 'positivist ... methodology' and 'the concept of scarcity'.

---

[5] A commentator on a previous draft of the material presented in this chapter accused me in writing of making a 'seemingly personal attack' on Fred Lee. But a critique confined to someone's academic statements is not a personal attack. I knew Lee for over thirty years before his tragic death in 2014. Although we often differed on points of economics and politics, we retained a mutual respect, and we never attacked one another personally. Lawson and I also have our differences, but we have remained mutually respectful friends for over thirty years.

But there are many unanswered questions of necessary clarification. Consider some of Lee's defining terms. For him, heterodoxy is partly defined by its rejection of scarcity, but there is no recognition that the word has different meanings (Daly, 1974). Lionel Robbins (1932) elevated scarcity as a central principle of mainstream economics but was imprecise about its meaning. Clearly some material things, such as water and oil, are globally scarce, in the sense of being finite and limited. Critics have pointed out that other important resources such as love, trust and honour are not scarce in this sense. Their provision may create still more of the resource: love creates love and so on. But this is not an argument to abandon entirely the notion of scarcity. It is an argument to be more precise about its possible meanings.

There is a key distinction between local and global scarcity. Local scarcity arises because of the time and resources required to make use of a resource. Even if something is readily available – such as water in a tap – it takes time, energy, cognitive activity and a drinking vessel to organize its consumption. Love, trust and honour may not be globally limited, but we all know from personal experience that they can often be in local short supply. Global scarcity does not apply to everything, but it remains important because of the finite resources on our planet. In contrast, local scarcity is a universal feature of the human condition: it is part of our daily struggle to cope and survive. Lee's blanket denial of the concept of scarcity is unnuanced and untenable.

Consider Lee's claim that the rejection of 'methodological individualism' is a requirement of heterodoxy. This term is frequently bandied about but is understood in very different ways (Hodgson, 2007). Both its advocates and its critics routinely treat it as if it had a well-established meaning. The widespread heterodox rejection of 'methodological individualism' rarely clarifies what is being rejected.

It is often confused with ontological individualism – the notion that individuals are the only entities that make up a society. Ontological individualism is false because social relations, and institutions such as language, are also vital to socio-economic phenomena, and these cannot be reduced to individuals alone (Hodgson, 2007; Epstein, 2015). Ontology is about *being*. Methodology is about *explanation*.

While advocating methodological individualism, the Marxist academic Elster (1982, p. 453) defined it as 'the doctrine that all social phenomena (their structure and their change) are in principle explicable only in terms of individuals – their properties, goals, and beliefs.' This attempted definition is clearer than many rivals, but it still falls at one crucial hurdle. It fails to clarify whether interactions between individuals or social relations are 'properties … of individuals' or not. If neither individual interactions nor social relations are 'properties of individuals', then Elster's notion of methodological individualism envisages explanations in terms of individuals alone. But it is unclear whether Elster means this or not. A great deal hinges on this issue: does methodological individualism simply point to the importance of individuals and their relationships in explanations of social phenomena, or does it insist that explanations should ultimately be reduced to individuals alone?

It turns out that many advocates of methodological individualism explicitly or implicitly require explanations in terms of individuals *and* social relations. Clearly-stated requirements of explanation in terms of individuals *alone* are rare (Hodgson, 2007). As Kenneth Arrow (1994) pointed out, successful explanations of social or economic phenomena in terms of individuals alone are unknown and unlikely, as social relations must always be brought into the picture as well. There are always structured communications and other interactions between individuals. Consequently, we must always seek explanations in terms of individuals *and* social relations.

With this realization, the beast of methodological individualism can be tamed. Given that social structures are typically defined in terms of social relations (Porpora, 1989), a 'methodological individualism' that calls for explanations in terms of individuals *and* social relations is equivalent to promoting explanations in terms of individuals *and* social structures. Adequate explanations of social phenomena should involve individuals as well as social structures or relations. Nothing is wrong with that, surely? Yet many of its advocates would define this stance as methodological individualism.

The remaining objection to this tamed and highly capacious version of 'methodological individualism' is that it is mis-labelled. While both individuals and social relations are involved, only individualism remains in its name. The fault here lies in the biased label, not necessarily in the accommodating substance (Hodgson, 2007).

Political individualism is a normative doctrine about the worth or rights of individuals; in some versions it proposes a limited role for government. Some advocates of what they call *methodological individualism* seem inclined to use the label because of their adherence to political individualism. Obversely, some opponents of what they call *methodological individualism* seem motivated by their opposition to political individualism. In fact, there is no logical connection between methodological and political individualism. Choosing or rejecting one does not necessitate the adoption or refusal of the other (Lukes, 1973).

In sum, Lee's claim that *methodological individualism* is a key characteristic of the mainstream is as imprecise and ambiguous as the term itself: there is no consensus on its meaning.

Consider Lee's accusation that orthodoxy uses 'fictitious concepts' while heterodoxy does not. The meaning of 'fictitious' is also imprecise. Some writers argue that many useful economic theories are 'fictitious' to the extent that they make simplifications that do not exactly correspond to reality (Mäki, 1992, 1994; Sugden, 2000). Given that a theory can never embrace all the details and complexity, abstractions and simplifications must always be made. This applies to heterodox as well as to orthodox theory.

In his important research on price theory, Lee promoted the theory of administered pricing that was developed by Gardiner C. Means in the 1930s. Lee co-edited a major collection of Means' writings (Lee and Samuels, 1992). These essays by Means are not without fictions. For example, Means wrote: 'As a device for simplifying the process of tracing through implications of rigid prices, four different abstract economies will be envisaged' (Lee and Samuels, 1992, p. 127). Surely this must be fictitious, because the described abstract economies have never existed, and are unlikely to exist in their simplified form?

Simply condemning 'fictions' is too blunt. It would be more sensible to suggest that, just as physicists often calculate velocities in an always-fictitious absolute vacuum, all theory must make some simplifications or abstractions of a kind. The real dispute is over what fictions are tolerable or appropriate.

Positivism – yet another of Lee's undefined characteristics of orthodoxy – is also a highly ambiguous term. *The Oxford English Dictionary* correctly defines positivism as: 'A system of philosophy elaborated by Auguste Comte from 1830 onwards, which recognizes only positive facts and observable phenomena, with the objective relations of these and the laws that determine them, abandoning all inquiry into causes or ultimate origins …'. With this reputable definition (Lenzer, 1998, p. xiv), little if any orthodox economics would qualify as positivist. Unlike the original, Comtean positivism, much orthodox economics is not about observable facts but mathematical models. When orthodox economics engages with facts, as it often does, then again, unlike Comtean positivism, it does not generally abandon the search for causal explanations of the phenomena. Orthodox economics is far from positivist in the original Comtean sense. But of course, the word *positivism* has been since twisted and turned in so many ways that anything might qualify as positivist, including much of heterodox economics. Lee's blunt account is of little help in guiding us through this mess.

ABANDONING PLURALISM: CRITICAL REALISM IS COMPULSORY

Other criteria fare little better. According to Lee, orthodoxy is 'deductivist' and heterodoxy is not. In philosophy, deduction refers to the logical process of establishing the validity of a conclusion from a set of premises which are assumed to be true. By *deductivism*, most philosophers mean the claim that logical deduction is the royal road to truth. Hence it could refer to the axiomatic or a priori approach that dominates much of mainstream economics, where assumptions are made, and mathematical models are built upon them. Some Austrian economists, such as Ludwig Mises (1949), defended another form of *a priorism* or deductivism that uses concepts and logic, but not mathematical models.

But in his influential account of *critical realism*, Lawson (1997, pp. 16–17) defined deductivism in a strikingly different manner, as presuming 'event regularities' or 'constant conjunctions of events or states of affairs' with regularities of the form 'whenever event *x* then event *y*'. This is a philosophically atypical definition of deductivism, because it refers to empirical regularities concerning events rather than logical deductions concerning propositions. Wade Hands (2001, p. 323 n.) noted that Lawson's use of the term *deductivism* 'is different from the way in which the term is generally used within the philosophical literature'. Hands (2001, p. 327) suggested, and Matthew Wilson (2005) argued more fully, that neoclassical economics does not fit Lawson's characterization of *deductivism*.

Although Lee (2016) himself tried to synthesize critical realism with other approaches, he saw the adoption of critical realism as an essential qualification for being a heterodox economist. This seems to allow for no dissent from critical realism among the heterodox. Are other philosophical approaches, including other versions of scientific realism, orthodox? So much for pluralism: the alternative options disappear when it comes to philosophy.

Notions of *open* and *closed* system are central to critical realism. Consider the meaning of *open system*. The distinction between an open and a closed system became prominent with the rise of systems theory, where, for pioneers in this field, a 'system is closed if no material enters or leaves it; it is open if there is import and export and, therefore, change of the components' (Bertalanffy, 1950, p. 23). The leading philosopher Mario Bunge (1979, p. 9) adopted a similar definition: 'A system that neither acts on nor is acted upon by any other thing is said to be closed'.

These definitions rest on fundamental ontological characteristics, rather than descriptions at the level of events.

In contrast, for all its emphasis on underlying ontology, critical realism adopts an event-level definition of one of its central concepts. Following Roy Bhaskar's (1975, p. 70) characterization of a closed system 'as one in which a constant conjunction of events obtains', Lawson (1997, p. 19) described closed systems in the terms of event regularities 'whenever event *x* then event *y*'. In a critical response, Victoria Chick and Sheila Dow (2005, p. 373) wrote: 'The difference between us and the critical realists lies in defining openness and closure in terms of the structure of the system versus its manifestation or outcome'.[6]

Lee asserted that mainstream economics adopts a 'closed-system methodology'. This would suggest an 'open-system methodology' as a defining heterodox alternative. But no one has yet adequately explained what an 'open-system methodology' would look like and how *any* theory could avoid some assumptions of isolation or closure (Mäki, 1992). Chick and Dow (2005) suggested that there are different open-system methodologies, depending on the sense in which a system is viewed as being open. An adequate picture of 'open-system methodology' has not yet been revealed. So far there is no consensus on what this means and how it would be deployed in practical cases. Yet Lee and other heterodox economists have insisted that an 'open-systems methodology' is a key characteristic of heterodoxy. Such statements seem more ceremonial than operational.

SOME MAJOR HETERODOX STREAMS HAVE GONE MISSING

Lee (2009, p. 7) concluded that heterodox economics comprises 'a group of heterodox theories – specifically Post Keynesian-Sraffian, Marxist-radical, Institutional-evolutionary, social, feminist, Austrian and eco-logical economics'.[7] His list was more inclusive than others. For instance, post-Keynesians are themselves divided on whether they

---

6   See Fleetwood (2017), Mearman (2006) and Pratten (2007) for further critical discussions of the meaning of an open system.
7   Feminist economics emerged in the 1980s (Waring, 1988). But this includes a range of theoretical approaches, including mainstream general equilibrium models, mainstream game theory and mainstream econometrics, as well as including strong insights that challenge mainstream assumptions (Woolley, 1993; Peterson and Lewis, 1999).

include work inspired by Sraffa (1960), Marxist economics or the Austrian School under their label.[8]

Despite ranging from Austrians to Marxists, some non-mainstream schools were excluded from Lee's heterodox listing. When Lee (2009, p. 7) mentioned 'institutional-evolutionary' approaches, he implied those inspired by the original institutionalists, such as those organized in the Association for Evolutionary Economics (AFEE) and in the European Association for Evolutionary Political Economy (EAEPE). Lee (2009) made no explicit mention of the new institutional economics or its leading authors. This suggests that his use of the term 'institutional' refers solely to the original institutional economics.

But by some criteria, leading 'new' institutional economists such as Douglass North, Ronald Coase, Elinor Ostrom and Oliver Williamson can also be regarded as heterodox. For example, Coase (1977, 1988) discarded utility maximization and was sceptical about the use of mathematics in economics. North (1990, 1994) in his later writings rejected neoclassical theory. Yet Lee does not mention any of them in his *History of Heterodox Economics*.

There is also no explicit mention of the 'evolutionary economics' of Richard Nelson and Sidney Winter (1982) in Lee's *History*. The irony here is that the original institutionalist Thorstein Veblen (1898a) coined the term 'evolutionary economics' and there are resemblances between the work of Veblen and that of Nelson and Winter (Eaton, 1984; Hodgson, 2004a).[9]

Given Lee's rejection of utility maximization, it is also strange that there is no reference in Lee's (2009) book to the behavioural economics of Herbert Simon. Simon (1957, 1959) was a strong critic of the rationality assumption in mainstream economics and to a degree his work was inspired by the original institutional economics (Rutherford, 2001;

---

[8] In 2014 the author asked leading post-Keynesians Philip Arestis, Fernando Carvallo, Sheila Dow, Gary Dymski, Geoffrey Harcourt, Mark Hayes, Mark Lavoie, Edward Nell and Engelbert Stockhammer whether they regarded Sraffian economics as part of post-Keynesianism. Six agreed, two answered in the negative, and another was unsure. Seven of the nine excluded Austrian economics from post-Keynesianism, despite the Austrians and Keynesians sharing a strong interest in uncertainty and expectations. The respondents were more evenly split on whether Marxian (three 'yes' versus four 'no') or institutional (four 'yes' versus four 'no') economics were included.

[9] 'Evolutionary economics' also has its own problems as an organizing label. See Chapter 4 below and Hodgson and Lamberg (2018).

Hodgson, 2004a). Similarly, Lee rejected 'equilibrium' but there is no mention of the classic work on *Anti-Equilibrium* by János Kornai (1971).[10]

Another major omission is the work of Amartya Sen (1977, 1979), who is another highly important critic of the behavioural assumptions of orthodox economic theory, including of rationality and maximization, and of their welfare implications.

Finally, Lee made little of the *régulation* school, which has been an important development in France and has had a significant broader influence (Boyer and Mistral, 1978; Aglietta, 1979; Orléan, 1994). Nevertheless, partly perhaps because of its leftist or Marxist overtones, the *régulation* school has inspired heterodox scholars in North America, Europe and Japan (Jessop, 1997a, 1997b, 2001; Boyer and Yamada, 2000). Although the French *régulation* school and Cantabrigian heterodoxy have a different genealogy and flavour, they both stress macroeconomics over microeconomics.

To his credit, Lee (1998) has given more attention than most heterodox economists to microeconomics. But even when the flaws in neoclassical microeconomics are listed directly in a journal article, to 'dispel ignorance ... of damning criticisms ... of neoclassical microeconomic theory', there is mention of neither Simon nor Sen (Lee and Keen, 2004, p. 170). Utility maximization is critiqued in one paragraph of this article, making the plausible but vague points that preference functions are 'socially constructed' and interdependent (Lee and Keen, 2004, pp. 174–5). But this is not nearly enough to overturn the postulate of utility maximization, particularly in the inclusive and more sophisticated versions presented by Samuel Bowles (2004) or by Herbert Gintis and Dirk Helbing (2015).

Lee is not alone. A similar (but not identical) pattern is repeated elsewhere by different heterodox authors. In their collection of interviews with heterodox economists Andrew Mearman et al. (2019) included a dialogue with evolutionary economist Ulrich Witt. But no one in the collection of interviews mentioned the work of Richard Nelson and Sidney Winter. It is possible (but not proven) that this silence is in part due to ideology, as Nelson and others have stressed the benefits of competition and markets, as well as their major limitations (Nelson, 1981, 2003, 2005).

---

[10] Kornai (2006) abandoned classical socialism and communism in the 1950s and moved towards a liberal position.

The only interviewee in the Mearman et al. (2019) volume to mention Herbert Simon was Esther-Mirjam Sent, who does not regard herself as a heterodox economist. Sen is given the briefest mention by one interviewee (S. Charusheela). Kornai is unmentioned throughout. The word *utilitarianism* does not appear, despite it being at the core of mainstream economics. By contrast, the name Marx (or derivatives) appears 130 times in the text and Keynes (or derivatives) appears 222 times. A notion that is central to mainstream economics, which might have been addressed critically, denoted by *utility functions* or *utility maximization* receives a scant mention of six times, three of which are by one interviewee (Anwar Shaikh). The omissions bear an uncanny resemblance to those found in Cambridge heterodoxy and in Lee's (2009) work. The dominance of Marx, Keynes and macroeconomics persists.

LEE AND THE STRUGGLE AGAINST CAPITALISM

The highly political nature of Lee's *heterodox economics* is obvious from reading his *History*. On many pages he documents past efforts to spread the teaching of Marxist economics outside as well as inside universities. He relates how Marxist and other socialist economists were persecuted for their beliefs, including under McCarthyism in the US. Symptomatically, his *History* is not confined to academia. For Lee, heterodox economics was not simply a scientific endeavour but also part of the global struggle against capitalism.

Lee's project was to bring a wide community of heterodox scholars together, with a view that the logic of heterodox criticism would lead to a critique of capitalism. For example, Lee (2002, p. 129) argued that 'radical Post Keynesians' – unlike Keynes himself – draw the conclusion that capitalism should be 'replaced': '[The] complete Post Keynesian macro-micro theory of capitalism portrays the state largely as a servant of the business community and the capitalist class. The implication that radical Post Keynesians draw from this is that capitalism cannot be made to work better, rather it must be completely changed.'

Lee conceived neoclassical economics as pro-capitalist, and saw heterodoxy as immanently impelled to take an anti-capitalist stance. But in his later accounts, Lee admitted the Austrian School into the heterodox camp, and these economists have typically defended a market economy. Lee was aware of this internal tension.[11]

---

[11] I knew Lee since 1980 and he often argued that Austrian economists were neoclassical. But sometime before 2008 he accepted them as heterodox.

Lee's political project is also evident from the (simplistic and inaccurate) way in which he linked different schools of thought in the history of economics to different, class-based ideologies. Hence Lee (2012, p. 344) claimed that 'neoclassical theory emerged in political opposition to classical economics' where the latter 'was providing aid and comfort to the class enemies of the larger property owners ... coupled to organized opposition to capitalism itself.' By this opposition to capitalism from 'classical economics', presumably Lee was referring to radical Ricardians such as Thomas Hodgskin and perhaps to the influence of the classical writers upon Marx.

Lee continued: 'Early neoclassical theory attempted to defend capitalism through its individualist, exchange-based approach in which economic actors are depicted as equals pursuing their interests through uncoerced mutually beneficial exchange.' Then, according to Lee (2012, p. 344), waves of heterodoxy began to challenge the prevailing capitalist order:

> Marxism, then Institutionalism and the left-wing Keynesians, and after 1970 heterodox economics argued that the social provisioning process can and should be altered in favor of the disadvantaged, the victims of discrimination, the unemployed and poorly employed, and the working and dependent classes of society. This would require more than economic efficiency; it would require altering state-property social relationships. It is this threat that emanates from heterodox theory which mainstream theory must counter; and this 'social duty' is inculcated into mainstream economists from the day they attend their first economics lectures. The critics fail to acknowledge this fundamental divide between mainstream and heterodox economics.

Hence Lee depicted mainstream economics as a defence of capitalism and heterodox economics as part of the struggle against it. He was not alone in this view. It was noted in the preceding chapter that Joan Robinson and John Eatwell (1973, pp. 47, 336) saw neoclassical economics as a defence of *laissez-faire*. Others take a similar view. For example, in an essay on 'neoclassical economics', Dimitris Milonakis (2012, p. 251) concluded: 'Deep down ... it is the very nature of the [capitalist] system and the ideological need for its justification that lies behind this type of theory.'

From the 1890s to the 1930s, the dominant form of neoclassical economics was Marshallian. There was greater pluralism within economics under Marshallian dominance. As Sheila Dow (2011b, p. 1158) put it: 'Marshall arguably had an open-system ontology, which led him to use only partial equilibrium models and to use verbal analysis.' She also pointed to Marshall's positive influence on Keynesian economics. There are strong grounds for a heterodox rehabilitation of Marshall, rather than his dismissal as a capitalist lackey (Hodgson, 2013b).

Yet Lee, Robinson, Eatwell, Milonakis and others saw mainstream economics as defending capitalism. On this basis, Lee saw few grounds for compromise: 'heterodox theory is fundamentally distinct from mainstream theory' and this alleged distinction operates on both theoretical and political levels (Lee, 2012, p. 347). This dramatic depiction of heterodoxy, as part of the class struggle to change capitalism, led Lee (2008, 2009, 2012) to suggest that heterodox economists should not engage with their mainstream colleagues: 'heterodox economics is not out to reform mainstream economics' (Lee, 2008). A similar stance is taken by the editors of *The Routledge Handbook of Heterodox Economics* (Jo et al., 2017).

Apart from the questionable analysis and politics behind this stance, it is challengeable as an academic strategy. Imagine a heterodox biology or physics that declared it did not want to change mainstream biology or physics. The mainstream scientists would give such heterodoxies short shrift. Critical engagement between orthodoxy and heterodoxy would decline, and the scientific development of heterodoxy through conversation would be impaired.

Lee's view of neoclassical theory as pro-capitalist sits uneasily with the widespread de facto adoption of neoclassical economics by advocates of socialism. Like his precursors from Cambridge, Lee gave little attention to the socialist calculation debate, where defenders of socialism used neoclassical general equilibrium models to make their case. Lee also overlooked the fact that other pioneering neoclassical economists, such as Oskar Lange, Abba Lerner and Kenneth Arrow (1978) were strong defenders of socialism.

Furthermore, Lee (like others) neglected the 'analytical Marxism' of Elster, Roemer, Wright and others, who used neoclassical models and game theory in efforts to sustain Marxist ideas and leftist policies (Elster, 1982, 1985, 1986; Roemer 1986a, 1986b, 1988; Wright, 1994). Despite their prominent academic efforts to develop and promote Marxism, neither Elster, Roemer nor Wright are mentioned in Lee's *History*. Awkward cases like this are simply ignored.

TONY LAWSON ON THE NATURE OF HETERODOX ECONOMICS

Lawson is the leading exponent and developer of critical realism among economists. He is also one of the most important economic methodologists to work at Cambridge University. He used Bhaskar's critical realism to develop a major critique of mainstream economic thought. Overall, Lawson's (2004, 2006) attempt to pin down the nature of heterodox economics is more systematic than Lee's.

Lawson's approach is based on ontological considerations, from which he drew conclusions concerning the use of mathematics, in situations where it is allegedly inappropriate. In contrast to Lee, he persuasively rejected the idea of defining orthodoxy in terms of support for 'status quo ideology', claiming that theories should not be classified exclusively in terms of the purposes or policies that they serve. Furthermore, as Lawson rightly recognized, the mainstream is itself highly diverse in ideological and policy terms.

Lawson also eschewed the view that mainstream orthodoxy can be defined in terms of one or more core assumptions. He rejected any definition of orthodoxy centred on rational, optimizing behaviour. Lawson (2006, p. 488) approvingly cited claims by John Davis (2005) and David Colander et al. (2004, p. 485) that mainstream economics is 'moving away from strict adherence to the holy trinity – rationality, selfishness, and equilibrium'. Even in terms of its core theory, mainstream economics is seen as mutable.

These arguments by Colander, Davis and others are contested in the following chapter. If the criticism there holds water, then Lawson's grounds for rejecting core assumptions such as utility maximization as defining for orthodoxy are undermined. But my main intention at this point is simply to register a concern with Lawson's quick dismissal of the possibility of defining orthodoxy in terms of some version of utility maximization.

Lawson's rejection of any definition of orthodoxy in terms of utility maximization, or any other basic assumptions, is necessary to clear the space for his crucial ontological argument. For Lawson (2006, p. 492) 'the mainstream project of modern economics just is an insistence, as a discipline-wide principle, that economic phenomena be investigated using only certain mathematical-deductive forms of reasoning. This is the mainstream conception of proper economics.' Lawson (2006, p. 493) claimed that 'mathematical methods are being imposed in situations for which they are largely inappropriate.' The 'formalistic models that economists wield mostly require, for their application, the existence (or positing) of closed systems'.

Lawson's 2006 article is an important extension of Lawson's (1997) earlier thesis on economic theory and reality. This argument has been widely debated.[12] As noted above, Lawson adopted unusual definitions of 'deductivism' and 'closed system'. Leaving these controversies aside, Lawson's (2006, pp. 493, 592) impressive and novel conclusion is that *'the essence of the heterodox opposition is ontological in nature'* and 'modern heterodoxy is, *qua* heterodoxy, first and foremost an orientation in ontology.'

This created an orthodox–heterodox demarcation, where the former imposes mathematical methods 'in situations for which they are largely inappropriate', and, by contrast, the latter either minimizes the use of mathematics, or it uses mathematics on the condition that a 'closed system' is approximated. Crucially, Lawson (2003, pp. 21, 178) also suggested that such approximations to a 'closed system' are 'seemingly rare' or 'rather rare' in reality.

Lawson (2003, pp. xix, 27, 178–9; 2006, p. 49; 2009, p. 19) has repeatedly insisted that he was not 'anti-mathematics' in principle. Instead, he is against the 'abuse' of mathematics and against the dogmatic insistence by the mainstream that mathematics must always be used.

But these statements have to be read alongside his own explicit criteria for when it is appropriate to use mathematics. He argued that mathematics would be appropriate for economics only in the extraordinary circumstances of approximation to what he called a 'closed system'. To repeat: Lawson (2003, pp. 21, 178) regarded the appropriate circumstances for the use of mathematics as 'seemingly rare' or 'rather rare'.

Lawson (2006) argued that while the heterodox camp is divided into multiple schools, they each make (explicit or implicit) ontological claims that imply that mathematical modelling is difficult or inappropriate. For example, post-Keynesians emphasize radical uncertainty (ruling out calculable probabilities),[13] the original institutionalists underline evolution in open systems (Kapp, 1976), and so on. Lawson accepted a division of labour within heterodoxy, where different heterodox strands commonly resist the pull of inappropriate mathematical formalization and together create a richer picture of 'open' economic reality.

---

[12] For critical views and responses see Chick and Dow (2005), Wilson (2005), Hodgson (2006b, ch. 7), Mearman (2006), Pratten (2007), Fullbrook (2009), Mohun and Veneziani (2012) and Fleetwood (2017). Objectors have argued that all (formalized) theory involves some assumption of closure or isolation, and some theories still manage to be useful, particularly as heuristics. Sugden (2000) argued that theory can be useful without claiming to represent or predict reality.

[13] We cannot discuss here the interesting claim by Brady and Arthmar (2012) that Keynesian uncertainty can be captured mathematically by an interval probability, in contrast to the point probability of a risk.

LIMITATIONS OF LAWSON'S ARGUMENT

Elsewhere I have put a lengthier case against Lawson's overall argument (Hodgson, 2006b, ch. 7). This section is a brief summary of the central points.

Lawson was right to emphasize that the real world is complex and open, and that its future evolution is uncertain (in the Keynesian sense). But this does not imply that any theory we use to analyse the real world must be complex, open or uncertain. In contrast, Lawson (2003, p. 22) suggested that theory must '"fit" with reality'. Yet theories are neither maps nor templates of reality, even if it is important that their assumptions resemble reality in some way. Instead, constructive theories are attempts to understand reality, which in turn may help us intervene in practice.

Lawson (2003, p. 12) based his critique of formalism on an ontological mismatch between formal models and reality: 'Few people ... would attempt to use a comb to write a letter ... or a drill to clean a window'. Of course, we use a pen to write a letter and a clean cloth to clean a window. Yet the ontology of pens is very different from that of letters, and there is also a big ontological difference between clean cloths and dirty windows. Lawson assumed, but made no argument, that the ontological characteristics of reality (such as complexity and openness) must be fully reflected somehow in the theory. But this assumption has no automatic warrant: theory and reality are different things.

I agree with Lawson's (2003, p. 12) implicit claim that theories are intellectual and practical instruments. But there is nothing in his appropriateness-of-tools argument that rules out using closed models to help to understand an open reality. He failed to establish that the openness of the real world requires us to adopt a theory that is 'open' in some sense.

Indeed, full openness in a theory may not be possible. All theory involves a degree of abstraction, isolation or closure – that is, some things must be left out of the picture (Mäki, 1992, 1994). Lawson (1997, p. 236) accepted part of this, but he attempted to force a distinction between 'isolation' and 'abstraction', depending on whether the omissions are 'temporary' or not. This distinction is spurious, because all theory can move on as a science develops, and hence potentially *all* omissions have a temporary character. Even if a theorist shuns the need to make the theory more comprehensive, then that does not make the omission permanent. Other researchers can fill gaps. Evaluation of a theory should not depend on whether the theorist intended at some stage to relax a restrictive assumption. That would be judging the personality of the theorist and not the suitability of the theory.

Lawson focused on the limitations of econometrics, which are very pertinent, given the complexity and openness of economic systems and the consequent and notorious difficulties of prediction. But he neglected the heuristic roles of many other formal models, which are not designed to predict, but to identify possible causal mechanisms that form part of a more complex system. Heuristics can be useful without necessarily making adequate predictions or closely matching existing data. Their purpose is to illustrate a plausible segment of a whole causal story, without necessarily giving an adequate or complete explanation of the phenomena to which they relate. Consequently, there is a role here for (closed) formal theory, despite the complexity and openness of the world (Sugden, 2000).

Lawson also neglected the use of formalism in internal critiques. Generally, the impact of an effective internal critique is negative rather than positive; it shows the limits of an existing theory rather than providing a new one. For example, in their critique of mainstream capital theory, Piero Sraffa (1960), Pierangelo Garegnani and others developed models with disaggregated physical capital and showed that relevant aggregate measures are dependent on profits, wages or prices. Consequently, any attempt to explain profits, wages or prices by means of such aggregated capital variables must assume that which it has to explain.

As another example, Rolf Mantel (1974) and others showed formally that even with the assumption of individual utility-maximization, there is no basis in standard general equilibrium theory for the assumption that demand functions are generally downward-sloping. Their devastating mathematical work brought the micro-foundations project in general equilibrium theory to an end (Kirman, 1989; Rizvi, 1994a). Such internal critiques do not themselves provide new theories, although they may establish some relevant pointers. Like heuristics, internal critiques are not claiming to map the real world. Instead, they are attempts to show that particular theories are inadequate or overly restrictive. Sometimes they indirectly play a positive role by getting science to search for a superior theory.

In sum, Lawson wrongly assumed that if reality is open (in some sense), then theories that are used to analyse reality must also be open. But it is neither possible nor desirable that theory should mirror reality in such a manner. Lawson provided no argument to sustain the proposition that ontological characteristics in reality should somehow be incorporated or reflected in a good theory. Even if we are concerned that theoretical assumptions should be as realistic as possible, then this does not mean that theory can be a mirror of reality. Theories are instruments of understanding and engagement: they are not reflections.

The potential value of heuristics and internal critiques further undermines Lawson's central argument. Such theoretical efforts are not intended to be realistic. Heuristics illustrate actual or possible mechanisms. Internal critiques show the limitations of existing theories in their own terms.

The problem with mainstream economics is not its use of mathematics as such, but its elevation of the development of formal techniques over the analysis and understanding of reality (Blaug, 1997). Lawson does not rule out the use of mathematics in principle, but his criteria for its possible inclusion – depending on approximations of 'closure' in reality – are overly restrictive.

WHO IS HETERODOX BY LAWSON'S FOREMOST CRITERION?

Further debate over the details of Lawson's significant contribution need not detain us here. Whatever the veracity of his argument, it is important to consider more fully its implications. Even if he is right, it has further consequences, which Lawson himself did not elaborate and the heterodox community might find unacceptable.

Consider first the example of Coase, who is described by Lawson (2006, pp. 492–3) in one passage as a 'mainstream contributor' alongside Ariel Rubinstein, Edward Leamer and Wassily Leontief. But unlike the other three, Coase did not use mathematics. In fact, Coase (1988, p. 185) ridiculed the excessive use of mathematics in economics: 'In my youth it was said that what was too silly to be said may be sung. In modern economics it may be put into mathematics.' Consequently, by Lawson's own argument, but contrary to Lawson's own designation, Coase would seem to qualify as a heterodox economist.

The problems do not stop there. The dominance of mathematical formalism in economics is relatively recent. Mark Blaug (2003) and others have dated its inception to the 1950s. In fact, few economists made much use of mathematics before the 1930s. Several prominent economists – including Marshall and his student Keynes – explicitly regarded mathematics as a highly limited tool (Hodgson, 2012). Lawson's criterion would seem to suggest that most economists, from Smith to Marshall, were 'heterodox'.

Even after the 'formalist revolution' of the 1950s, a substantial number of influential economists have concentrated on words rather than equations. As with Coase, there is little mathematics in the works of Douglass North, Oliver Williamson or Elinor Ostrom, all of whom won Nobel Prizes for their research in the new institutional economics. The works of Richard Posner are also frequently cited in leading economics journals: but he made little use of mathematics.

Others made some use of mathematics but also saw its limitations. Several of Milton Friedman's works made relatively little use of mathematics, and he complained that 'economics has become increasingly an arcane branch of mathematics rather than dealing with real economic problems' (Friedman, 1999, p. 137). Frank Hahn (1991, p. 50) predicted a state of diminishing mathematical returns for future economists: 'less frequently for them the pleasures of theorems and proof. Instead the uncertain embrace of history and sociology and biology.'

We may add numerous additional examples. By Lawson's criterion, there is a case for regarding most pre-1930 economists and at least some work by many famous and lauded post-1930 economists as 'heterodox'. Yet, whatever the merits of Lawson's classification, names such as Coase, Hayek, North, Ostrom and Williamson are rarely regarded as 'heterodox economists'. Lawson's logic leads to heterodox boundaries very different from those described by Lee.

Consider the contrasting criteria of heterodoxy proposed by Roger Backhouse (2000, p. 149). According to him, a heterodox economist must claim 'to be working in a way that does not fit in with the dominant way of doing economics, or to be offering an alternative that is incompatible with this'. Consequently, 'the new institutional economics fails the self-identification criterion and is arguably based on some core beliefs about the economy that are shared with most orthodox economists.' In contrast, Lawson's criteria would put Coase, North and Williamson down as heterodox.[14]

Despite the strong explicit backing of critical realism within the heterodox community, there seems much less support for Lawson's definition of heterodoxy. Lawson's exclusion of Sraffian and post-Keynesian mathematicians from the heterodox camp contrasts with their widespread (but not universal) inclusion, by Lee and others. There are

[14] Backhouse's (2000) argument over-simplifies, because, as noted above, Coase (1977, 1988) spurned the assumption of utility maximization and North (1990, 1994) eventually criticized what he described as 'neoclassical' theory. But, keen to maintain orthodox respectability, many new institutional economists who draw inspiration from Coase or North make less of these rebellious outbursts.

many economists, notably from Cambridge as well as elsewhere, who are critical of mainstream theoretical approaches but use mathematics or econometrics. They dislike being classified as orthodox. Other concerns would arise if it were realized that the logic of Lawson's argument would also include Nobel Laureates such as Coase, Hayek, North, Ostrom and Williamson as heterodox.

More than a decade has passed since two of Lawson's (2004, 2006) key articles on this topic and it does not seem that his definition of heterodoxy has become widely adopted. Contrary to his ontological demarcation, mathematical modelling and econometrics are still widespread among those who describe themselves as heterodox.

In a later paper, Lawson (2013, p. 979) noted the presence of critics of the mainstream 'who prioritise the goal of being realistic, and yet who fail themselves fully to recognise or to accept the limited scope for any … approach … that makes significant use of methods of mathematical deductive modelling'. This is an admission that a significant part of the heterodox community does not conform to Lawson's own strictures.

For their book entitled *What is Heterodox Economics?* Mearman et al. (2019) interviewed sixteen economists. They found that three (Edward Fullbrook, Joan Martinez-Alier and Esther-Mirjam Sent) rejected the *heterodox* label as a description of their position. Lawson was one of the thirteen interviewees who accepted the heterodox description. Only one of the remaining twelve (Sheila Dow) expressed agreement with Lawson's argument that the difference between orthodoxy and heterodoxy is fundamentally ontological and it concerns the (mis)use of mathematics. By contrast, another of these twelve (Gary Mongiovi) explicitly disagreed with Lawson's argument. Despite every interviewee being asked their view of what heterodox economics is, and how it differs from mainstream economics, none of the remaining ten mentioned Lawson or critical realism.

Consider *The Routledge Handbook of Heterodox Economics*. Neither *critical realism* nor *ontology* appear in its index, but there is a brief discussion of ontological issues at the end, where Lawson's work is mentioned (Jo et al., 2017, pp. 523–6). Otherwise, Lawson's argument has little explicit impact in the *Handbook*. Whatever its merits, Lawson's argument concerning mathematics is not widely accepted, even in the heterodox community.

Even among avowed critical realists there are several who disagree with Lawson and adopt mathematical methods or models. Paul Downward (2000, 2003) and John Finch and Robert McMaster (2002) defended a more extensive use of some econometric techniques. They pointed to concrete instances where econometrics has been or can be usefully deployed. While declaring his support for both critical realism and Marxism, Erik Olin Wright (1994, pp. 183–9) strongly advocated the use of 'explicit abstract models, sometimes highly formalized as in game theory' and other 'rational choice models'. This compounds the problem of defining the orthodox–heterodox distinction in Lawson's terms.

THE POLITICAL UNDERCURRENTS OF CRITICAL REALISM

Unlike Lee, and to his credit, Lawson did not attempt to relate his definition of heterodox economics to any political position or policy stance. Lawson is a Marxist, but he does not wear his politics on his sleeve. But Bhaskar and others have claimed that critical realism leads logically to full-blooded socialist politics.

Bhaskar (1986, p. 169) wrote of the 'essential emancipatory impulse' of the social sciences. Andrew Collier (1994, p. 172) summarized Bhaskar's argument: 'To say that some institution causes false beliefs is to criticise it.' Critical realists describe this as an 'explanatory critique'. In short, the revelation of underlying social causes or mechanisms is bound to lead to attempts to improve or replace the system. Although I would not express it in the same way, I agree that social science can have an emancipatory role.

But Bhaskar and Collier then argued that adequate explanations in social sciences imply fully-socialist policy stances. Bhaskar (1989, p. 6) rejected social-democratic compromises with capitalism. Instead, Bhaskar and Collier (1998, p. 392) saw critical realism as implying undiluted socialism: 'Critical realism shows the fallacy of several of the classical arguments against socialism and supports the *possibility* of a form of socialism which is neither a market economy nor a command economy nor a mix of the two, but a genuine extension of pluralistic democracy into economic life.'

Critical realism is thus tied to a hard-boiled socialism in which there is no place for markets. Given the fact that markets have existed for many thousands of years, and much longer than capitalism itself (Hodgson, 2015b), this agoraphobia (fear of markets) is rash and extreme. The argument by Bhaskar and Collier is brief, crude, questionable, uncritical and hardly realistic.

Contrary to Bhaskar and Collier, the possibility of this extreme socialism, while retaining any semblance of human emancipation, is not successfully demonstrated, by critical realism or any other doctrine. Like many others, Bhaskar and Collier ignored the socialist calculation debate and the failed real-world experiments in full-blooded socialism. They made no case whatsoever concerning the feasibility of their socialist vision. The scholarly mask of critical realism has dropped, to reveal its hard-left ideological face.[15]

Evidently, the attempts by Lee and Lawson to define heterodox economics have discernible political undercurrents. As far as I am aware, they have not disassociated themselves from the extreme and implausible political statements made by leading and founding critical realists. Consequently, they have aligned themselves by default with the hard-left political baggage of critical realism.[16]

THE ROUTLEDGE HANDBOOK OF HETERODOX ECONOMICS

Moving on from the contributions of Lee and Lawson, *The Routledge Handbook of Heterodox Economics* gives several indications of the de facto nature of current heterodoxy, although it too fails to define its meaning. The volume contains 37 essays by 44 authors, covering 531 pages of main text. The subtitle of the *Handbook* is *Theorizing, Analyzing, and Transforming Capitalism* (Jo et al., 2017).

A table in the opening essay by the editors shows that 28 of the 37 essays are by scholars said to be 'representing ... Post Keynesian ... and Sraffian' approaches (but not necessarily to the exclusion of other schools). It also shows that 26 of the 37 essays are by scholars said to be 'representing' Marxist approaches. Despite its claim to incorporate 'a wide range of theoretical traditions within heterodox economics', other schools and approaches are less-well served (Jo et al., 2017, pp. 3–6). For example, while it is mentioned on a few pages, there is no essay by a member of the Austrian School. Also, despite its importance for policy, there is no discussion of the socialist calculation debate.

A search of the index entries confirms the familiar bias toward Keynesianism and Marxism. The index reports that Marx or Marxism are mentioned on 96 pages and Keynes or (Post) Keynesianism on 95 pages.

---

[15]   For extensive criticisms of socialism in theory and practice see Hodgson (1999a, 2018, 2019c).

[16]   Other critical realists have also revealed their leftist ideological leanings. Clive Spash (2012) invoked the Bhaskar–Collier argument in his critique of pluralist strategies in ecological economics. Spash and Ryan (2012, p. 1092) promoted an ideologically-driven economics that empowers 'a challenge to ... dominant neoliberal market structures'. On the other hand, some adherents of critical realism embrace neither socialism nor Marxism. But they seem to be in a minority.

References to Sraffa or the Sraffian school are on 25 pages. Concerning individuals, there are 31 pages referring to Kalecki and 28 to Veblen. In its commissions and omissions, the *Handbook* largely replicates the profile of classical Cantabrigian heterodoxy, with a few added ingredients.

The *Handbook* does cite the work of Amartya Sen in two of its main essays. But the focus is on Sen's theory of capabilities and his contributions to development economics, not on his critique of utility maximization or his alternative view of human motivation. Others fare less well. Neither Herbert Simon, *behaviouralism, bounded rationality*, nor *satisficing* appear in the index. References to Richard Nelson, Sidney Winter and *evolutionary economics* are absent as well. Both Nelson–Winter evolutionary economics and behavioural economics are excluded.

There is no developed critique of utility maximization in the *Handbook*, and neither *utility* nor *maximization* appear in the index. There is very little discussion of alternative understandings of human motivation or of the importance of psychology. There is more in the *Handbook* about macroeconomics than microeconomics. These classic omissions of Cantabrigian heterodoxy are replicated here.

The editors of the *Handbook* deliberately favoured younger 'emerging scholars' in their choices of authors, and they threw the net wide, recruiting authors from six continents (Jo et al., 2017, pp. 6–7). But there is little of the innovative freshness of youth in the volume. It addresses concerns and approaches largely similar to those developed by ageing economists in the ancient University of Cambridge over half a century ago.

ANDREW MEARMAN'S REJECTION OF A 'FIXED DEFINITION' OF HETERODOXY

Mearman and his co-authors have explored the problem of defining heterodox economics in depth (Mearman, 2011, 2012; Mearman et al., 2019). Mearman concluded that among heterodox economists, there is no consensus on what heterodox economics means. But rather than trying to resolve this matter by finding a definition, Mearman (2012, p. 407) argued that a 'fixed definition' of heterodoxy is undesirable, and its meaning should be left 'purposefully vague'.

For Mearman (2012, p. 407), 'strict, fixed, simple definitions' are unacceptable because they 'suffer from problems of dualism'. On *dualism* he drew from the work of Dow. Dow's (1990, pp. 143–4) argument was cautious and qualified. She admitted that 'as a means of labelling, or categorising, dualism would seem to be necessary to any attempt at theorising'. She also pointed out that to insist on universal non-dualism is itself dualist: 'the category "dualism" itself implies its opposite, "non-dualism".' She was aware that *dualism* could not be used as a dismissive criterion *tout court.*

She went on to clarify that her critique of dualism was aimed at 'a particularly restrictive use of labelling'. Such restrictions might involve the unwarranted application of the law of the excluded middle (where something is either *X* or not-*X*). In defiance of this law, categorization must occasionally accept undecided, uncertain or hybrid cases. Another reason for rejection of dualism was its assumed 'fixity of meaning of categories'. But while making these important warnings, Dow did not argue that definitions or categorizations should be entirely abandoned. After all, she accepted that *dualism* was itself a category. My interpretation of Dow's argument is that labels or classifications can be acceptable, as long as they are capable of revision, and as long as unwarranted exclusions of undecided, uncertain or hybrid cases are avoided. Dow realized that to be effective, any critique of dualism had to be limited rather than universal.

Without acknowledging these nuances, Mearman (2012, pp. 408, 414) claimed that attempted definitions of heterodox economics (HE) 'display an unwarranted dualism'. He continued:

> They often create unjustifiably strict distinctions between the categories ... dualist definitions also tend to become unnecessarily and unjustifiably fixed, mutually exclusive and exhaustive. ... The main evidence of this problem is the extent of anomalies created by current definitions of HE. In turn, these anomalies result from the simplicity of many definitions of HE, a simplicity which underplays the complexity of HE. Yet, there appears to be a desire to use strict distinctions between HE and mainstream economics ... a rhetoric of distinction. ... Overall, we can see that there are no grounds for treating HE as a fixed object and therefore giving it a fixed definition.

There are several major problems with this argument. First let us accept with Mearman the possibility that the law of the excluded middle does not apply, and that there are types of economics that do not fit into any reasonable categorization of orthodox or heterodox: their status is undecided, uncertain or somehow intermediate. Let us also emphasize alongside Mearman that both orthodoxy and heterodoxy are in constant development and flux. In other words, they are not fixed objects.

Given these reasonable assumptions, I still argue that Mearman's case is unconvincing. Evidence of 'the extent of anomalies created by current definitions of HE' does not make Mearman's case against definitions as such. It calls for renewed efforts to find a suitable definition. Biologists did not cease to talk about species when it was realized that there was no clear and robust rule that always served to demarcate one species from another. They accepted fuzzy boundaries and worked around them.

Mearman's claim that 'these anomalies result from the simplicity of many definitions of HE' is also unpersuasive. Simple definitions – such as that of a mammal – do not necessarily create anomalies, even when the reality is complex and evolving. Furthermore, making definitions more complex could easily create additional anomalies, because of the greater number of criteria involved. Toward the end of this chapter I shall propose a very simple way of identifying orthodoxy in economics that is relatively free of anomalies.

Mearman also suggested that change and complexity disallow 'fixed definitions'. This repeats a common misunderstanding of the nature and purpose of definitions or classifications (Hodgson, 2019a). Consider Max Weber's concept of an *ideal type*. In a 1904 essay, Weber (1949, p. 107) argued that conceptual precision was required not *despite but because of* the changing, tangled and complex nature of socio-economic reality: 'it is *because* the content of historical concepts is necessarily subject to change that they must be formulated precisely and clearly on all occasions.' Real-world muddle is no excuse for a muddled conceptual model. Clear concepts were especially necessary to deal with a messy and changing reality. Similar observations apply to taxonomic or classificatory defin-itions. It is a common misconception that a changing or muddled reality must be tackled with changing or muddled concepts.

The social embeddedness of science means that communication and understanding are vital. Scientists need to interact with one another and establish common understandings, including of the terms being used. This transmission of meaning is vital for scientific advance. Some vagueness is unavoidable, even necessary. But the communication of meaning also requires repeated efforts of clarification.

For example, investigation of the (true or false) claim that 'capitalism generates inequality' requires an adequate common understanding of what is meant by 'capitalism' and 'inequality'. There has been some dispute over whether to include (say) prehistoric trade, ancient Rome, or the former Soviet Union under the category 'capitalist'.[17] Consequently,

---

[17] Such wide-ranging inclusions under the category 'capitalism' have been suggested, by McCloskey (2010, pp. 16, 259), Runciman (1983) and Cliff (1955) respectively. See by contrast Hodgson (2015b), where a narrower definition of capitalism is presented. It focuses on well-developed financial institutions and markets, which became dominant in the West no earlier than the seventeenth century.

attempts to critique or justify the inequality claim could be confounded by major differences over what entities were being analysed. This would frustrate the search for possible generic mechanisms that might explain capitalist inequality.

Consider further the definition of a mammal. The famous definition of 'an animal that suckles its young' is extremely simple. Yet it covers a huge class of evolving, complex entities. There are odd boundary cases, such as the duck-billed platypus, which lays eggs like a reptile but still suckles its young. But recently the definition of a mammal had to be changed to deal with burgeoning fossil evidence, where the existence or non-existence of mammary glands is difficult to detect. But note that this change in definition was a result of the need to deal with additional types of evidence, not because mammals are evolving or complex (which of course they are). Taxonomic or classificatory definitions are pragmatic tools to aid communication and the search for explanation in a scientific community.[18]

Scientists must first establish an agreed rough understanding of the phenomena they are investigating. Then they try to focus on the problem, using a taxonomic or classificatory definition as a means of demarcation. They sometimes change this definition, in the light of new theories or new evidence. But workable definitions matter at every stage.

It is possible to turn Mearman's argument against itself: the very idea of rejecting a 'fixed definition' is also 'dualistic'. All definitions must in a sense be fixed, at least for a while, because some fixity is essential to transmit meaning. But they are never fixed in the sense of being unalterable: new theories or new evidence may lead to a change of definition. Hence definitions, in some senses, are both fixed and not-fixed.

Consider the *Heterodox Economics Directory*. This large and expanding online publication has gone through several editions (Kapeller and Springholz, 2016). It is useful for those who regard themselves as heterodox economists because it provides global lists of:

- 'Further readings in heterodox economics';
- PhD, Masters or undergraduate programmes featuring 'heterodox economics';

---

[18]   The leading palaeontologist Kemp (2005, p. 3) defined mammals as 'synapsids that possess a dentary-squamosal jaw articulation and occlusion between upper and lower molars with a transverse component to the movement.' In Kemp's view, this criterion is sufficient to identify the clade originating with the last common ancestor of both *Sinoconodon* (an early type of mammal found as fossils in China) and more recent mammals.

- regular conferences and summer schools involving 'heterodox economics';
- publishers who publish works on 'heterodox economics';
- book series in 'heterodox economics';
- 'heterodox economic journals';
- associations involving 'heterodox economists'; and much else.

All these classifications in the *Directory* are dualist. An entity *X* is either on a list, or it is not. There is no 'undecided' or 'uncertain' category. The team producing the *Directory* has used some explicit or implicit 'fixed' definition of heterodoxy to compile these lists. The criteria may change later, but they must be more-or-less fixed when they are used, to establish adequate coherence and consistency.[19]

Similarly, the *Heterodox Economics Newsletter* (which at the time of writing is regularly broadcast via email by Jakob Kapeller) lists some events, journals and calls for papers, but excludes others. Dualism reigns. Hence the meaning of *heterodox economics* is unavoidably being established, sometimes blindly and haphazardly, in practice. Yet at present the outcome signals little more than the preferences and possible prejudices of those compiling these lists. It is undisciplined by explicit definitional guidelines, because these are not agreed. Establishing guidelines for inclusion or exclusion would amount to defining the nature and scope of heterodox economics.

In sum, Mearman's argument against a 'fixed definition' of heterodox economics fails. It is undermined in practice by the ongoing attempt by heterodox economists to organize themselves as a community and to share information on useful heterodox resources. This implicit strategy defies Mearman's recommendation that the meaning of heterodox economics should be 'purposefully vague'. A *Vaguely-Heterodox Economics Directory* would include many-fold more readings, courses, conferences, journals and so on, and it would be much less useful as a result. For practical effect, lines must be drawn somewhere, even if they are to be redrawn later.

---

[19] Consider some anomalies. Several items on these lists in the *Directory* have labelled *themselves* as 'heterodox' (such as the Australia-based Society for Heterodox Economics (SHE)). But with some other listed items this is not the case. Consider the *Journal of Economic Methodology* and the *Journal of Institutional Economics*, both of which appear on the *Directory* list of 'heterodox economic journals'. I know from close personal experience that those who run these two journals do not wish them to be promoted as *heterodox*, although both these journals willingly publish much material that might be described as such, by Lee's, Lawson's or other prominent criteria.

A NEGLECTED POSSIBLE DEFINITION OF HETERODOX ECONOMICS

As pointed out above, the problem of defining heterodox economics is just the flip-side of the same problem of defining orthodox economics. Identify one and you can then recognize the other. Asserting that heterodoxy has a 'vague' and flexible meaning implies that one's understanding of the nature of orthodoxy is similarly vague and flexible.

Yet an obvious definition of orthodox economics exists. I suggest that it can be defined in terms of the centrality of the assumption of utility-maximizing agents with preference functions, otherwise known as Max U. It is well known that Max U derives from a version of individualistic utilitarianism, inspired by the seminal work of Jeremy Bentham. This postulate of maximization dovetails with the widespread use of equilibrium analysis: maximization occurs when an equilibrium is reached.

In the following chapter I give evidence of the strong persistence of the Max U assumption and the related idea of preference functions. Even the rise of behavioural economics has not displaced Max U: the new behaviouralists treat evidence that contradicts Max U models as deviations from strict maximization, due to agent errors or to inadequate information. Unlike the original and more radical behavioural economics of Simon (1955, 1957), the evidence of deviation is not used to overturn Max U in principle.

I also argue in the following chapter that Davis (2005) and Colander et al. (2004) were wrong to suggest that mainstream economics as a whole was moving away from Max U. Instead, orthodoxy may be usefully defined by its retention of the Max U assumption.

Another possible way of defining orthodoxy is the assumption of a 'field' ontology, where infinite adjustment of all or many variables and gross substitutability between them are possible (Mirowski, 1989; Potts, 2000). The problem here is game theory – it assumes a structured world without this gross substitutability. All game theory would be heterodox by the criterion of gross substitutability. But game theory is clearly *mainstream* these days, in the sense that it 'is taught in the most prestigious universities and colleges, gets published in the most prestigious journals, receives funds from the most important research foundations, and wins the most prestigious awards' (Dequech, 2007, p. 281). Much (but not all) game theory assumes Max U. If Max U were the criterion of orthodoxy, then much of game theory would be orthodox. Max U covers a wider mainstream domain than the assumption of gross substitutability. This is an argument for using Max U as the main criterion of orthodoxy.[20]

When Max U became prominent in economics in the latter part of the nineteenth century, it was often in a version that assumed narrow self-interest. This self-regarding version of Max U prevailed in mainstream economics until the 1990s. Since then, several economists have argued for 'other-regarding' or 'social' preferences to explain altruism or other apparently unselfish behaviour (Becker, 1976b; Charness and Rabin, 2002; Fehr and Fischbacher, 2002; Bowles and Gintis, 2011). These authors propose a version of Max U with individual preferences that are partly 'other-regarding' and not purely 'self-regarding'.

Originally, Max U enabled a particular type of mathematical formalism in economics, often including calculus. Although it was not directly measurable, utility seemed an ideal candidate for uni-dimensional quantification. In different ways and to different degrees (Jaffé, 1976), the turn toward utility was manifest in the seminal marginalist treatises of William Stanley Jevons (1871), Carl Menger (1871) and Léon Walras (1874).

One of the contemporary arguments for the adoption of Max U in the late nineteenth century was its facilitation of mathematics. For Jevons (1871, pp. 50, 52, 70), economics 'must be pervaded by ... the tracing out of the mechanics of self-interest and utility.' He believed that 'all economic writers must be mathematical so far as they are scientific at all.' His reduction of behaviour to utility maximization circumvented psychology and opened the door to mathematics.

Similarly, defending the idea that individuals maximize their own utility or pleasure, Francis Edgeworth (1881, p. 15) argued that '*the conception of Man as a pleasure machine* may justify and facilitate the employment of mechanical terms and Mathematical reasoning in social science.' Irving Fisher (1892) promoted Max U, relating it to 'mechanical analogies' that enabled the greater use of mathematics. Similarly, Vilfredo Pareto (1897, p. 490) saw 'rational mechanics' as a suitable approximation for economic phenomena, which in turn justified 'a place for mathematics'.

The mention by Jevons, Edgeworth, Fisher and Pareto of mechanics was no accidental turn of phrase. As with Walras (1874), the search for usable mathematical techniques had quickly gravitated towards physics (Mirowski, 1989). Late nineteenth-century physics provided specific

---

[20] Consequently, evolutionary game theory and parts of the new institutional economics (which do not assume maximizing behaviour) may be regarded as *mainstream* but not *orthodox*.

formalisms (particularly those involving calculus) that guided the general approach to modelling, enshrined the preoccupation with equilibria and elevated the supreme goal of prediction.[21]

Although Lawson (2006, p. 488) was wrong to follow the mistaken claim of Colander and others that mainstream economics is 'moving away' from Max U, he was right, like Marshall and Keynes before, to identify the problem of excessive formalism in economics. But I would put it differently. Orthodoxy is characterized by Max U: he invokes a crude, one-dimensional view of human behaviour that cannot do justice to multiple facets of human motivation – particularly moral motivation – that are relational rather than purely individual (Wilson, 2010; Hodgson, 2013a; Smith, 2013; Smith and Wilson, 2019). In turn, Max U marginalism has enabled a particular kind of mathematical formalism. More recently, Max U has escaped the confines of marginalism and he lives on in parts of game theory, involving a different kind of mathematics.

In sum, the best definition we have for heterodoxy is an economics that rejects Max U with his preference function. But although we can find cases of heterodox economists, from or inspired by Cambridge, who challenge the assumption of Max U (Robinson, 1964a, p. 48) it is not a prominent critical theme in heterodox research of Cambridge pedigree. Unlike the separate heterodoxy of evolutionary economics, Cantabrigian heterodoxy has been more involved with macroeconomics. Its excursions into microeconomics have given more attention to pricing analysis than to the psychological underpinnings of human behaviour.

Although Veblen (1898a, 1909) established a forceful critique of utility maximization, the strongest challenges to the Max U assumption in the second half of the twentieth century have come from scholars neglected by the Cantabrigian heterodox community. In particular they have come from Nobel Laureates Simon (1947, 1955, 1956, 1957, 1979) and Sen (1973, 1977). Yet, as established earlier, Simon and Sen have been absent from many prominent attempts to identify prominent elements of heterodox economics.

Why is a critical focus on Max U not a principal theme of heterodoxy? The answer is not entirely clear, but some connected hypotheses come to

---

[21]   See Mirowski (1989). Marshall is depicted as an orthodox villain by some heterodox economists (Fine and Milonakis, 2009; Milonakis and Fine, 2009). But Marshall's approach was different. Although he was responsible for the grand synthesis of marginalist theory in Max U and partial equilibrium terms, in some respects he differed from other Max U proponents. As noted in Chapter 1 above, Marshall wanted to include ethical principles as well as utility maximization. He warned also against over-obsession with mathematical formalism and his chosen metaphor was biology, not physics (Hodgson, 2013d).

mind. These hypotheses are suggested for future investigation: they are not regarded as sacrosanct.

The most obvious argument is that the heterodox neglect of micro topics such as Max U reflects an uppermost concern for macroeconomic policy. This would suggest that heterodox economics is as much policy-driven as theory-driven. That is not necessarily a bad thing. But policy alone cannot define the nature and scope of heterodoxy because orthodox economic theory does not sustain any one particular policy direction.

Furthermore, as noted in the preceding chapter, the provision of a more complex theory of human motivation does not necessarily lead to anti-market policy conclusions. An emphasis on morality and duty, for example, is found in conservative as well as socialist and liberal strands of thought. The uncertain policy destination of Max U critiques may help to explain why this area is neglected.

Finally, the closeness of much heterodox economics to Marxism may have an effect. The theory of motivation in Marxism is material self-interest. It is not explicitly utilitarian, but the form and results are very similar. Like the utilitarians, Marx separated ends from means. The end of socialism was proclaimed as both desirable and inevitable, and all means towards that end were justified.[22]

Addressing mainstream economics, Veblen famously (1898a, p. 389) lampooned the utilitarian individual as a 'lightning calculator of pleasures and pains ... a homogeneous globule of desire.' But Veblen found a related flaw in Marxism. Veblen (1906, p. 583) wrote that 'the doctrine of class struggle ... is of a utilitarian origin ... and it belongs to Marx by virtue of his having borrowed its elements from the system of self-interest.' In Marxism, social classes are treated much as self-interested individuals, but writ large. Veblen (1909, p. 623) also criticized the Marxist use of the 'hedonistic calculus', whereby 'human conduct is conceived of and interpreted as a rational response to the exigencies of the situation in which mankind is placed.'[23]

---

[22] Lukes (1985) forcefully criticized Marx's 'extreme consequentialism' – which amounts to a neglect of any moral evaluation of the means, as long as they serve the ends. See also Hodgson (2013a).

[23] But while Marx's analysis has utilitarian features, including an enlargement of self-interest, Marx (1976, pp. 758–9 n.) distanced himself from Benthamism and the concept of utility. The Benthamite impulse is found more broadly in socialism. Keynes (1931, p. 291) wrote: 'Nineteenth-century State Socialism sprang from Bentham'. Similarly, Allen (1998, p. 141) noted that 'the utilitarian forms of liberalism can be turned, as ... in the case of Bentham, into schemes of collectivist control and reorganisation.' Hence the use of neoclassical economics in attempts to show the feasibility of socialism.

There are several puzzles surrounding the failure of heterodoxy to agree on a shared definition of its nature and its avoidance of a rather obvious (Max U) criterion for making the orthodox–heterodox distinction. Some possible explanations appear when we consider the leftist ideological undercurrents within the self-described heterodox community.

CONCLUSION: THE NEED FOR A *RAISON D'ÊTRE*

The failure of heterodox economics to establish a consensus over its identity is an immense disempowerment. How can paradigm change be attempted when there is inadequate agreement on the nature of the required change, and no agreement on the kind of alternative theories that are to replace orthodox ones?

Stating that heterodox economics is a de facto community is a grossly inadequate response. Such a group has to justify its separate existence. To attract newcomers, it has to explain why it is congregated. It has to have a common mission. It cannot simply sing, like soldiers in another war, to the tune of *Auld Lang Syne*, 'we're here because we're here because ...'.

Any viable academic school of thought should have a shared *raison d'être*. This may be defined in terms of:

a. the study of a specific zone of enquiry or a set of phenomena in the real world; or

b. the promotion or development of a particular theoretical approach (such as utility maximization, or the use of evolutionary theory, or whatever); or

c. the promotion or development of a particular set of analytical techniques (such as econometrics, or game theory, or agent-based models, or whatever); or

d. the promotion or development of policies in a defining problem area (such as the environment, peace, or economic development).

The *raison d'être* may consist of one of these, or a combination of more than one.

Lee's (2008, 2009, 2012) definition of heterodoxy fits largely into category (b), by listing sets of acceptable and unacceptable theoretical assumptions for heterodoxy. Lee also entered the policy area (d) by suggesting that heterodox economics is critical of modern capitalism. Lawson's (1997, 2003, 2004, 2006, 2013) definition of heterodoxy entails (a), with his insistence that the socio-economic world is 'open', with implications concerning types of theoretical approach (b) and appropriate analytical techniques (c).

The hitherto unacknowledged strategy of identifying orthodoxy with Max U and developing alternatives to it would also fit largely into category (b). But unlike Lee's account, it would be much more focused, by targeting a central assumption and developing alternative theories of human motivation. It would have to show that these alternative theories not only provide a more plausible and psychologically grounded analysis, but that these alternatives have an impact on policy design. This is one of several possible heterodox strategies considered in the final chapter of this book.

3. Rumours of the death of Max U are exaggerated

> There is no reason to suppose that most human beings are engaged in maximising anything unless it be unhappiness, and even this with incomplete success.
>
> Ronald Coase (1988)

Mainstream economics has gone through several major changes since the Second World War. There was the 'formalist revolution' of the 1950s (Backhouse, 1998; Blaug, 1999, 2003; Weintraub, 2002), which increased the frequency and prestige of mathematical techniques. There was the rise, and 1970s theoretical breakdown, of the 'sound micro-foundations' project, followed by the vigorous rehabilitation of game theory in the 1980s (Kirman, 1989; Rizvi, 1994a, 1994b).

By the 1990s, approaches in experimental economics (Smith, 1992) and behavioural economics (Camerer et al., 2004) were well-established in leading journals and prestigious departments of economics. Since then we have seen neuro-economics (Glimcher, 2003; Zak 2004, 2011a, 2011b; Camerer et al., 2005), happiness economics (Di Tella and MacCulloch, 2006), identity economics (Akerlof and Kranton, 2010) and much else. There has been a broad empirical turn in economics since the 1990s, leading to a higher preponderance of applied papers in leading journals (Hamermesh, 2013; Backhouse and Cherrier, 2017). Finally, the old idea of 'economic man' as entirely greedy and self-regarding has been challenged from within economics itself, by research on 'other-regarding' and 'social' preferences, including discussions of altruism (Becker, 1976b; Charness and Rabin, 2002; Fehr and Fischbacher, 2002; Bowles and Gintis, 2011).

The pace of change and growing diversity of the discipline are impressive. The rise of behavioural economics and other developments have made it possible to question some basic assumptions, when beforehand to raise such doubts was to exclude oneself from the discipline. But these shifts pose greater challenges for heterodox critics, who have to fire at multiple, moving targets.

There has been an important debate about the nature, extent and evolution of economics since 1990 (Colander, 2000a, 2000b, 2005a, 2005b; Colander et al., 2004; Davis, 2006, 2008). Several authors have argued that the 'neoclassical' paradigm – involving its core concepts of rationality and equilibrium – is in decline within mainstream economics, and it is being replaced by a variety of different approaches.

David Colander's analysis of the discipline was based on interviews with graduate students in the most esteemed departments of economics, principally in the USA. He announced the 'death of neoclassical economics' as a useful label (Colander, 2000a) and argued that mainstream economics was 'moving away' from its 'holy trinity' assumptions of 'rationality, selfishness and equilibrium' (Colander et al., 2004, p. 485; Colander, 2005b, p. 930).

There have been quarrels over whether or not *neoclassical* is a useful or appropriate term, or (more esoterically) whether or not its current usage corresponds to that of Veblen, who coined it in 1900 (Aspromourgos, 1986; Fayazmanesh, 1998; Colander, 2000a; Lawson, 2013; Morgan, 2016). A problem with the *neoclassical* label is that it might misleadingly suggest that the *classical* economists formed a coherent school or approach, and that *neoclassical* economics is a new version of that older school. As Joseph Schumpeter (1954, p. 919) observed: 'there is no more sense in calling the Jevons-Menger-Walras theory neoclassic than there would be in calling the Einstein theory neo-Newtonian.'

Another point against the use of the *neoclassical* label is that it is widely and wrongly assumed (often by its critics and sometimes by its exponents) that the economics to which it refers automatically leads to pro-market policies. Yet leading proponents of 'neoclassical' economics, with utility-maximizing agents and equilibrium models, including Oskar Lange, Abba Lerner, Kenneth Arrow and John Roemer, favoured a socialist economy dominated by common ownership. The focus on the utility-maximizing individual does not necessarily imply market policies. Many models with utility-maximizing individuals have been developed in non-market contexts.

Indeed, mainstream economics has been inadequate in its grasp of basic trading institutions such as private property and the market (Hodgson, 1999b, ch. 2; 2015b). Serious definitions and institutional analyses of the market are relatively rare, as Nobel Laureates George Stigler (1967, p. 291), Douglass North (1977, p. 710) and Ronald Coase (1988, p. 7) have all pointed out. Adequate concepts of property, contract, exchange and market are also absent from standard neoclassical theory (Sened, 1997; Heinsohn and Steiger, 2013; Hodgson, 2015b, 2015c; Steiger, 2008). It is far too charitable to describe neoclassical economics as the economics of the market, because neoclassical analysis is deficient in its analysis of market institutions.

Given this controversy and confusion, there are good reasons to prefer Deirdre McCloskey's (2008, 2016) inspired 'Max U' label instead. Max U refers to the core ideas of utility maximization and equilibrium.

Another prominent term is 'the economic approach'. This typically involves a focus on maximizing behaviour by individuals, taking into account costs and benefits. Gary Becker (1976a, pp. 5, 14) wrote: 'The combined assumptions of maximizing behavior, market equilibrium, and stable preferences, used relentlessly and unflinchingly, form the heart of the economic approach as I see it ... all human behavior can be viewed as involving participants who maximize their utility from a stable set of preferences'.[1]

Whatever its label, the key issue here is the theoretical core. Colander rightly highlighted the basic assumptions of 'rationality, selfishness and equilibrium'. He argued that mainstream economics was 'moving away' from these assumptions. Colander (2000a, pp. 135–6) made even bolder (and more questionable) assertions: 'Few modern economists today accept utilitarianism; most see it as a quaint aspect of the past. One sees very little operational use of utility theory in modern economics.' Also 'general equilibrium models are seldom used.'

In the following section I contest the claim that these core ideas are being side-lined, even if they are rivalled by other developments. But I agree with some important aspects of Colander's argument. In particular, the shift towards game theory has radically changed microeconomics, the relaxations of the assumptions of perfect information and omniscience have been dramatic, and there has been a strong turn towards greater use of empirical data, partly driven by the emergence of new databases and the rapid advance of computer technology.

But while economics has continued to innovate and change, the accounts by Colander and Davis overlook important elements of theoretical continuity at the core. I argue below that the degree of continuity of these core elements has been underestimated.

Colander (2000a, p. 137) emphasized (with approval) that '*the modelling approach to problems is the central element of modern economics.*' But with disapproval, Tony Lawson (1997, 2006, 2013) famously argued that mathematical model-building in economics is inappropriate for the 'open systems' that economists typically address. Both authors proposed

---

[1]   Becker (1976a, p. 15) also described his work as 'an application of neo-classical economics' to a wide range of phenomena, including the family.

that the prevalence of modelling in economics has eclipsed any other major continuity at the theoretical core. I dispute this shared conclusion, while fully accepting that model-building (for good or ill) is well-entrenched in economics. It is also evident that particular kinds of model-building have been facilitated by the enduring assumption of Max U.

If these preliminary indications and arguments hold water, then they have major implications, including for the efforts by Amartya Sen (1977, 1985a, 1985b, 2004), John Davis (1995, 2003), Deirdre McCloskey (2006, 2008, 2016) and others to promote a more nuanced and multi-faceted picture of the economic agent, at least within the academic boundaries of economics as a discipline. They suggest more pessimistic conclusions concerning the possibility of changing the core assumptions of economics and thereby establishing a new paradigm (Davis, 2008; Earl, 2010). Heterodox economists may have to choose to live with Max U, or to abandon the academic power structures of economics altogether.

MAX U AND BEHAVIOURAL ECONOMICS

Colander (2005b, p. 930) rightly identified the theoretical core of micro-economics as the zone where any fundamental change would occur in the discipline as a whole. Microeconomics sustains basic assumptions about individuals, their motivation, and their modes of interaction with others. Supporting his thesis that Max U assumptions were moving out of fashion, he claimed to identify a shift toward Herbert Simon's version of behavioural economics. Here, according to his argument, we should expect further signs of development:

> Herbert Simon's work ... provides a map for the direction in which I am predicting economics will evolve. ... Simon was neglected ... Today, however, his work and approach are beginning to be considered more carefully, as the profession catches up with his vision of the way in which one can understand the economy.

But this overlooked the transformation of 'behavioural economics' itself. The original version of Simon (1957, 1959) adopted insights from psychology and subverted the notion of rational, optimizing, behaviour. By contrast, mainstream versions of 'behavioural economics' since 1990 are typically seen as modifications in the orbit of ever-tenacious Max U.

Simon was awarded the Nobel Prize in Economics in 1978 for his work in this area. But 'behavioural economics' did not take off in the highly-ranked economics journals and departments until about twenty years later, and only after major modifications. Simon's radical message had to be toned down and some of his major insights jettisoned (Sent, 2004; Earl, 2010).

Although Matthew Rabin (1998) announced the return of psychological insights into economics – after decades of economists shunning them with their 'people act *as if* they are maximizing utility' reasoning – the acceptance of psychological ideas within economics has proved to be severely limited. As Nathan Berg and Gerd Gigerenzer (2010, p. 133) pointed out:

> For a research program that counts improved empirical realism among its primary goals, it is startling that behavioral economics appears, in many cases, indistinguishable from neoclassical economics in its reliance on as-if arguments to justify 'psychological' models that make no pretense of even attempting to describe the psychological processes that underlie human decision making.

Sheila Dow (2011a) considered in particular the highly limited use of psychology by behavioural finance, which misses some of the major psychological drivers of financial volatility. Peter Earl (2010, pp. 216–17) commented more generally: 'There is no systematic attempt to bring psychology into economics; instead, constrained optimization is modified to allow for preferences and/or perceptions to be distorted by "heuristics and biases" uncovered in empirical work. ... Simon's approach remains almost completely invisible within the new literature'.

As a witness, Earl (2010, p. 317) called the 740-page reader on behavioural economics edited by Colin Camerer et al. (2004). Earl noted that within this hefty volume, Simon is mentioned only four times: the first three refer to his notion of 'procedural rationality', with no references. Only the last appearance cites any of his work and makes any connection with his concept of satisficing (for which there is no index entry). Bounded rationality appears on only three pages (all in the same paper).

Camerer and his colleagues made it clear that the new behavioural economics was an adjustment to the reigning Max U paradigm, rather than an attempt to overthrow it. Camerer et al. (2004, p. 1) insisted that behavioural economics 'does not imply a wholesale rejection of the neoclassical approach to economics based on utility maximization, equilibrium, and efficiency.' Accordingly, Daniel Kahneman (2003, p. 1469) wrote: 'Theories in behavioural economics have generally retained the basic architecture of the rational model, adding assumptions about cognitive limitations designed to account for specific anomalies'.

The massive text on behavioural economics by Sanjit Dhami (2016) is a *tour de force*, and it mentions Simon's work several times. The concept of satisficing appears on six of its 1700 pages. But the text mostly replicates the current practice of using utility maximization as a reference point. And there is no mention at all of the behavioural theory of the firm developed by Richard M. Cyert and James G. March (1963), which continues to receive attention from academics in business schools and is closely connected to evolutionary economics (see the following chapter).

One of the key offshoots of behavioural economics is the theory of 'libertarian paternalism', where key information is presented in a way to 'nudge' people to make more efficacious decisions (Thaler and Sunstein, 2008). In a widespread interpretation, the 'nudge' is designed to help people to maximize their utility and overcome cognitive biases or other 'errors'. Max U serves as the normative standard of behaviour, while deviations from that norm have to be 'corrected' by a nudge.

Overall, there is little evidence that the new 'behavioural economics' has passed Colander's (2005b, p. 930) Herbert Simon Test. So far, there is no discernible indication that 'his work and approach are beginning to be considered more carefully' or the profession are beginning to catch up 'with his vision of the way in which one can understand the economy'. For instance, Simon's core concept of satisficing behaviour, which he adapted from psychology and administrative science, and which he regarded as more realistic than maximization or optimization, rarely appears in the new version of behaviouralism. Simon's radical ideas are largely side-lined.

Indeed, Max U has reconquered some territory that was conceded in the initial bubble of enthusiasm for the new behaviouralism. While promoting more sophisticated and accommodating Max U formulations, Herbert Gintis (2005) showed that experimental evidence by behavioural economists and psychologists that seemed to challenge utility-maximizing rationality, does not in fact refute it, once more sophisticated (typically 'social' or 'other-regarding') preference functions are introduced. Unrefuted by evidence, Max U returns.

THE UNFALSIFIABILITY OF MAX U

But is there any evidence that could falsify Max U? To see why Max U is capable of conquering unlimited behavioural territory, we need to appreciate that utility maximization is consistent with *any* data concerning the behaviour of anything. In other words, utility functions can be modified to fit any data on manifest behaviour. *Particular* utility or preference functions may be falsified because they are unable to predict some observed behaviour, but Max U *in general terms is unfalsifiable* (Hodgson, 2013a; Steele, 2014). Despite being noted by some leading authors, this unfalsifiability is still insufficiently acknowledged.

When the young Paul Samuelson (1937, p. 156) discussed utility maximization, he understood that 'all types of observable behavior might conceivably result from such an assumption.' Many experiments show that people sometimes do not maximize monetary rewards. But that does not show that they are not maximizing their utility. Because utility is unobservable, all kinds of behaviour can be 'expressed' in terms of utility maximization, without fear of refutation. As Sidney Winter (1964, pp. 309, 315), Harvey Leibenstein (1976, p. 8), Lawrence Boland (1981) and others have argued, no evidence can possibly refute the theory that agents are maximizing some hidden or unknown variable (such as utility).[2]

Many experiments show that participants do not maximize expected monetary (or other visible) payoffs. But payoff maximization is not the same as utility maximization. Although it is often assumed that payoffs and utility are monotonically related, experimental economists such as Vernon Smith (1982, p. 929) admitted that this monotonic correspondence cannot be guaranteed, partly because preferences and utility are 'not directly observable' (Siakantaris, 2000). Consequently, if we have evidence that payoffs are not being maximized, then this does not imply that utility is not being maximized.

If experiments show that some consumers appear to prefer a monetary reward that is less than the expected outcome, or appear to have intransitive preference orderings, or defy the von Neumann–Morgenstern independence axiom, then we can always get around these problems, and make the evidence consistent with utility maximization, by introducing other variables or states of the world into the utility function. For example, apparent preference inconsistency can be explained away by the fact that the apparently inconsistent choices are always made at different times and in (at least slightly) different circumstances.[3]

Given that we can never in principle demonstrate that some unobserved variable (like utility) is *not* being maximized, then an accommodating Max U is invulnerable to any empirical attack. The general core of expected utility theory is unfalsifiable. But it is not a tautology (in the logical sense) because it is *conceivably false*. Logical tautologies and

---

[2]   See the useful methodological discussions in Dow (2013) and Crespo (2013).
[3]   See Hodgson (2013a, ch. 3) and my debate with Gintis and Helbing (2015) in Hodgson (2015a).

unfalsifiable propositions are often confused, but they are quite different. Logical tautologies are true by logical inference or definition. By contrast, even if we cannot observe it, it might really be the case that utility exists, and some individual may not be maximizing it. But no empirical evidence can ever establish this for certain, as long as utility is unobservable.

This does not necessarily mean that the utility-maximization framework is useless or wrong. Neither tautological nor unfalsifiable statements are necessarily meaningless or unscientific.[4] They can play a framing or organizing role in scientific thought, in which falsifiable propositions are proposed and tested. In economics, Max U has played a prominent role in these terms, just as there are other key frameworks that structure enquiry in other sciences.

But the unfalsifiable nature of Max U in general is rarely admitted. Is this truth avoided because of worries that it might risk Popperian accusations that Max U is not scientific? Yet Karl Popper himself did not require all science to pass the falsifiability test (Ackerman, 1976, pp. 30–31). Or is the truth eluded because it would undermine the frequent claim that Max U leads to specific testable propositions? Frameworks that are unfalsifiable can predict an unbounded range of possibilities, because they can be made compatible with all of them.

In fact, when predictions are made with Max U models the auxiliary assumptions constrain possibilities and do much of the predictive work. As Mark Blaug (1992, p. 232) put it: 'The rationality hypothesis by itself is rather weak. To make it yield interesting implications, we need to add auxiliary assumptions.' In a critique of Gary Becker's claim that Max U yielded useful predictions, Robert Pollak (2003) showed that Becker's predictions always depend on auxiliary assumptions, which constrain the otherwise-unbounded possibilities for prediction with Max U.

It seems that to provide it with predictive credentials, news of the unfalsifiability of Max U has to be suppressed. Consequently, devotees of Max U can set about their tasks of showing that apparently 'anomalous' results can be predicted within a Max U framework, either as deviations from a particular Max U model, or via complete incorporation in a more sophisticated Max U model that 'explains' the deviations as well.

---

[4] It is widely accepted in the philosophy of science that some unfalsifiable propositions are necessary. These include the principle of determinacy (every event has a cause) and the assumption of the uniformity of nature. Without these prior assumptions, science is impossible.

THE SURVIVAL OF MAX U

Camerer (2003, p. 101) elucidated the aim and practice of behavioural economics as 'to find parsimonious utility functions, supported by psychological intuition, that are general enough to explain many phenomena in one fell swoop, and also make new predictions'. The parsimony criterion makes the task more difficult, and successful fittings of functions to data are then more impressive. Predictions are made to test the fitted function. But what is being tested here is not Max U in general, but particular and parsimonious formulations of a utility function. If the test fails, then Max U is not abandoned, but the search is triggered to find another tolerably parsimonious function to fit the augmented dataset. And so it goes on.

While the new behavioural economics thrived, the gravitational pull of Max U did not allow any escape from its orbit. If anything, the Max U force field has become more powerful in recent years. Gerardo Infante et al. (2016) documented how some behavioural economists have claimed to have rediscovered an inner *homo economicus* within everyone. Deviations from this inner rationality are put down to mistakes, to misinterpretations of evidence or to missing information. Max U returns, once his or her mistakes and misperceptions are corrected.

Max U has exerted influence over neuro-economics as well. As soon as it became possible to garner extensive data on brain activity, pioneering neuro-economists (Platt and Glimcher, 1999; Glimcher et al., 2005) claimed to discover the utility function exists as a physiological reality inside the brain. This prompted Gintis (2009, p. 2) to write: 'Neuroscientists increasingly find that an aggregate decision process in the brain synthesizes all available information into a single unitary value.' Indeed, if utility could be directly measured in the brain, then utility would become observable and Max U would be falsifiable.

But Jack Vromen (2010) argued that at best the neurological evidence exhibits consistency with the predictions of expected utility theory. There is no evidence of actual computation of utility in the brain. Given the argument here that any observed outcomes can be made consistent with some utility function, the consistency claim is hardly powerful or surprising. But the existence claims are unsupported. The whole argument shows that Max U still preoccupies influential economists. If they had abandoned utility functions, then they would not be looking for them.[5]

---

5   See also Vromen (2008) and McMaster and Novarese (2016).

Max U can jump species too. Experimental work with rats and other animals (Kagel et al., 1995) 'revealed' that animals have downward-sloping demand curves, supposedly just like humans. Becker (1991, p. 307) proposed that: 'Economic analysis is a powerful tool not only in understanding human behavior but also in understanding the behavior of other species.' Similarly, Gordon Tullock (1994) claimed that organisms can be treated as if they have the same general type of utility function that is attributed to humans in the microeconomics textbooks. Seemingly, we now have 'evidence' of the 'rationality' of everything in evolution from the amoeba onwards. As a consequence, Max U cannot express what is specific to human nature, human motivation or human society. Its very weakness, at least when applied to the human domain, stems from its excessive scope.

The persistence of Max U and of allied terms such as 'the economic approach' does not mean that economic theory as a whole has not changed. For example, the shift from general equilibrium to game theory in microeconomics has had a major impact on the discipline. As Davis (2008, p. 358) put it, game theory rejects the formerly standard 'competitive model of indirect interaction solely through the price mechanism to focus on scenario-driven direct interaction.' In some versions of game theory, the notion of rationality becomes difficult to specify in a single, obvious sense (Sugden, 1991). Actors in agent-based models and in prominent versions of evolutionary game theory are formulated in terms of strategic algorithms rather than in conventional Max U terms. For this reason, evolutionary game theory may be considered *mainstream* but not *orthodox*. Max U does not prevail over all contemporary economic theory. But departing from his orbit carries risks: game theory begets multiple equilibria, and agent-based models illustrate multiple, often radically different, outcomes. Max U often provides a more secure theoretical world. Consequently, he still prevails, and rumours of the death of Max U are grossly exaggerated.

Rival approaches are neglected. For example, Matteo Richiardi and Roberto Leombruni (2005) pointed out that agent-based models are very rare in 20 highly-rated journals in economics. They have made up only 0.03 per cent of published articles in these journals since 1988. Richiardi and Leombruni reported common arguments against agent-based models – that they are often difficult to generalize, interpret or estimate. Some high-priesthood resistance to agent-based modelling may also stem from its non-reliance on Max U formulations. The growth of agent-based models will be more significant for economics when it has achieved greater penetration into its leading journals.

Colander (2000a, p. 136) is also wrong to say that 'general equilibrium models are seldom used'. Dynamic stochastic general equilibrium (DSGE) models (with their core Max U assumptions) are still widespread in macroeconomics. So too are the rational expectations and efficient markets hypotheses. These ideas persist even after the economic crash of 2008, when they were subjected to severe public criticism. As Alan Kirman (2009) noted: 'Thus both the development of the DSGE model and the evolution of the efficient market hypothesis share a common feature – despite the empirical evidence and despite their theoretical weaknesses, their development proceeded as if the criticism did not exist.'

Justin Fox (2009, p. 310) similarly remarked: 'While behavioralists and other critics poked a lot of holes in the edifice of rational market finance, they haven't been willing to abandon that edifice.' Max U has survived the Great Crash of 2008, and he still prospers in macroeconomics as well as in microeconomics.

Colander was involved in two major surveys and sets of interviews, in 1985 and 2004, with graduate students at seven top-ranking graduate economics programmes (University of Chicago, Columbia University, Harvard University, Massachusetts Institute of Technology, Stanford University, Yale University and Princeton University). To gauge how the discipline had changed, similar questions were asked on both occasions.

Some of Colander's statistics undermine his own claims. Colander's (2005a, p. 188, Table 5) data show that those graduate students regarding the assumption of rational behaviour as 'very important' remained on average at 51 per cent from 1985 to 2004. Those seeing it as 'important in some cases' increased on average from 41 per cent to 43 per cent. On the rational expectations hypothesis, those seeing it as at least 'important in some cases' increased on average from 70 per cent to 83 per cent. Colander's own data show that, if anything, Max U had become slightly more entrenched over the 19 years between the two surveys (although the frequencies and changes are radically different at different leading universities).

Figure 3.1 shows bibliometric evidence that Max U is still alive and influential. Using the JSTOR database, some key words were searched in 10 leading journals of economics from 1960 to 2014.[6] The vertical axis shows the percentages of articles in any given period in which any one of

---

6   The journals were the *American Economic Review, Econometrica, Economic Journal, Economica, Journal of Economic Literature, Journal of Economic Perspectives, Journal of Political Economy, Quarterly Journal of Economics, Review of Economic Studies* and *Review of Economics and Statistics.* The data were collected on 20 May 2018. In some cases, data were unavailable in the years 2013–14, because of JSTOR access horizons. But as the frequency (rather than the absolute number) of appearances was measured this deficit is less serious.

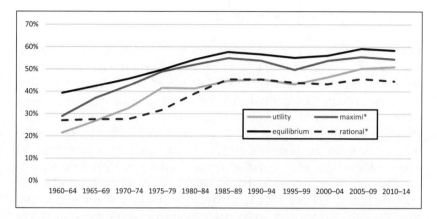

Figure 3.1   Frequencies of key terms in leading economics journals

the key terms appeared. In two cases the wild card (*) allowed for variations (such as maximise, maximize, maximization and so on).

Figure 3.1 shows that, contrary to rumours that Max U was on the way out, the use of terms such as utility, maximization, equilibrium and rationality have increased in frequency from the 1960s to the most recent period. All four terms reach their highest frequencies in 2005–09 or 2010–14. There is no sign here of any impact of the Great Crash of 2008 on the tenacity of Max U. Of course, some of the appearances of these terms may have been in criticism rather than by adoption, but they still dominate the agenda, nevertheless. Furthermore, there is little sign of alternative terms making headway against them. Searches for 'satisfic*' found appearances below 1 per cent frequency for the entire 1960–2014 period. Searches for ('bounded rationality' OR 'boundedly rational') never got above a frequency of 4 per cent.

The data in Figure 3.1 suggest that the Formalist Revolution of the 1950s led to a consolidation of the hard-core assumptions of Max U, despite ongoing technical and formal innovations, such as game theory. Max U has survived the 2008 crisis without any wounds, and he seems alive and well.

As noted in the previous chapter, early Max U came with a 'field' ontology, where infinite adjustment of variables and gross substitutability between them are possible (Mirowski, 1989; Potts, 2000). This allows, of course, the use of calculus. But game theory sheds this baggage, assuming a structured world without gross substitutability. Nevertheless, for much (but not all) contemporary game theory, Max U remains. Despite other major underlying changes, Max U still dominates.

WILL MAX U BE REPLACED?

John Davis (2006, p. 2) rightly warned us that 'the question of change in any science or system of ideas is an extremely complicated one, and that historians and philosophers of science are hardly in agreement over what constitute criteria for identifying change.' Among other outcomes, Davis (2006) considered the possibility of a 'maturity' scenario where 'neoclassical' economics persists but is no longer dominant. There may be something in his suggestion that Max U economics has completed its major contributions and theoretical returns to this paradigm are diminishing. But the case of behavioural economics gravitating back to Max U after 1990 suggests that Max U survives not simply because it is a relic from the past. Furthermore, the limited bibliographic evidence in Figure 3.1 suggests that Max U is as dominant as it has ever been.

Davis (2008) addressed the possibility of a shift from the current 'pluralism' toward a new orthodoxy. Again, the degree of persistence of Max U may have been underestimated, leading to some overstatement of the extent of current pluralism and an overestimation of the possibilities of the rise of a new orthodoxy. Like Colander, Davis pointed to behavioural economics as a harbinger of possible change. Like Colander, Davis seemed to have underestimated the degree to which behavioural economics has retained Max U, principally as an enduring measuring rod to detect 'deviations' from it.

To set the scene for a possible new orthodoxy, Davis (2008, p. 353) pointed to long-run historic changes in the reigning paradigm of economics: 'For example, classical economics was preceded by physiocracy and mercantilism, and succeeded by neoclassicism.' Is a major shift toward a new paradigm already underway and gaining ground in the twenty-first century?

I do not rule out this possibility, but I wish to bring another major factor into the argument – that is the professionalization of the economics discipline in the modern university. In the Anglophone world, professionalization in research-oriented universities was under way by about 1880 and accelerated in the twentieth century. In economics, the top departments and journals became established and recognized (Maloney, 1985; Coats, 1993; Kadish and Tribe, 1993; Fourcade, 2006).

Remarkably, for the entire period since 1880, despite enormous other changes, Max U has endured and dominated the core. The original promoters of Max U also insisted upon a particular kind of mathematical formalism (Mirowski, 1989). It is possible that, as economics became professionalized, institutionalized and formalized, Max U served as its lodestone. More than anything else, the discipline defined itself in terms of Max U and his utilitarian trappings. Max U has provided a framework for the organization and operation of particular kinds of mathematical formalism in economics.

The professionalized discipline sets down fundamental parameters that are difficult to change. As the prophet of scientific revolutions put it: scientific 'professionalization leads ... to an immense restriction of the scientist's vision and to a considerable resistance to paradigm change' (Kuhn, 1970, p. 64). Even if homage to Max U becomes little more than ritual, it could remain totemistic for the discipline for the conceivable future. If this account of Max U's defining function in the context of the professionalization of the discipline is true, then the chances of changing economics (at least from within) diminish significantly.

In some respects, Max U and its attendant assumptions have served as *hard core* in the sense of Imré Lakatos (1970). It is a guiding framework of analysis that serves to identify the discipline and channel its research. Early behavioural economics challenged this core but their successors retreated into a position of accommodation with it.

Given the strong additional empirical turn in the discipline, it may become even more difficult to challenge the Max U theoretical core. The unfalsifiability of Max U makes it invulnerable to evidence. Empirical work has a steep uphill task if trying to take on the Max U theoretical core, in addition to providing robust empirics. Earl (2010, p. 221) pointed out that 'if empirical work is based on unfamiliar economic theory it will be disadvantaged, if only because papers may need to be far longer in order to introduce the theory to referees and readers.' To get the empirical study published it is often best not to challenge hard core theoretical assumptions as well. Ultimately the empirical turn in economics may have made Max U stronger – at least in some ceremonial and discipline-defining sense – rather than weaker.

The increasing internal specialism within economics also frustrates challenges to any hard-core assumptions or ceremonial shibboleths (Cedrini and Fontana, 2018). The greater and deeper the specialisms, the more difficult it is to broaden the argument and shift the discourse away from the silos and toward taken-for-granted general principles.

A prominent view is that the theoretical core of a science becomes weakened when accumulating data and failures of explanation stretch the reigning paradigm to its limits. Anomalies accumulate to the point where normal science is undermined, creating the conditions for a 'scientific revolution' (Kuhn, 1970). The Darwinian revolution in biology, the Copernican revolution in cosmology, and the Newtonian and Einsteinian revolutions in physics are given as examples.

But the unfalsifiability of Max U at the core of mainstream economics places this discipline in a position different from others. Anomalies appear, not as a threat but as a challenge for those who will adapt preference functions in ever-more complex ways to fit the data. They then declare in triumph that Max U lives on. With suitable ingenuity this always can be done. Neither utility nor preferences are directly observable, and they themselves are not directly subject to empirical scrutiny.

Has there been a scientific paradigm in another discipline that is largely defined in terms of unfalsifiable claims, and a revolution that overthrew a scientific core that was largely unfalsifiable? Some have said that Darwinism is unfalsifiable, but this turned out to be mistaken.[7]

The efforts to make Max U fit the data, by making preference functions more elaborate, incorporating 'other-regarding' or 'social' preferences, are reminiscent of the conservative efforts of Ptolemaic astronomers to protect their theory that the Earth was the centre of the universe. To account for why heavenly bodies appear from Earth to move in circles, the Ptolemaic model incorporated 39 'wheels' to carry the sun, moon, planet and stars in cycles and epicycles. As John Milton put it in *Paradise Lost:* 'when they come to model heaven and calculate the stars, how they … contrive to save appearances, how gird the sphere with centric and eccentric scribbled o'er, cycle and epicycle, orb in orb'. This erection was cumbersome and without causal explanation. But it was predictively accurate enough to be used in navigation. And it kept the reigning dogma intact (Koestler, 1959). Similarly, adaptable Max U remains at the centre of the universe of orthodox economics, despite its limited explanatory power. Max U survives because epicycles (more complex preference functions) are brought in to 'save appearances'. Max U is endlessly modified to fit the incoming data.

In the end, the Ptolemaic view was not overthrown by data. The Copernican paradigm was adopted because it hugely simplified the picture, by assuming the sun was at the centre of the solar system. In addition, once Isaac Newton and others analysed the forces governing planetary orbits, the change of paradigm was irresistible (Kuhn, 1957).

But even this case is different in key respects from Max U in economics. Max U is already highly simplified. An adequate alternative account of the forces behind human motivation is likely to be more

---

[7] Popper (1976, pp. 151, 168) once argued that Darwinism was unfalsifiable. But he then changed his mind (Popper, 1978, pp. 344–6). Darwinism is neither tautological nor unfalsifiable: the fittest are not defined as those who survive, and the fittest do not always survive. In any case, the term 'survival of the fittest' came from Herbert Spencer and was rarely used by Darwin.

complex and to fail some empirical tests. The alternative theory may be more useful in analytical and policy terms, but if the focus is instead on mathematical prowess, then there is little incentive to switch from one paradigm to another. In this respect the role of Max U in economics seems unique. His unfalsifiability and simplicity are reasons why he lives on, and why a Kuhnian scientific revolution in economics is unlikely, at least in the foreseeable future.

The enormous empirical challenges mounted by experimental and behavioural economics since the 1980s have led to major positive developments, but they have ultimately left the Max U hard core intact. The 'anomalies' have disappeared through adjustment of the utility functions, or by their treatment as temporary deviations from the Max U norm.

This is quite unlike other sciences. For example, in chemistry, the phlogiston theory held that a fire-like element called phlogiston is contained within combustible bodies and released during combustion. But experiments in the laboratory revealed anomalies that were met by numerous contradictory refinements to the theory. The theory remained dominant until the 1780s when Antoine-Laurent Lavoisier showed that combustion requires a gas that has mass (oxygen) and could be measured by means of weighing closed vessels. These experiments set the stage for the oxygen theory of combustion. The idea of phlogiston was eventually abandoned. This paradigm shift occurred because the evidence fitted much better with the oxygen theory. By contrast, Max U can be adapted to fit any behavioural evidence.

As another example, it had long been observed that the planet Mercury had a solar orbit that deviated from that predicted by Newtonian equations. This alone was not enough to dethrone Newtonian physics. Change began when it was shown that Albert Einstein's alternative theory accurately predicted the orbit of Mercury. This led to Arthur Eddington performing a famous experiment in 1919 to test Einstein's prediction that light rays were bent by the sun. Paradigm change was fuelled by empirical refutation of an old theoretical system when combined with an empirical confirmation of a new one. In economics, there is no such dance of conjecture and refutation around its enduring Max U core.

If at all, radical change at the heart of economics is more likely to come slowly, as accumulating empirical work and context-specific theory are gradually acknowledged as more important than any ceremonial attachment to Max U. The unfalsifiability and infinite empirical plasticity of its core idea might eventually become more widely understood, and Max U might be seen less as triumphal vindication of disciplinary machismo, and more as ceremonial and dispensable ritual. A deeper desire to understand human motivation and psychology may begin to eclipse ritual efforts to represent all human behaviour in Max U terms. Then things will change. But there is little sign of that happening yet. Despite the 2008 shock of the biggest global financial crisis since the 1930s, these questions are not yet widely asked.

The current shift toward 'complexity economics' (Colander, 2000c, 2000d; Gallegati and Kirman, 2012) might move the discipline further away from simplistic formulations of interactive systems, heroic assumptions of representative agents, and much else. Some of this work may use agent-based models and other devices that are consistent with Max U but not necessarily derived from it. But the evidence from Richiardi and Leombruni (2005) cited above showed that agent-based models had made little penetration of the top-rank journals. Some infiltration of the citadels of the discipline may happen, but this process of change may be slow, and it does not necessarily follow that Max U will be removed from the high altar.

BRINGING REAL HUMANS BACK IN

The unfalsifiability of Max U sustains an *epistemic* critique. But it does not clinch the matter. One has also to consider the *theoretical* limitations of this stance. Max U falls down for at least two further reasons. First it side-lines the problem of *explaining the causes* of behaviour. Second it fudges the question of the individual *development* of capacities and dispositions. Both of these are vital in policy terms: they affect the design of incentives and popular education in aspects of public policy. They also affect the theoretical foundations of welfare economics (Steedman, 1980).

Max U is 'good' at prediction because, for reasons given above, it can envisage any conceivable behaviour. But Max U falls down when it comes to *explaining* behaviour. In the first volume of *Capital* Marx (1976, pp. 758–9 n.) noted the explanatory emptiness of Bentham's utilitarian argument:

> To know what is useful for a dog, one must investigate the nature of dogs. This nature is not itself deducible from the principle of utility. Applying this to man, he that would judge all human acts ... according to the principle of utility would first have to deal with human nature in general, and then with human nature as historically modified in each epoch.

Over a century later, Ronald Coase (1977, p. 488) focused on the crucial issue of motivation: 'To say that people maximize utility tells us nothing about the purposes for which they engage in economic activity and leaves us without any insight into why people do what they do.'

Relatedly, Amartya Sen (1977, p. 325) pointed to the circularity of explaining behaviour 'in terms of preferences, which are in turn defined only by behaviour.' Sen (1987b, p. 73) noted elsewhere that the description of choices in terms of utility 'does not give any independent evidence on what the person is aiming to do or trying to achieve.' This is why the use of Max U as a mere summary of behaviour is inadequate. Fitting utility functions to behavioural data does not amount to an explanation of motivation or action.

Max U offers an ex-post rationalization or 'expression' of behaviour – rather than an empirically grounded causal explanation. A utility function may serve a limited purpose as a formalized preference ordering. Such formal constructions can have some theoretical benefits in some contexts. They can be useful shortcuts, for modelling or explanatory purposes. But they do not enhance our understanding of human motivation.

The lack of an adequate explanation of human motivation, behaviour and development diminishes the utility of Max U for policy design. If human motivation is irreducible to one variable, such as money, happiness or utility, then policy design should also focus on multiple incentives, including an appreciation of their possible interdependence and mutual adaptation. If human motivation is multi-dimensional and multi-modular, and driven by multiple, potentially conflicting habits (James, 1890; Veblen, 1914; Dewey, 1922; Plotkin, 1994; Hodgson, 2004a, 2010), then particular motivations that are triggered in particular circumstances must be identified. Hopefully, this point will become clearer when we discuss the issue of moral motivation shortly below.

Inspired by Adam Smith (1759), Amartya Sen (1977, 1985a, 1985b, 1987a, 1987b) argued that human agents are not purely self-interested but have a measure of *sympathy* for others. Sen also stresses the concept of *commitment*, defined as a practical reason for an action that is independent of any gains or losses for that actor. Sen (2002, 2004) later added the concept of *identity* to his multi-faceted view of human nature. We choose an identity to make sense of our actions and to project a persona upon others. This cue was followed up by Davis (2007), Akerlof and Kranton (2010) and several others. For Sen, the reduction of human motivation to utility maximization neglects crucial issues surrounding individual capabilities, agency, and choice.

The experimental economist and Nobel Laureate Vernon Smith has become increasingly persuaded that the new behaviouralist game of fitting utility functions to data avoids the subtleties of human personality, including those revealed by Adam Smith (1759), who 'saw the individual as not even defined except in a social context' (Smith, 2013, p. 6). By contrast, the new behaviouralists attempted to force relational phenomena between individuals into preference functions attributed to separable agents. Rejecting this, Vernon Smith (2013, pp. 4–5) wrote:

> In my view, utilitarianism cannot be rescued by adding arguments to the utility function without undermining human sociality as relationship. ... Preferences cannot be 'social' (or 'pro-social') because relationship processes matter, with judgment of conduct emerging from the context, and from its propriety and ecological fitness with the order of rules defining social conventions.

Note that the article that carries the above quotation was published in a relatively minor heterodox journal. Despite his Nobel status, Smith has not so far published these anti-Max U arguments in a leading mainstream journal in economics. For similar reasons, also addressing experimental evidence, Bart Wilson (2010) argued that 'social preferences aren't preferences'.[8] Explanations of human behaviour cannot be devolved upon individuals (with or without preferences) alone. What matter too are social relations, and the rules that are embodied in social institutions.

THE NATURE AND IMPORTANCE OF MORAL MOTIVATION

Human nature is multi-faceted. For the purposes of this chapter I focus on our capacities for moral feelings and judgements. As Adam Smith emphasized, these are important components of human motivation. To repeat: behaviour guided by moral motivations can be subsumed under, and 'predicted by', Max U. But Max U theory fails to recognize the separate power and irreducibility of moral motivation: hence it offers an impoverished theoretical explanation and weakened policy guidance.

Moral motivation is not necessarily the same as altruism or other-regarding preferences. We may give to others, or show concern for others, for reasons other than morality. Furthermore, the Max U preference functions that accommodate altruism or other-regarding behaviour still treat individuals as if they are maximizing *their own* utility, and for this reason they may be regarded as selfish too. Even other-regarding Max U is acting selfishly. By breaking from Max U entirely, more genuine notions of moral motivation are able to overcome this limitation.

---

[8]   Wilson (2010) is also published in a journal with a heterodox history.

Many controversies divide moral philosophers. The best we can do here is to select a few prominent descriptions of the nature of moral judgement. The leading philosopher Richard M. Hare (1952) argued that morality was subject to reason and one cannot hold contradictory ethical judgements. As John L. Mackie (1977, p. 33) put it in his classic account, a moral judgement 'is not purely descriptive, certainly not inert, but something that involves a call for action or for the refraining from action, and one that is absolute, not contingent upon any desire or preference or policy or choice, his own or anyone else's.'

In his impressive philosophical account of the *Evolution of Morality*, Richard Joyce (2006, p. 70) argued on the basis of considerations in the philosophical literature that morality has most or all of the following characteristics:

1. Moral judgements express attitudes (such as approval or contempt) and also express beliefs.
2. The emotion of guilt is an important mechanism for regulating moral conduct.
3. Moral judgements transcend the interests or ends of those concerned.
4. Moral judgements imply notions of desert and justice.
5. Moral judgements are inescapable.
6. Moral judgements transcend human conventions.
7. Moral judgements govern interpersonal relations and counter self-regarding individualism.

These characteristics do not establish a *valid* morality; they instead help us to identify what is a *moral judgement*, whether acceptable or otherwise. In other words, the argument here concerns descriptive rather than normative ethics: there is no attempt here to identify the 'right' morality, but instead to identify the basic nature of a moral claim. Most religions uphold moral claims, but that does not make them all right or just.

Like others, Joyce emphasized the role of the emotions as well as deliberation in making moral judgements. Joyce's point (1) establishes that a moral judgement must involve both beliefs and sentiments and is not reducible to either alone. If an action is impelled *purely* by emotion and sentiment, then it cannot amount to moral motivation. Deliberations and beliefs are also vital but are themselves insufficient because they must be backed by sentiments or emotions: acting morally is more than calculated conformity to moral rules.

Moral judgements may be rationalized in various ways, but they are more than matters of reason or logic. Defiance of shared moral rules in a group is often met with emotional hostility. Conformity to them may sometimes bring an emotional glow. The emotional dimension of moral rules plays an important role in their evolution and their survival. Guilt (point (2)) is a particularly important emotion that sometimes emerges after breaches of moral rules, and it too plays a part in the evolutionary process.

Joyce's points (3) through (7) reveal the limitations of typical Max U approaches. Moral judgements are not simply expressions of an individual's interests, preferences, sentiments or beliefs. They are also universal claims, which are deemed to have force irrespective of the interests, preferences, sentiments or beliefs of those to whom they are supposed to apply.

As both Mackie and Joyce insisted, morality surpasses questions of preference. It is a matter of right or wrong, or of duty, of 'doing the right thing', irrespective of whether we like it or not. This is part of what makes us human: we are capable of considering moral rules and understanding that their observance is more than a matter of personal whim or satisfaction. As Charles Darwin (1871) pointed out, no other species has a developed morality, and its unique evolution is a vital matter for scientific research (Hodgson, 2013a, 2014a). A number of writers have explored how morality evolved uniquely among humans, building on capacities for empathy or sympathy among our primate ancestors (Sober and Wilson, 1998; De Waal, 2006; Joyce, 2006; Kitcher, 2011; Boehm, 2012). But Max U covers all species, and the uniquely human and genuinely moral dimension is missing. Moral values are either ignored or subsumed under matters of utility or preference.

This has important consequences for policy design (Hodgson, 2013a). For example, in creating policies for taxation, for health provision, or to deal with climate change, it is often insufficient to rely on pecuniary incentives alone. It is also vital to make a moral appeal, concerning the need for social solidarity and our duty to care for others, including for future generations. Such moral appeals transcend questions of individual benefit. They speak to our senses of duty, solidarity and nobility, rather than simply offering a 'warm glow' of extra utility, derived by doing good and feeling satisfied.

There is a fundamental difference between moral rules and other (normative) rules. 'Murder is wrong' does not carry the same connotations as 'splitting infinitives in English is wrong' or 'in Britain one must drive on the left side of the road'. Linguistic and traffic rules are matters of convention or local convenience. Murder is much more than a breach of convention.

Threat of punishment or respect for the law are each insufficient to explain the relatively low frequency of murder. Most of us abstain from murder not simply because the probability of severe punishment out-weighs any expected benefit. Most of us refrain from murder because we believe that it is *morally wrong*; we would desist even if we lived in a country where murder went unpunished. Most people obey laws, when they perceive them as legitimate, for moral rather than instrumental reasons (Tyler, 1990).

It is a commonplace observation that what may be a moral rule for one culture may not be so for another. But this does not mean that moral rules are reducible to conventions. They become moral rules because many people believe in them as such, and they jointly uphold them as more than matters of convenience, self-interest or convention. The cultural specificity of some moral judgements does not justify a *normative moral relativism*, where one person's morality is deemed as good as any other.

A moral judgement is more than mere convention; it is inescapable and transcends individual preferences or interests (Smart and Williams, 1973). Of course, when faced with moral dilemmas, people do often weigh up one option against the other. But to describe all this as utility maximization or a matter of preference misses the point. If people are always acting in a way that ends up maximizing *their own* utility, then they cannot be seen as truly altruistic or moral: instead they are psychopaths or sociopaths, manipulating circumstances for their own benefit, behind appearances of kindness.

Drawing on what I believe is the majority view among moral phil-osophers, I maintain that *moral dispositions cannot be adequately summarized by any preference function*. It is thus no accident that Adam Smith resisted the utilitarianism of his friend David Hume. Smith insisted on transcendent values such as justice and the common good that cannot be reduced to mere pleasure or happiness. But as modern economics has developed, a lesser place has been given to such values or moral considerations.

Figure 3.2 shows how the usage of terms beginning in 'ethic' or 'moral' (but excluding appearances of 'moral hazard') has declined in articles in ten leading Anglophone journals of economics relative to the use of the term 'utility'.[9] The number of articles containing terms beginning in 'ethic' or 'moral' were searched, and the number of articles

---

[9] This figure is taken from Hodgson (2013a). The ten journals surveyed were the *American Economic Review, Econometrica, Economic Journal, Economica, Journal of Political Economy, Oxford Economic Papers, Quarterly Journal of Economics, Review of Economic Studies, Review of Economics and Statistics* and the *Southern Economic Journal*. The oldest of these journals started in 1886 and the newest in 1938. Economists use the term 'moral hazard' to describe inefficiencies that occur when risks are displaced. It has minimal resemblance to the concept of morality in ethics.

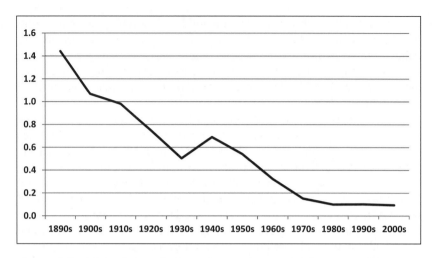

*Figure 3.2   The relative decline of 'morality' in leading economics
            journals*

containing the word 'utility' were also found. The graph shows the
former figure divided by the latter for each decade. Before 1910 terms
such as 'ethics' or 'morality' were more common than 'utility'. After the
First World War, 'utility' took the lead and stayed ahead. By the 1970s,
articles with 'moral' terms were less than 20 per cent as frequent as those
with 'utility,' and from the 1980s they were around 10 per cent. In an era
where mathematical expression matters most, morality had been largely
subsumed under utility.

CONCLUSION: OBITUARIES FOR MAX U ARE PREMATURE

The principal argument in this chapter is that Max U has been more
durable in recent decades than some scholars have argued. This is despite
the major changes in theoretical approach, technique and diversity in
economics since 1980. Key developments – such as the kind of post-
Simon behavioural economics that emerged in the 1990s – still show the
gravitational pull of Max U. There are exceptions, such as work on
complexity, evolutionary game theory or agent-based modelling, but so
far these have been insufficient to dislodge the dominance of Max U in
the discourse of the most prestigious journals of economics. Neither has
the increasing use of empirical methods and data undermined the reign of
Max U.

In part, Max U survives because utility maximization is unfalsifiable. There is no way of demonstrating that agents are not maximizing the hidden variable of utility. But unfalsifiable propositions can have a framing or organizing role in scientific thought, and Max U plays this part to the full. To a large degree this explains its persistence. It has returned to behavioural economics, where it serves as a benchmark.

Bibliometric and other evidence counters the (Colander et al., 2004, p. 485; Colander, 2005b, pp. 930–31) claim that mainstream economics is moving away from its 'holy trinity' assumptions of 'rationality, selfishness and equilibrium'. On the contrary, Max U is still god. He has adorned new clothes, including 'social' and 'other-regarding' preferences – all while his own selfish U is still being maximized.

To underline the explanatory limitations of Max U, this chapter has considered the human capacity for moral judgement and the possibility of moral motivation. A number of moral philosophers suggest that a moral judgement is different from a convention or preference because it entails a claim to universality.

For policy design, models such as Max U that *predict* behaviour are far from enough. Policies should be informed by richer *explanations* of motivational dispositions and behaviour. Moral motivation is important in this regard. Policy design can often appeal to moral values as well as pecuniary incentives. But, apart from the work of Sen and a few others, there is little sign of economics moving in this direction, and fully rehabilitating the 'moral sentiments' of Adam Smith.

Unfortunately, as established in Chapters 1 and 2 above, this development is indiscernible in orthodox economics and it is absent from much of heterodox economics as well. Although self-described 'heterodox' economists sometimes complain about Max U they rarely begin the task of constructing an alternative explanation of human behaviour. But generally, Max U is an important part of the enduring core of orthodox economics, and most heterodox critics have overlooked this prime target.

Even if it were unlikely to divert mainstream economics from its tracks, an organized, focused and sustained criticism of Max U by a network of scholars could have some positive influence. But while such criticisms could have rich policy conclusions, they would not necessarily be aligned to what is currently described politically as the left. The restoration of moral sentiments would be a project for traditional conservatives or advocates of free-market economics, as well as other liberals or socialists. The potential political ambiguity of the assault by moral sentiments on Max U is perhaps a reason why it is largely absent from existing 'heterodox' networks, which have generally been inclined to the left.

4. The separate heterodoxy of evolutionary economics

with Juha-Antti Lamberg

> The premises and the point of view required for an evolutionary economics have been wanting.
>
> Thorstein Veblen (1898a)

The term 'evolutionary economics' was coined by Thorstein Veblen (1898a), who argued that economics should take account of the widespread impact of Darwinism on the social as well as the natural sciences.[1] But Veblen's 'post-Darwinian' approach was largely abandoned after his death, even by his closest followers (Rutherford, 1998; Hodgson, 2004a). At least until the 1970s, the derogatory but partially mythological label of 'social Darwinism' blocked much further exploration (Bannister, 1988; Hodgson, 2004b, 2006b).

After decades when the word was taboo in the social sciences, since 1980 the word 'evolution' and claimed 'evolutionary approaches' have proliferated, particularly in areas related to business, organization studies and innovation research. From economics (Boulding, 1981; Nelson and Winter, 1982, 2002; Hayek, 1988; D. Friedman, 1991; Hodgson, 1993, 1998a, 1999b, 2006b; R. Nelson, 1995; Nelson et al., 2018; Witt, 2003), the terms 'evolution' and 'evolutionary' have spread to other disciplines including organizational, innovation and management research (Aldrich and Ruef, 2006; Durand, 2006). Some scholars (Aldrich, 1999; Geroski, 2001) have argued for a meta-theoretical 'evolutionary perspective', to express the conceptual and theoretical core and unite separate disciplinary approaches. But as yet there is little agreement on what should make up this core.

---

[1]   This chapter uses material from Hodgson and Lamberg (2018). Further information is found in that journal article, including a more detailed version of the results presented in Figure 4.2, and data plots for different 5-year periods in the 1986–2010 time-span. See also Hodgson (2019b).

The modern wave of evolutionary economics was launched with the classic study by Richard Nelson and Sidney Winter (1982). This book, along with a number of other related works, has spawned an impressive global network of research that rivals any other heterodox movement. But unlike 'heterodox economics' elsewhere, evolutionary economics did not spring from Cambridge or from dissident Marxist economists, and it is less ideological in tenor. Furthermore, Nelson and Winter (1982) did not mention Veblen, despite striking resemblances in these approaches (Eaton, 1984; Hodgson, 2004a). Veblen applied Darwin ideas to economics. Nelson and Winter (1982) then mentioned Darwin only once, and in passing.

It is important to emphasize that the word *evolution* is highly vague, and it does not necessarily mean Darwinism. Nor should it. There are rival conceptions of what evolution means, such as in the differing accounts of Herbert Spencer or Joseph Schumpeter. Neither the etymology nor the past usage of the word *evolution* require us to use it in a Darwinian sense. In fact, in the first edition of the *Origin of Species*, Darwin did not use the word *evolution* and he wrote *evolved* only once.

Nevertheless, although Nelson and Winter (1982) avoided any explicit Darwinian connection, their theoretical approach builds on the Darwinian triplet of variation, selection and inheritance. Hence Veblen's original claim about the importance of Darwinism remains pertinent. Yet the issue of Darwinism remains largely unrecognized and unresolved within the Nelson–Winter tradition of evolutionary economics. The congenital homage to Schumpeter has endured instead. Furthermore, the word *evolution* is used liberally and persistently, with little attempt to clarify the intended meaning.

Accordingly, despite the success and impact of Nelson and Winter's 1982 book, it did not establish a clear over-arching paradigm for theoretical research. Its impact was more inspirational than constitutive, particularly in applied studies. The failure to resolve these general questions of meaning and substance within *evolutionary economics* has been exacerbated by the subsequent fragmentation of this field and its dispersal to multiple disciplinary locations within academia.

Although the stream of research stemming from Nelson and Winter (1982) has had a big impact on business economics, organization studies and innovation research, it still does not appear on the radar screen of many heterodox economists. This estrangement from the rest of heterodoxy makes it an outsider. It is a 'separate heterodoxy' in another sense, because since the 1990s it has largely developed outside departments of economics.

Unlike other economic heterodoxies, Nelson–Winter evolutionary economics manages to be highly policy-oriented and pragmatic, but less overtly ideological. The numerous researchers inspired by Nelson and Winter adopt a number of very different policy stances, ranging from support for less-regulated markets to recommendations for substantial state intervention in a mixed economy. But while policy stances range from libertarian free-market to social democratic, and while Karl Marx remains an influence alongside Schumpeter and others, I am not aware of any evolutionary economist in the Nelson–Winter tradition who advocates wholesale common ownership and full-blooded socialism, in the manner of (say) Joan Robinson, Frederic Lee or Roy Bhaskar.

The theoretical explanation of this socialist lacuna is straightforward. Despite diverse opinions, evolutionary economists emphasize uncertainty, complexity, bounded rationality, tacit knowledge and other factors that together make comprehensive and effective central planning impossible (Hodgson, 2019c). Perhaps rival heterodox economists are aware of this, and it is a reason why they pass over Nelson–Winter evolutionary economics?

Although evolutionary economists diverge in theoretical and policy terms, there is general agreement among its participants on some basic ideas. First, evolutionary economics addresses a world of change. But this change is not merely quantitative or parametric: it involves qualitative changes in technology, organizations and the structure of the economy (Veblen, 1919; Schumpeter, 1934; Dosi et al., 1988; Hayek, 1988).

Second, an important feature of economic change is the generation of novelty. Variety and its replenishment through novelty and creativity is a central theme of contemporary evolutionary economics (Foss, 1994; Witt, 1992). Third, evolutionary economists stress the complexity of economic systems. Complexity involves non-linear and potentially chaotic interactions, further limiting predictability (Dosi et al., 1988; Arthur et al., 1997).

Fourth, human agents have limited cognitive capacities. Especially given the complexity, uncertainty and ongoing change in the real world, agents are unable to fully understand what is going on. As Herbert Simon (1955, 1957) put it, there is 'bounded rationality'. Indeed, unlike the remainder of heterodox economics, Simon's concept of bounded rationality is central to evolutionary economics in the Nelson–Winter tradition. Finally, complex phenomena can emerge through self-organization or piecemeal iteration as well as through design. Just as Darwin showed that intricate and complex phenomena can emerge without God, evolutionary economists adopt the insight of Hayek (1948, 1988) and others that many human institutions and other social arrangements evolve spontaneously through individual interactions, without an overall planner or blueprint.

These five points are widely if not universally accepted among evolutionary economists. But beyond this point some major divergences begin. There is little further agreement on a core theoretical approach.

If orthodoxy is defined in terms of the adoption of Max U, as suggested in Chapter 2, then these five points clearly make the majority of work in evolutionary economics heterodox, despite many influential heterodox economists having neglected this stream of thought.

A BIBLIOMETRIC ANALYSIS OF EVOLUTIONARY ECONOMICS

Evolutionary economics seems more susceptible to bibliometric analysis than other forms of heterodoxy.[2] Within its networks, much discursive interconnection hinges on the word *evolution*, despite its vague meaning. This provides a means of identification of widely dispersed works, to explore their connections with prominent texts in evolutionary economics.

This chapter reports a broad bibliometric analysis of 'evolutionary' research in the disciplines of management, business, economics and sociology over 25 years from 1986 to 2010. It confirms that Nelson and Winter (1982) is an enduring nodal reference point for this broad inter-disciplinary 'evolutionary' field.

The bibliometric evidence suggests that evolutionary economics has benefited from the rise of business schools and other inter-disciplinary institutions, which have provided it with a home, but it has failed to nurture a strong unifying core narrative or theory, which in turn could provide superior answers to important questions and generate an over-arching positive heuristic of research.

This bibliometric evidence also shows that no strong cluster of general *theoretical* research immediately around Nelson and Winter (1982) has subsequently emerged. It identifies developmental problems in a partly successful but fragmented field. Future research in evolutionary economics needs a more integrated research community with shared conceptual narratives and common research questions, to promote conversation and synergy between diverse clusters of research.

---

[2] Bibliometric methodology has been employed in strategic management (Martinsons et al., 2001; Ramos-Rodriguez and Ruiz-Navarro, 2004); economics (Cahlik, 2000; Pieters and Baumgartner, 2002); entrepreneurship (Ratnatunga and Romano, 1997; Busenitz et al., 2003); organization studies (Usdiken and Pasadeos, 1995); inter-organizational relationships (Sobrero and Schrader, 1998); marketing (Hoffman and Holbrook, 1993; Pasadeos et al., 1998); management information systems studies (Culnan, 1986); and research and development studies (Tijssen and Van Raan, 1994).

Modern evolutionary economics of the Nelson–Winter variety has had more impact on research in business schools and departments of innovation studies than in departments of economics. This is confirmed by evidence that it receives more citations from business and management journals than from core journals of economics. This is neither surprising nor necessarily alarming, as the analytical perspectives of mainstream and evolutionary economics are quite different. But this bibliometric study also confirms the fragmentation of developments in evolutionary economics, and highlights problems for this stream of research.

Because of changes in the character of mainstream economics and the growth of inter-disciplinary academic arenas such as business schools, many practitioners of Nelson–Winter type evolutionary economics emigrated from departments of economics. This exodus was most pronounced in the United States and other Anglophone countries, where business schools expanded rapidly. The development of business schools was not uniform globally, and other countries tell a different story. In Italy, for example, evolutionary economics retains a stronger footing in departments of economics.

Residence in business schools, departments of innovation studies, or departments of science policy created both opportunities and problems for the theoretical development of this field. The successes are apparent in the rapid impact of evolutionary economics in empirical studies of technological change, national innovation systems, and science policy (Dosi et al., 1988; Nelson et al., 2018). On the other hand, theoretical cohesion and communication are more difficult to develop with researchers located in multiple disciplines or sub-disciplines. In such contexts, a developmental problem for evolutionary economics is that of enhancing its theoretical core through trans-disciplinary conversations.

These trans-disciplinary and trans-departmental features gave evolutionary economics a unique character. The lack of a consensus over a clearly identified theoretical core, combined with the well-known communication barriers between disciplines, mean that the standard sociology of scientific disciplines (Whitley, 1986, 2000) is inadequate to deal with evolutionary economics. As Anthony Van Raan (2000) argued, bibliometric analysis can at least have a preliminary diagnostic role in dealing with the problems of inter-disciplinarity, by making communicative 'maps', identifying key actors, works and research areas, and showing structural changes in the field through time.

The theoretical fragmentation of this field has been noted by other authors (Verspagen and Werker, 2003; Witt, 2008), but the bibliometric analysis reported here is more extensive. It addresses published 'evolutionary' research in the fields of business studies, economics and sociology by combining co-citation analysis (Small, 1973; Griffith et al., 1974) with cluster and document-centrality analysis.[3]

Two earlier studies were confined to evolutionary economics (Dolfsma and Leydesdorff, 2010; Silva and Teixeira, 2009). Witt (2008) built on an opinion survey of meanings of the word 'evolutionary' adopted by users in the field. Another study confined itself to innovation and technology research in the context of evolutionary economics (Verspagen and Werker, 2003). Bhupatiraju et al. (2012) applied network analysis to a citation database confined to the fields of entrepreneurship, innovation studies, and studies in science and technology. While these three fields have links with evolutionary economics, they exhibit independent trajectories and are no more than segments of its whole field.[4]

Only two earlier systematic reviews took a longitudinal bibliometric approach and attempted to show the evolution of the field through time (Dolfsma and Leydesdorff, 2010; Silva and Teixeira, 2009). Dolfsma and Leydesdorff (2010) considered the years 2000–05 and 7534 journals citing or cited by the *Journal of Evolutionary Economics.* Silva and Teixeira (2009) addressed the 1958–2008 period and used 2510 journal articles for their survey.

Our study covered 1986–2010. It accessed 8474 articles, which in turn cited 349 750 further usable works. This is by far the largest bibliometric study of the 'evolutionary' field to date. This is also the first systematic bibliometric analysis covering economics, sociology, management and business. Because of its multi-disciplinary scope and time span, it is able to address the development of such key problems as fragmentation and disciplinary division to an unprecedented depth and degree. In particular, the nodal role and lack of development of immediate offshoots with continuous theoretical rapport with Nelson and Winter (1982) is much clearer in this study.

---

[3]   A wider research focus to include additional disciplines (such as politics and history) would have limited our ability to study the structure of the field effectively. Increased heterogeneity would have made the identification of different research streams trickier. Also, the available software restricted the number of articles and the number of cited pieces of work. The 350 000 potential citation objects approached the performance limits of the Sitkis software. As shown in Figure 4.1, by a good margin the most important areas using 'evolutionary' terminology are management, business and economics.

[4]   Bhupatiraju et al. (2012) found that citations between the fields of (1) entrepreneurship, (2) innovation studies, and (3) studies in science and technology are scarcer than citations within the fields. Although the three fields share research topics and themes, they have developed largely on their own and in relative isolation from one another. This further confirms the problem of spanning different research communities.

Our analysis mapped the research field, including the most influential authors, publications and research areas. It identified a diversity of 'evolutionary' research clusters, of which few cross disciplinary boundaries. A crucial problem highlighted by our study is for this 'evolutionary' field to maintain a common research agenda and momentum across these boundaries. Unless they are defined more sharply, vague terms such as *evolution* and *selection* are insufficient to retain connectedness and inter-disciplinary conversation, while enhancing theoretical development, across a highly diverse field of study.

RESULTS OF THE BIBLIOMETRIC ANALYSIS

Figure 4.1 portrays the rapid rise since 1980 in research employing 'evolutionary' terminology. It reveals its particularly strong usage in management, business and economics. It is not claimed that all uses of 'evolutionary' terminology can be described as evolutionary economics. But a later figure confirms the supreme nodal significance of Nelson and Winter's (1982) work, and its multiple connections across different clusters of research.

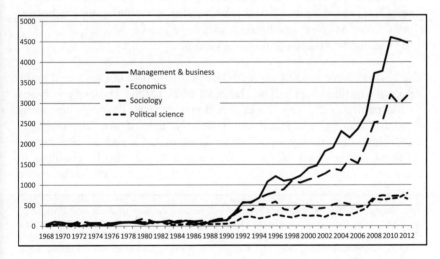

Note: Number of publications in Clarivate Analytics (formerly Thomson Reuters) Web of Science with 'evolution' or derivative in the title, abstract or keywords.

Figure 4.1 *'Evolutionary' publications in management, economics, sociology and politics*

An important institutional factor is the rapid growth of business schools after 1980, particularly in the US and UK.[5] Our co-citation analysis shows how the seminal and nodal work of Nelson and Winter (1982) has been linked most strongly to areas of business-related research. As discussed in the following section, its success is partly due to its implantation in business schools and other multi-disciplinary milieux.

Several key clusters of research are described as follows:

- Cluster A   Industrial evolution and product life-cycles
- Cluster B   National innovation systems
- Cluster C   Economic sociology
- Cluster D   Endogenous growth theory
- Cluster E   Qualitative research methods
- Cluster F   Socio-genetic evolution
- Cluster G   Evolutionary game theory
- Cluster H   Genetic algorithms (not shown on Figure 4.2)[6]
- Cluster I   Organizational ecology
- Cluster J   Evolution of technology and dominant designs
- Cluster K   Resource and capability-based views
- Cluster L   Organizational learning and behavioural approaches
- Cluster M   New institutional sociology
- Cluster N   Transaction cost economics

The clusters were formed via the bibliometric algorithm mentioned in the Appendix to this chapter. The choice of titles for the clusters was based on the nature of the key works that dominate each cluster, often using standard terminology. Note that relatively few of the clusters span established disciplinary boundaries. Clusters C, I and M are largely confined to sociology. Clusters D, G and N are largely confined to economics. Other clusters relate to specialist groups of researchers with

---

[5]   In the US, for example, the number of graduate degrees (masters and doctorates) conferred in business increased from 9.1 per cent of the total in 1970–71 to 21.2 per cent of the total in 2010–11 (National Center for Education Statistics, 2017, Tables 323.10 and 324.10). In absolute terms, the number of such degrees increased almost sevenfold in the same period. *The Economist* (1996, p. 54) reported that 'the number of business schools in Britain has risen from 20 in the early 1980s to 120' by 1996. By 2012–13, 23.1 per cent of all postgraduate degrees in the UK were in business or administration (Higher Education Student Statistics UK, 2018).

[6]   Cluster H appears in other Figures in Hodgson and Lamberg (2018). The same lettering of clusters as found in the Hodgson and Lamberg paper is preserved here, for ease of cross-referencing.

their own institutional niches in academia. So Clusters A and J relate to technology studies, Clusters I and L to organization science, and Cluster K to business strategy.

Figure 4.2 maps the clusters and presents the structure of evolutionary research during the whole period 1986–2010. The size of the node represents the relative citing frequency of the document. The thickness of the line connecting two documents indicates the strength of the link between the documents.

Figure 4.2 clearly illustrates the central and the enduring nodal role of Nelson and Winter's (1982) classic book. This work has a significant connection with Giovanni Dosi's (1982) seminal essay on technological paradigms, and with various works on organizational learning and the original behaviouralism (March and Simon, 1958; Cohen and Levinthal, 1990; March, 1991). But more than creating an immediate and dense cluster of spin-off research, the seminal role of Nelson and Winter (1982) has been to serve as a point of reference for other clusters. It seems that Nelson and Winter's work stimulated a dispersed array of semi-detached enquiries but did not lead to the further development of a closely related and distinctive evolutionary theory in that genre. This result is confirmed by other studies (Witt, 2008; Silva and Teixeira, 2009).

Notably, there is no qualifying cluster on evolutionary theory. A group of works on evolutionary theory in economics, including the famous papers by Armen Alchian (1950) and Milton Friedman (1953) (which both appear in Figure 4.2) did not meet the threshold level that was set for cluster status. Other connected papers in this area did not meet the threshold citation levels for appearance in the figure.

The work of Nelson and Winter (1982) was most closely linked with Cluster L on organizational learning and behavioural approaches, with Cluster I on organizational ecology, with Cluster M on new institutional sociology, and (more remotely) with Cluster B on national innovation systems. Research in these areas appears infrequently in departments of economics and it is much more prominent in business schools.

Further evidence of the detachment of Nelson–Winter style evolutionary economics from its originating discipline of economics is the absence of significant interchange between evolutionary economics and evolutionary game theory (Hodgson and Huang, 2012). Consider also the weak ties between Nelson–Winter evolutionary economics and endogeneous growth theory in Cluster D, which is dominated by two works by Nobel Laureate Paul Romer (1986, 1990). Romer's models supported an active role for technology policy, as Nelson, Winter and many others working with them have done. But the model-centred style of endogenous growth theory is different from the less-formal theorizing found in

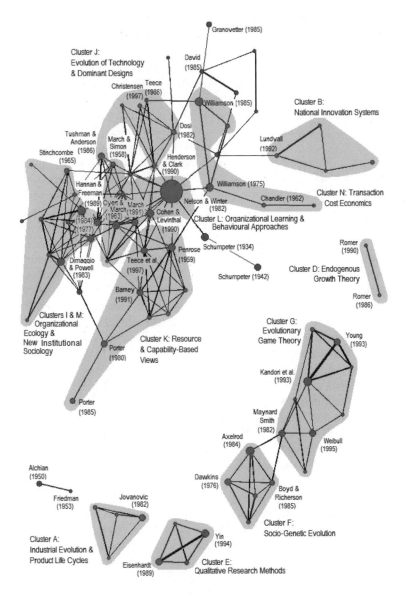

Notes: The size of the node represents the relative citing frequency of the document. The thickness of the line connecting two documents indicates the strength of the link between the documents. All nodes and links are subject to minimum thresholds for inclusion. Not all nodes are labelled in this version. This figure is a simplification of a more detailed version found in Hodgson and Lamberg (2018).

Figure 4.2   Evolutionary clusters and co-citations 1986–2010

Nelson–Winter style evolutionary economics. This may partly account for the limited connections between the two. Mainstream evolutionary game theory and endogenous growth theory are both dominated by what Nelson and Winter (1982) describe as 'formal theory'. This contrasts with the less-formal 'appreciative theory' that Nelson and Winter regard as crucial. The higher regard for 'appreciative theory' may help to explain the level of neglect of Nelson–Winter evolutionary economics by mainstream economists.

There are stronger citation links between Nelson and Winter (1982) and the pioneering work in transaction cost economics by Coase (1937) and Williamson (1975, 1985). But transaction cost analysis has also moved its centre of gravity away from economics and towards business schools, as evidenced by a detailed analysis through time of references in Williamson's publications (Pessali, 2006).

While Nelson and Winter's work remained relatively marginal in its source discipline of economics, it became very popular in management. This shift is reflected in citations. In the years 1983–89 inclusive, there were 142 citations to Nelson and Winter (1982) from journals listed under 'economics' in the Clarivate Analytics (formerly Thomson-Reuters) database, compared to 82 citations from journals in business and management. In 1990 the number of citations to this book from economics was roughly equal to those from business and management journals. Subsequently citations from business and management increased rapidly, while the number of citations from economics grew much more slowly. In the years 2006–12 inclusive, there were 515 citations to this book from journals listed under 'economics' compared to 1766 citations from journals in business and management. This shows a dramatic migration from the home discipline of economics in the 1980s to the new home in business and management by about 2012. As the evolutionary economics of Nelson and Winter (1982) has become more influential, it has become detached from mainstream economics while being cited much more in the business school sector.[7]

---

[7] Further evidence suggests an even deeper divergence. The three journals citing Nelson and Winter most often since 1983, which are listed under 'economics' in the Clarivate database, are *Industrial and Corporate Change* (accounting for 3.0 per cent of all citations to Nelson and Winter (1982)), the *Journal of Evolutionary Economics* (2.6 per cent), and the *Journal of Economic Behavior and Organization* (2.2 per cent): none of these is by any account a mainstream journal of economics. The six other journals citing Nelson and Winter most since 1983 are *Research Policy* (5.7 per cent), the *Strategic Management Journal* (5.7 per cent), *Organization Science* (3.7 per cent), *Management Science* (2.1 per cent), the *International Journal of Technology Management* (1.9 per cent), and the *Journal of Management Studies* (1.8 per cent).

This change of home discipline has allowed Nelson–Winter evolutionary economics to prosper but it has created additional problems for its development. In particular, it is more difficult to maintain intensive conversations across multiple clusters and research programmes. Unlike departments of economics, business schools are multi-disciplinary and often heavily compartmentalized. Analysis of curricula in business schools has noted very limited success in linking separate disciplines, except for the use of common mathematical and statistical tools (Dunning, 1989; Starkey and Madan, 2001).

Our analysis provides further evidence that disciplinary designations and boundaries have reduced linkages. For example, work in Clusters I and M was not as close to Nelson and Winter's nodal work as it could be, despite the strong evolutionary and selectionist theme in much work on organizational ecology (Hannan and Freeman, 1989) and the work on the evolution of organizations by Aldrich (1999) and others. Michael Hannan, John Freeman and Howard Aldrich were all trained as sociologists and are often labelled as such.

Our analysis also shows an enduring disconnection of research gathered around Nelson and Winter (1982), from evolutionary anthropology (Boyd and Richerson, 1985), from evolutionary psychology, from work on the evolution of cooperation (Axelrod, 1984), and from the evolutionary theory of Darwin (1859) himself – see Cluster F. Given that the core theory of Nelson–Winter style evolutionary economics may benefit from further development, this lively, theoretically-rich and relevant evolutionary literature would be obvious places to turn for inspiration. So far this has not happened to any great degree.

In sum, while our analysis identifies Nelson and Winter (1982) as an enduring nodal point in the evolution of the field, it indicates that this work has not inspired major subsequent development of the core evolutionary theory. Instead it serves as an historic 'concept marker' (Case and Higgins, 2000) with 'conceptual symbolism' (Small, 2004, p. 71) for a diverse, inter-disciplinary and fragmented field of specialized evolutionary studies of particular economic and business phenomena. This also suggests that this evolutionary field lacks an integrated, developing meta-theoretical perspective, which can help to generate shared ideas and research questions for empirical investigation. These issues are likely to be significant for its further development.

PROBLEMS OF IDENTITY AND STRATEGY

As noted in Chapter 2, any viable discipline or school of thought must have a *raison d'être*. This can be defined in terms of one or more of the following:

a.   the study of a specific zone of enquiry or a set of phenomena in the real world; or
b.   the promotion or development of a particular theoretical approach; or
c.   the promotion or development of a set of analytical techniques; or
d.   the promotion or development of policies in a defining problem area.

Starting with the first option, evolutionary economics is difficult to define in terms of (a) – a specific zone of enquiry or a set of phenomena in the real world. While it has emphasized innovation and technological change, these topics are insufficient to define the essence of evolutionary economics. Evolutionary economists stress that innovation and change are pervasive phenomena, so they do not identify a specific zone of enquiry.

Turning to (d), while Nelson–Winter type evolutionary economics has made important policy contributions, particularly in regard to science and technology, these varied contributions to policy development are also insufficient and too diverse to define evolutionary economics. Hence (d) alone does not provide a *raison d'être*, while it has been a major area of contribution.

This leaves us with (b) or (c) as potential *raisons d'être* for evolutionary economics. Different opinions may exist on this. A core theoretical approach is evident in Nelson and Winter (1982). But as we have noted, it has received limited further theoretical development at the foundational level. On the other hand, some evolutionary economists have adopted and promoted specific techniques, such as Stuart Kauffman's (1995) NK model. But again, this has not taken off as a defining attribute. In neither case does this bibliometric evidence point to extensive post-1982 development of these theories or techniques. Whatever the *raison d'être* of evolutionary economics, this bibliometric analysis fails to detect its defining developmental traces in post-1982 publications. This does not mean that there have been no developments in technique or core theory since 1982 in this field. But none of these have established strong bibliometric traces in the citation record. This absence is significant.

Consider one possible reason for this, among others. We hypothesize that the migration of evolutionary economics from departments of economics to business schools and other multi-disciplinary institutes has exacerbated its ongoing fragmentation and thwarted the development of its identity, in terms of theory or technique – (b) or (c). This relocation has also created great opportunities, particularly on the policy front. But the rewards of policy influence simply helped to postpone the development of a core identity.

Success in these inter-disciplinary milieux has been a major blessing, but also in part a curse. Akin to oil-rich countries enjoying prosperity but failing to invest revenues in long-lasting and productive assets such as infrastructure and education, evolutionary economics has failed to invest in a viable theoretical core or provide another suitable *raison d'être*.

This book emphasizes that science is a social process and it works partly through the creation and ongoing amendment of established positions in a scientific community (Merton, 1942; Polanyi, 1962; Kuhn, 1970; Kitcher, 1993; Collins, 1998). It involves 'epistemic communities' and institutionalized 'machineries of knowing' (Knorr-Cetina, 1981).

In any scientific community there is a trade-off between diversity and consensus. Sufficient variety of opinion is necessary for advance, so that inadequate or flawed beliefs can be challenged by alternatives. Some sufficient (but not absolute) agreement is also required to avoid endless criticism and unceasing demolition of core beliefs (Polanyi, 1962; Kitcher, 1993). Otherwise science cannot progress.

The Nelson–Winter wave of evolutionary economics established some conversational forums and consensus-preserving institutions. They include the International Joseph Schumpeter Society formed in 1986. There are allied or sympathetic international journals such as the *Journal of Evolutionary Economics* and *Industrial and Corporate Change*. These entities have helped to keep evolutionary economics together, on a global scale.

But otherwise, and within particular universities, reputational and other incentives have been lacking. Migrating from economics, evolutionary economics took hold in other, multi-disciplinary environments. Here goals and incentives are more diverse, emanating from multiple disciplines. In such contexts, most evolutionary economists have to advance their individual careers in compartmentalized research fields such as innovation studies, business economics, science policy or organization studies. This has consigned evolutionary economics to fragmented environments, where plural incentives and overlapping structures were less aligned to any unifying mission.

The necessary degree of consensus is more difficult to sustain in such contexts. Researchers have vested interests based on time investments and incentives – including those of promotion, status and publication –

that are largely compartmentalized by the institutional and departmental structures of academia (Weingart and Stehr, 2000). Specialization within disciplines compounds this problem further. Any inter-disciplinary research programme has to provide additional incentives – including common questions of interest – to escape multiple, narrow, specialist confinements (Cedrini and Fontana, 2018).

The success of evolutionary economics in maintaining fruitful conversation among its practitioners has been very much against the stream. It is down to the enduring vitality of several international networks (including the International Schumpeter Society and allied journals) and some national scholarly associations. But the bibliometric evidence presented here reveals insufficient further development of a theoretical core. Studies of scientific research from the philosophy and sociology of science suggest that additional institutionalized incentives are necessary.

SUMMARY AND CONCLUSION

The bibliometric analysis reveals a combination of growth, diversification and deepening fragmentation, caused in large part by disciplinary boundaries that cannot be dissolved simply by the use of vague words such as 'evolution', 'evolutionary' or even 'selection'. This diverse 'evolutionary' field has been described as an 'invisible college' (Verspagen and Werker, 2003). But it has striking differences from 'invisible colleges' studied elsewhere. Classically the term applied to 'an elite of mutually interacting and productive scientists within a research area' (Crane, 1972, p. 348). Although the 'evolutionary' field in economics, sociology and management has an elite group of highly cited researchers, their works are also divided by disciplinary and sub-disciplinary frontiers. The identity and boundaries of its 'research area' are unclear. It is a peculiarly diverse and segmented elite, making relatively few widely shared references to core theoretical works appearing after 1982.

In this diverse context, the narrower stream of evolutionary economics lacks an adequate theoretical 'hard core' in the sense of Imré Lakatos (1970). The bibliometric analysis clearly establishes that the work of Nelson and Winter (1982) is a dominant node for evolutionary research, but there is a lack of subsequent identifiable literature developing a core theoretical framework. Its enduring presence among the citations in the field seems as much a ceremonial and 'symbolic payment of intellectual debts' (Small, 2004, p. 71), as of anything else.

Each individual cluster in the field manifests a high degree of historical path dependence and a good measure of isolation (Lucio-Arias and

Leydesdorff, 2008). The silo effect (Lewin and Volberda, 1999) refers to an outcome of specialization and fragmentation, where sub-fields become less capable of reciprocal operation with related sub-fields. Our evidence suggests that evolutionary economics may be moving dangerously in this direction.

To counter the silo effect, fragmentation and specialization have not been matched by fruitful development of overarching theory, a common conceptual vocabulary, and common research questions promising answers that demonstrate the superiority of the approach. If evolutionary economics is to develop in the future it needs to find ways to:

1. Further facilitate inter-cluster communication by developing shared theoretical arguments with a common vocabulary, and shared empirical questions.
2. Promote conversation or integration between clusters.
3. Generate prominent research questions with potential 'evolutionary' answers that are superior to those produced by prominent rival approaches.

Communication is currently inhibited by insufficient shared terminology. Organizational ecologists use some specialized vocabulary that differs from that of evolutionary economists. There is also the lack of a shared overarching 'evolutionary' theoretical framework. Words such as 'evolution', 'co-evolution', 'evolutionary' or 'selection' are used in very different ways, with chronically insufficient attempts to establish shared meanings (Hodgson, 2013c; Dollimore and Hodgson, 2014; Hodgson and Stoelhorst, 2014).

An obvious longstanding candidate for a shared theoretical evolutionary framework, deploying sharper meanings of these terms, is the generalization of Darwinian principles to the socio-economic domain (Veblen, 1898a, 1899; Campbell, 1965; Hayek, 1988; Hull, 1988). But work in this area has been resisted or ignored by many researchers within Nelson–Winter type evolutionary economics. Despite much effort since the turn of the century, it is far from universally accepted by researchers in this field (Aldrich et al., 2008; Stoelhorst, 2008, 2014; Hodgson and Knudsen, 2010; Breslin, 2011; Hodgson and Stoelhorst, 2014).

Peter Murmann et al. (2003) wrote an essay on the state and future of 'evolutionary' research in management and organization theory. This article illustrates the problems as well as the potentialities. Darwinism is mentioned only once, when noting that Schumpeter rejected its application to social evolution – as if that ended all discussion on that issue. The idea of generalizing Darwinism to socio-economic evolution – which goes back to Veblen and others – does not appear. This is strange because the concept of 'selection' appears many times. But notably the authors fail to give it a sufficiently clear meaning. There is little elaboration of what is being selected, of what selection mechanisms are involved, and what kind of selection outcomes need to be identified. While pointing to the importance of empirical work, the key concepts to be deployed in analysing evolutionary phenomena remain vague. The recommended immersion in empirics cannot serve as a research programme, especially if it is conceptually blind. The article is evidence of a conceptual vagueness, and a failure to establish a clear theoretical hard core.

There is little sign since of these defects being adequately addressed. In a retrospective essay, significantly oriented to management scholars as well as economists, Sidney Winter (2017) mentioned terms like *evolution* and *selection* frequently, but he never defined what they mean.

In 2018 nine leading evolutionary economists (including Dosi, Nelson and Winter) published a collection of essays to serve as an introduction to *Modern Evolutionary Economics* (Nelson et al., 2018). It is a very useful book, and it can be highly recommended as a guide to work in the field. But the reader will search in vain for an adequate, unifying conceptual framework to replace orthodox economics. There is no discernible development in the theoretical hard core beyond Nelson and Winter (1982). Some previously prominent core ideas are even dropped. For example, the concept of selection is mentioned merely as an aside (Nelson et al., 2018, p. 208), and it does not even appear in the index of the book. There is avoidance rather than development of the theoretical core.

Key connections are missed. For example, there is no mention in the volume of the evolutionary work on organizational selection by Michael Hannan and John Freeman (1989). Especially given the migration of evolutionary economics to business schools, omissions such as this are blinkered and damaging.

In the lead essay, Nelson saw evolutionary economics as 'to a considerable extent inductive in nature' (Nelson et al., 2018, p. 10). In response, we are reminded of the statement by Marshall (1885, p. 168) that 'the most reckless and treacherous of all theorists is he who professes to let facts and figures speak for themselves.' As Albert Einstein said to Werner Heisenberg during a lecture in 1926 in Berlin: 'Whether you can observe a thing or not depends on the theory which you use. It is the theory which decides what can be observed' (quoted in Salam, 1990, pp. 98–101). Empirically-oriented research is commendable and necessary, but it can never be theory-free. Theory always plays a role on framing the questions, establishing the concepts and guiding the enquiry.

The idea that theory can spring inductively and unaided from mere data is an illusion.

Some authors within *Modern Evolutionary Economics* try to give the impression that evolutionary economics is already well-defined. Virtually vacuous statements such as 'there is a consensus that the process should be understood as evolutionary' pepper the text. There are also upbeat claims that 'an evolutionary perspective' has taken root in other disciplines (Dopfer and Nelson, 2018, p. 225). But because the word *evolution* is used therein in an extremely vague sense, meaning little more than (any kind of) transformational change, then claims of the widespread incidence of 'evolutionary perspectives' are hardly surprising.

Evolution and *evolutionary* are highly imprecise words. This does not necessarily mean that they should be given more precise meanings. But they do not intrinsically constitute or even signal a theory. The authors raise important issues, including a stress on innovation and change and the importance of moving beyond standard equilibrium theory. But these statements do not amount to a theory that remotely approximates the overarching power and resilience of the neoclassical paradigm (which is not to ignore its grave weaknesses).

An effective rival theory would have to displace the entire neoclassical corpus and ontology, which is based on utility maximization and gross substitutability, and is wrapped up in the formalisms and metaphors of nineteenth-century physics (Mirowski, 1989). A rival ontology would have to be adopted and rival metaphors deployed (Potts, 2000). These are formidable tasks.

Yet the final essay, by Nelson and Kurt Dopfer, tries to create the impression that the book has achieved an adequate theoretical exegesis. They refer to 'master' theories that 'influence strongly the orientation of theories focused more narrowly on particular phenomena and questions' (Nelson et al., 2018, p. 229). But no adequate master theory is outlined in the book.

Strategic issues, relating to power and influence in the academy, are also neglected. It is not claimed here that theory must be mathematical. Any 'master' theory is unavoidably conceptual, even if it uses mathematics. Nelson and his colleagues are right to emphasize that what is required is a combination of 'formal' and 'appreciative' theorizing (Nelson and Winter, 1982). But if the strategy is to persuade economists, then given the current state of the discipline, the 'master' theory *would* have to find a mathematical expression. Like it or not, mainstream economics today speaks the language of mathematics. *Modern Evolutionary Economics* retains an orientation towards economics and persuading economists. Such a strategy of engagement with the mainstream would also mean addressing mainstream developments such as evolutionary game theory and endogenous growth theory. This entry price is not paid. An alternative strategy would be to address an audience outside economics. These vital strategic dilemmas are not considered.

There are numerous citations in Nelson et al. (2018) of publications in management and innovation studies. But there is no attempt as yet to engage with evolutionary anthropology (Boyd and Richerson, 1985), evolutionary psychology (Cosmides and Tooby, 1994; Buss, 1999), or work on the evolution of cooperation (Axelrod, 1984; Hammerstein, 2003; Bowles and Gintis, 2011). Darwinian evolutionary ideas could be drawn upon to develop an alternative and morally enriched theory of human motivation to replace Max U (Sober and Wilson, 1998; De Waal, 2006; Joyce, 2006; Kitcher, 2011; Boehm, 2012; Hodgson, 2013a, 2014a). None of this is evident.

Darwin is mentioned a few times in the Nelson et al. (2018) volume, including once where Richard Nelson (p. 25) accepted that evolutionary economics 'has something in common with the perspective of Darwinian evolutionary biology'.[8] But always there are the cautionary additions that the processes of 'evolution' (whatever that means) in the biological and social worlds are very different. Of course they are. And the processes of evolution of molluscs are very different from those of orangutans, as are those of grasses from those of pine trees. The whole point of Darwin's 'master theory' is that it elaborates basic principles of selection, variation and inheritance that apply to all such highly varied replicating populations. The claim of writers such as Veblen and Donald T. Campbell (1965) was that the same overarching principles can act as a 'master theory', to help guide further theorizing to understand the evolution of human society.

Is this considered further? No. While Veblen is mentioned several times in the book, his promotion of an evolutionary economics guided by Darwinian principles is overlooked. Campbell is mentioned once in a footnote, but the substance of his major foundational contribution toward a Darwinian and evolutionary social science is also neglected. There is no mention in Nelson et al. (2018) of recent attempts – following Veblen and Campbell – to generalize Darwinian principles to socio-economic evolution (Aldrich et al., 2008; Stoelhorst, 2008, 2014; Hodgson and Knudsen, 2010; Breslin, 2011; Hodgson and Stoelhorst, 2014).

---

[8]   Nelson and Winter (1982) did not admit this. Instead they then claimed that they were Lamarckians. Without any explanation, this claim was not repeated in Nelson et al. (2018). On the misleading notion that socio-economic evolution is Lamarckian see Hodgson and Knudsen (2010, ch. 4).

In the decades since Nelson and Winter (1982), much has been achieved, particularly in applied areas. But one has to look hard to find any evolution of its theoretical core. Without such integrative theoretical developments, evolutionary economics is likely to suffer further fragmentation, albeit with substantial innovation and progress within its individual fragments. A core theoretical framework is necessary to show that the broad approach has improved answers to pressing research questions, whereby it can claim its superiority over rival approaches.

Some promising links have yet to be developed between evolutionary economics and other complementary streams of evolutionary research. While evolutionary economists, organizational ecologists and institutional economists have often distanced themselves from narrow versions of rationality and have been strongly influenced by behaviouralist pioneers such as Herbert Simon (1957) and Richard M. Cyert and James G. March (1963), much less attention has been given to evolutionary psychology and the evolution of cooperation. The missing links with classic works in these areas are clearly evident from the bibliometric analysis discussed above.

There is no recipe that guarantees success, but above all evolutionary economics needs a much clearer identity and *raison d'être*. This bibliometric analysis identifies the failure to develop a prominent and widely cited theoretical core. This is not to belittle the many important achievements of evolutionary economics, but to point to gaps that may need to be addressed in the future. Despite its achievements, evolutionary economics, like the rest of heterodox economics, has failed to establish sufficient consensus around a theoretical nucleus.

While other streams of heterodox economics have been overly politicized, Nelson–Winter evolutionary economics has not shared this problem, despite its effective involvement in policy analysis. Evolutionary economics demonstrates that ideology is not the only problem with heterodoxy. All heterodoxies lack adequate spheres of power within academia, where sufficient agreement over core issues can develop and motivate cumulative research. Despite its successes in several applied areas, Nelson–Winter evolutionary economics has fragmented. The heterodox institutional problem of building sufficient consensus for theoretical development is addressed in the following chapter.

APPENDIX ON THE DATA AND METHODOLOGY EMPLOYED IN THE BIBLIOMETRIC ANALYSIS

Citation analysis is a powerful tool for the identification of intellectual bases and underlying research streams (Usdiken and Pasadeos, 1995; Pasadeos et al., 1998; Schildt and Mattsson, 2006).[9] Citation analyses divide into 'macro' approaches that focus on the overall structure of disciplines and develop principles governing the evolution of science, and 'micro' approaches that describe retrospectively the structure and historical development of schools of research and their interdependencies (Gmür, 2003). This study fits with the micro stream of research.

Critics of the use of citation analysis address citation biases, including a focus on published articles and books only. They also point to the technical limitations and imperfections of citation indices and bibliographies (Macroberts and Macroberts, 1989; Osareh, 1996). With improved databases, some of these shortcomings have been reduced (Sillanpää, 2006). Important limitations remain, but we have done our best to address possible biases and to remove errors from our extensive database.

The approach reported here combines co-citation and cluster analysis (Schildt et al., 2006; Sillanpää, 2006; Schildt and Mattsson, 2006). Co-citation analysis reveals the closeness of two pieces of work in a common discourse. Cluster analysis and network analysis enable further structuring of the research field under study. Highlighting the structure of the field by both cluster analysis and network analysis (which produce highly similar results) mitigates the biases in any individual research method.

We used data from the Social Science Citation Index (SSCI) of the Clarivate Analytics Web of Science, which is a massive multi-disciplinary index to social sciences journals. It indexes over 1720 journals across 50 social science disciplines; and individually selected, relevant items from over 3300 of the world's leading scientific and technical journals.

Within the database we conducted searches for the word *evolution* and its derivatives. Further searches confirmed the result of Bernhard Dachs et al. (2001) that related search words (for example *Schumpeter, biological, biology, genes*) yielded a much smaller number of retrieved articles, compared to *evolution* and *evolutionary*. To narrow down the number of hits (over 20 000), and to confine our study to business-related issues, we refined the search to cover documents related to the following

---

[9]   This technical Appendix omits some of the further details found in the Appendix to Hodgson and Lamberg (2018).

fields only: management, business, economics and sociology. The search was further refined to cover articles only, thus excluding book reviews, notes and editorial announcements.

The start date of the searches was 1 January 1986 (the first accessible year on the Clarivate database) and the end date was 31 December 2010. Before 1986 far fewer articles discussing 'evolution' were published in the social sciences (Hodgson, 1998a). To identify changes for the whole period we retrieved 8474 articles: 217 were published during 1986–90, 954 during 1991–95, 1637 during 1996–2000, 2172 during 2001–05, and 3494 during 2006–10. These were all possible citation sources.

Sitkis computer software (Schildt, 2004) was used to download data on possible citation objects from the Web of Science to a Microsoft Access database. The articles in the whole period cited another 373 848 texts, of which 24 098 were discarded by the program. The program reported disregarded citations and all of these were checked manually. Most referred to newspapers, trade journal articles or statistics and were deemed tangential to this analysis. A small number of corrections were made.

Clarivate data are not entirely accurate. Because of the large number of total references, it was impossible to check every one. Schildt (2002) argued that correcting citation data for the top 20–50 authors or documents is sufficient to provide reliable and usable results. But we imposed higher standards by checking in excess of 400 documents in each of the 5-year periods from 1986 to 2010. References made to reprints and book-editions were combined as references to one, original article or book. But citations to compiled book editions were left unaltered.

A co-citation involves a link between two documents that is created by a later document (Griffith et al., 1974). A co-citation measures 'the frequency with which two documents are cited together' (Small, 1973, p. 265). If two articles are cited in the same text, then they may be closely related to each other either because they are part of the same topic area or because their topic areas are closely connected (Small, 1973; Cawkell, 1976). Although some co-citations are between unrelated references, a sufficiently large sample of cited articles enables researchers to mitigate this problem (Schildt and Mattsson, 2006).

Using Sitkis software, we produced a co-citation network. A threshold level, based on the frequency with which the citing articles cited the references, was used to exclude references that did not have a serious impact on the study (Schildt et al., 2006). A series of two-dimensional (citer–cited) networks were then produced in order to determine the best threshold level. In a two-dimensional network, the citing articles were the first dimensions, and the cited texts acted as their affiliations. When the threshold was raised, the number of remaining cited documents decreased, and the number of citing articles also declined. After testing the series of networks, the threshold was set at a point at which lowering the threshold level by one would bring the maximum marginal increase in the number of cited articles. Below this threshold the heterogeneity of the cited documents increased considerably, leaving additional documents outside the core of the field.

Co-citation data were normalized to emphasize proximate relationships between similar references that are not cited as often as the most common references (Gmür, 2003). The normalized co-citation strength measure, *S*, for individual pairs was calculated by means of the Jaccard index (Small and Greenlee, 1980). The co-citation link strength *S(A,B)* between papers *A* and *B* was defined as follows:

$$S(A,B) = \frac{a \cap b}{a+b-a \cap b}$$

where *a* represents the number of citations to document *A*, *b* the number of citations to document *B* and $a \cap b$ the number of co-citations of *A* and *B*.

We employed cluster analysis to classify objects into clusters that maximize homogeneity within clusters and heterogeneity between clusters (Culnan, 1987; Hair et al., 1998). We employed Johnston's average-link hierarchical algorithm, as in the UCINET 6 software (Borgatti et al., 2002), to produce clusters from the co-citation network data. In the average-link algorithm, the distance between two clusters is the average dissimilarity between members (Borgatti et al., 2002). According to Sillanpää (2006), the average-link method produces clusters more continuously than other hierarchical methods.

UCINET NetDraw software was used to draw network figures from the co-citation network data. To make reading of the networks easier, we reduced the number of visible links by imposing an arbitrary cut-off level of co-citation strength. The links below the cut-off level (of 0.1) were left out of the figures, as well as documents isolated by the procedure. The NetDraw software then arranged the remaining documents according to geodesic distances.

We performed the cluster analysis for documents in co-citation networks for the 1986–2010 period. As there is no unique way to identify clusters, their identification involves some interpretation: we used similarity levels calculated by the algorithm as guidelines. We set two rules for the identification of clusters from the tree diagrams. First, an independent cluster or sub-cluster must consist of at least two documents.

Second, main clusters were separated at a similarity level that produced a moderate number of clearly identifiable clusters.

5. Heterodox economics as a scientific community

> The innovating theoretician needs a ruthless self-belief. He must overturn the intellectual dwelling-places of hundreds of people, whose first instinct will be resistance and revenge. Yet reconstruction must inevitably use much of the old material. Piety is not only honourable, it is indispensable. Invention is helpless without tradition.
>
> George L.S. Shackle (1967)

Heterodox economists have been working hard to improve economics for several decades. They have published thousands of articles in reputable academic journals and taught many more thousands of students. But their progress in changing economics has been limited. If anything, despite the embarrassment of mainstream economics by the 2008 Crash, they have less power within the most prestigious departments of economics and less of a presence in leading journals of economics than they did in the 1970s. To understand this shortfall, we must examine economics not merely as a set of doctrines, but as a system of organized authority, requiring strategies of power to transform it.

We need to apply the analytical tools of science to understand science itself. This chapter makes use of work in the philosophy, sociology and social epistemology of science to suggest that the traditional emphasis by heterodoxy on pluralism, while valid, is one-sided. It neglects the roles of power and authority within science, and it overlooks the need to build up an empowered community of scientists sharing some common assumptions and with some agreement on key issues.

While diversity and pluralism are desirable, innovating schools of thought also rely on some degree of consensus, around positions of academic power. Of course, the existence of a consensus does not validate any shared belief, and the possibility of challenging orthodoxy must remain, but some kind of authoritative agreement is essential for science to move forward, and to create cumulative progress.

These and other insights help us understand the limited progress of 'heterodox economics' since its consolidation in the 1970s, and its chequered esteem in terms of quality. They help us appreciate why the 'heterodox' project often does not build cumulatively on its own past achievements, and consequently has made relatively little advance, despite a global economic crisis from 2008.

SCIENTIFIC COMMUNITIES AS DECENTRALIZED COORDINATION SYSTEMS

After the work of Robert Merton (1942), Michael Polanyi (1962), Thomas Kuhn (1970), David Hull (1988), Philip Kitcher (1993) and others, the social embeddedness of scientific enquiry has become more widely understood. Instead of the picture of the lone, reflective observer or experimenter, there is a growing understanding that effective enquiry requires an interacting network of researchers. Science consists of coordinated practices performed in a structured social community.

Michael Polanyi was a pioneer of the scientific study of science. He was a younger brother of the famous Karl Polanyi, author of *The Great Transformation* (Polanyi, 1944). Trained as a chemist, Michael also made important contributions to economics and to the philosophy of science. As Mary Jo Nye (2011, p. xviii) put it in her intellectual biography of Michael Polanyi: 'Karl's stress on the role of institutions in economic systems eventually found an echo in Michael's work on the social dimensions of science.'[1]

Michael Polanyi criticized the idea that the central planning of science was possible or desirable. In a pioneering series of works, he described science as a community of individuals and practices, working through a partly unplanned division of labour. The nature of specialist knowledge in science, much of it being tacit and dispersed, meant that meaningful and progressive planning of science as a whole was impossible.

Because of the overwhelming scale and complexities of any science, and the immense amount of information involved, individual scientists cannot make sound judgements on everything. They depend on the screening capacities of others and they necessarily rely on good measures of competence, trust and mutual respect. Some sharing or coordination of

---

[1]   While Karl Polanyi was a classical socialist, Michael Polanyi was a Keynesian liberal who advocated substantial and redistributive inheritance taxes. Although Michael attended the first meeting of the Mont Pèlerin Society in 1947, he had drifted away by 1955, stressing its inadequate consideration of the problems of unemployment and economic inequality, and its promotion of a narrow view of liberty as the absence of coercion, thus neglecting the need to prioritize human self-realization and development (Burgin, 2012, p. 116; Jacobs and Mullins, 2016).

knowledge is necessary to keep science together, scrutinize research, establish results and enable progress. As Polanyi (1962, p. 60) argued:

> [While] scientists can admittedly exercise competent judgment only over a small part of science, they can usually judge an area adjoining their own special studies that is broad enough to include some fields on which other scientists have specialised. We thus have a considerable degree of overlapping between the areas over which a scientist can exercise a sound critical judgment. ... Scientific opinion is an opinion not held by any single human mind, but one which, split into thousands of fragments, is held by a multitude of individuals, each of whom endorses the other's opinion at second hand, by relying on the consensual chains which link him to all the others through a sequence of overlapping neighbourhoods.

Polanyi saw science as a cognitive organism of intersecting individual knowledge, bound together by 'consensual chains' in 'overlapping neighbourhoods'. This implies clusters of specialists, working interactively within scientific communities on particular projects and problems.[2]

Polanyi's arguments about the irretrievably dispersed nature of scientific knowledge are reminiscent of those of Friedrich Hayek (1935, 1944, 1948) against central planning.[3] The two authors knew one another, and Hayek took the term 'tacit knowledge' from Polanyi. Although he did not coin the term 'spontaneous order', Michael Polanyi (1948) used it before Hayek and possibly inspired the Austrian's adoption of the expression.[4]

Although Polanyi (1944, 1962) used the term 'market for ideas', unlike others he did not pursue it literally.[5] For him it was a useful metaphor among others: in discussing science he also used analogies from politics and religion. His 1962 paper also describes science as a 'republic'. The market metaphor expresses the competition in science for precedence,

---

[2] Lindblom and Cohen (1979, p. 100) saw Polanyi's (1962) approach as valuable but flawed because Polanyi 'finds interaction among scientists alone to be the chief guidance of the coordination system' thus neglecting interactions between scientists and others, including practical problem solvers and government officials. We need to take account of interfaces between the scientific community and the outside world as well as the interactions within.

[3] Polanyi's 1962 essay is his classic summary statement on the nature of science. Polanyi (1940, 1941, 1951, 1958) made numerous earlier important declarations on this topic. Polanyi (1945) also made contributions to economics from a Keynesian standpoint.

[4] See Jacobs (2000), Bladel (2005), D'Amico (2015), Jacobs and Mullins (2016). McQuade (2007) and McQuade and Butos (2003) applied Hayek's (1948, 1988) theory of spontaneous order to the operation of science.

[5] By contrast, addressing 'the market for goods and the market for ideas' Coase (1974, p. 389) wrote: 'There is no fundamental difference between these two markets'. Neither of the Polanyi brothers took this view. See Mäki (1999) and Hodgson (2019d) for criticisms of Coase and others in this area.

status, approval and other rewards. But it can be misleading because most ideas are not literally traded in scientific communities. The market analogy also downplays the key role of authority, and of admission by institutional qualification to the concourse of ideas. Like his brother Karl Polanyi (1944, pp. 41–3, 56, 68–72 ctc.), Michael was clear that true markets use explicit prices. By contrast, scientific communities rely on additional and often more important criteria of evaluation.

Nevertheless, Michael Polanyi argued that organized science and complex, large-scale economic systems share some features. These include the devolved and dispersed nature of knowledge and the reliance on decentralized systems of coordination. As Polanyi (1962, p. 57) argued: 'the coordinating functions of the market are but a special case of coordination by mutual adjustment'. Science is one such coordination system. The polity is another. The legal system is yet another. Civil society involves others. True markets are still others. Because they all share the feature of dispersed knowledge, which cannot adequately be retrieved and processed by a central authority, none of them can be planned comprehensively by the centre. But while these decentralized coordination systems have common features at some abstract level, the detailed institutional structures and mechanisms are often very different.[6]

There has been related research on the social and contextualized nature of knowledge and cognition. Instead of assuming that individuals proceed largely by building representative models of their world in their brains, psychologists and others argue that human cognition also depends on its social and material environment and the cues provided by structured interactions with individuals and artefacts. Human cognitive capacities are thus irreducible to individuals alone: they also depend upon social structures and material cues. This is true for science as much as any other organized human activity. Science becomes institutionalized, to create 'epistemic communities' and 'machineries of knowing'.[7]

---

[6] János Kornai suggested the term 'decentralized coordination mechanism' to me in an email on 17 April 2018, indicating that they may be universal in (large-scale) human societies, while markets are not. I have replaced 'mechanism' by 'system'.

[7] The quoted phrases are from Haas (1992) and Knorr-Cetina (1981) respectively. See also, for example, Toulmin (1972), Fuller (1988), Longino (1990), Lave and Wenger (1991), Hutchins (1995), Wenger (1998), Nooteboom (2000), Lorenz (2001), Nelson and Nelson (2003), Fuller and Collier (2004), Nonaka et al. (2006) and Rolin (2008).

With only one brief mention of Polanyi, Philip Kitcher (1993) applied social epistemology to the scientific community.[8] Scientific knowledge is developed by institutionalized communities of investigators that scrutinize others in their area and play a crucial role in the advancement or rejection of particular approaches to understanding. The academic institutions of the scientific community mould the conceptual language, identify the questions that are deemed important, establish acceptable modes of explanation, determine the issues due for experimentation and observation, and highlight the exemplars of acceptable scientific reasoning.

For both Polanyi and Kitcher, the scientific project is an ongoing search for truth, and scientific communities are machines for revealing and testing possible truths. Both authors adhered to philosophical realism, believing that there is a social and natural world beyond our perceptions, which can be appraised by the methods and institutions of science. It is important to emphasize this, because there has been a contrasting turn in the social studies of science, when objective truth was sometimes denied, and science was made equivalent to a form of religion (Sokal and Bricmont, 1998; Parsons, 2003; Nye, 2011). Kitcher's (1993) work was in part a response to such arguments.

SCIENCE AS A SYSTEM OF POWER

Polanyi emphasized that science is a system of power. To function effectively and to create a community of mutual trust and esteem, science must be organized. It should screen new entrants and require specific qualifications. It requires a community of scientists who share some fundamental assumptions and with some consensus on key issues. Some accord over basic ideas is essential to monitor quality, to maintain standards, to avoid ongoing critical discussions of potentially everything, and to establish shared principles and questions that can then be appraised extensively by multiple, interacting researchers in the face of accumulating empirical data.

Of course, the mere existence of a consensus does not validate any shared belief. But some agreement is essential for science to move

---

[8]   While Kitcher's approach is very useful, there are several points of dispute, including his emphasis on rationality (while ignoring many of the problems and ambiguities surrounding that concept), his all-too-quick rebuttal of the problem of theory-ladenness of observation, and his gravitation towards an analytical framework that in some respects resembles neoclassical economics (Mirowski, 1995). But much of his core argument can survive the removal of these flaws. Michael Polanyi's work does not have these defects.

forward. Progress in any school of thought requires social institutions to establish interlinked concentrations of expertise that can help monitor quality, synergize insights and channel debate.

Separated by particular skills, scientists dig down into their specialist areas. All scientific fields face the unrelenting challenge of what Eli Noam (1995, p. 248) called the 'inexorable specialization of scholars' as research digs deeper and deeper into specific, separate problems (Blau, 1994; Wenger, 1998; Cedrini and Fontana, 2018).

Especially given this necessary and unrelenting specialization, it is impossible for any scientist (or team of scientists) to check every result or claim upon which their research is based. As Polanyi (1958, p. 216) wrote: 'The organisation of the scientific process is so vast that any single person can properly understand only a small section of it.' Nevertheless, through institutions involving power and rewards, functioning on measures of mutual trust and respect, scientists manage to come together to sustain a system of power, which is necessary for science to function: '[This] group of persons – the scientists – administer jointly the advancement and dissemination of science. They do so through the control of university premises, academic appointments, research grants, scientific journals and the awarding of academic degrees which ... open up the possibility of academic appointment.' (Polanyi, 1958, p. 216).

Furthermore, these scientists establish what is, and what is not science, and who qualifies as a scientist. The whole science system in modern democratic societies in turn depends on sufficient public acceptance of their legitimate authority in this area, despite the fact that scientists are not elected by the public at large. All functioning sciences are elitist – they proceed by authority, consensus and constructive dissent, not by democratic votes.

In his seminal study of tacit knowledge, Polanyi (1967, p. 62) noted that the transmission of knowledge, including in science, required some acceptance of hierarchy and seniority. There has to be some trust in experts and teachers: 'confidence in authority is indispensable for the transmission of any human culture'. The institutions of the scientific community must establish some accord and authority upon which the progress of science depends.

A suitable metaphor for science is neither a central planning system nor a market. Science combines competition with hierarchical authority, the enforcement of rules, and limited entry. Science is more like a football league, or an association for basketball, baseball or other competitive team sports. It is competitive yet closed, devolved yet hierarchical, pluralist yet reliant on authority. It is a genuine hybrid of competition with hierarchy, involving both cooperation and rivalry, between multiple agents in organized structures.

THE VITAL INTERACTION OF PLURALISM AND CONSENSUS

It is well established that much innovation in science comes from the synthesis of ideas from different topics or disciplines (Peirce, [1882]1958; Koestler, 1964; Laudan, 1977). But scientific innovation requires not only diversity, but also a sufficiency of consensus and community, with shared understandings and conceptual language, to make such synergy possible.

Some internal pluralism or diversity within any academic community is vital. Internal debate is necessary for theoretical advance: diversity and dissent provide the fuel for theoretical innovation. But pluralism must be housed within some kind of consensus over what common problems are to be faced, over what is within or beyond the scope of the group of researchers and over what is deemed important and interesting. Without some consensus, progress is impaired by endless dispute over fundamentals. As Randall Collins (1998, p. 845) noted in his prodigious account of intellectual change: 'At times the density of warring factions floods the attention space with contending positions' leading to a curtailment of intellectual progress. Sheila Dow (2007, p. 448) argued similarly, that an 'unstructured pluralism or eclecticism, understood as an absence of selection criteria, or "anything goes", is antithetical to the building up of knowledge': it would lead to chaos or stagnation.[9]

Previously Robert Merton (1942, p. 126) had stressed the importance of 'organized skepticism' in science. Going further, Polanyi (1962, p. 59) stressed the indispensability of both conformity and innovation in any science, and how they may interact with one another:

Both the criteria of plausibility and of scientific value tend to enforce conformity, while the value attached to originality encourages dissent. This internal tension is essential in guiding and motivating scientific work. The professional standards of science must impose a framework of discipline and at the same time encourage rebellion against it. They must demand that, in order to be taken seriously, an investigation should largely conform to the currently predominant beliefs about the nature of things, while allowing that

---

[9] See also Dow (2008).

in order to be original it may to some extent go against these. Thus, the authority of scientific opinion enforces the teachings of science in general, for the very purpose of fostering their subversion in particular points. ... The authority of scientific standards is thus exercised for the very purpose of providing those guided by it with independent grounds for opposing it.

Accordingly, Polanyi captured the vital interplay and mutual necessity of criticism and consensus, and of pluralism and authority. Science must combine both conservative and revolutionary forces. Conservativism retains the authority, integrity and credibility of the scientific community. The revolutionary spirit spurs innovation and pluralism.

Like Polanyi, Kitcher (1993) emphasized the importance of both consensus and variety within the scientific community of a discipline. Sufficient agreement is a requirement for a critical mass of attuned scholars, with a division of labour to scrutinize and guide emerging research, and to provide essential criticism and expertise.

Other writers have used social epistemology to show that some consensus is essential to establish a working bedrock of assumptions and results. For example, Kristina Rolin (2008, p. 115) developed a 'contextualist theory of epistemic justification to argue that scientific communities have an interest in collective knowledge because it enables them to establish a context of epistemic justification.'

A consensus requires incentives to be sustained. Leaders in a scientific community must have sufficient power over career opportunities, academic promotions, academic journals, and grant-awarding bodies to provide reputational and pecuniary rewards, to encourage respect for existing scientific claims, and to discourage endless or excessive criticism of the vital consensus. Consensus-retaining incentives must counterbalance the sceptical and critical spirit.

The obvious danger here is that the group becomes overly conservative, hence rebutting sensible criticism and stifling innovation. But the absence of agreement is also damaging: endless criticism and unrestrained innovation would inhibit cumulative advance in the healthiest areas of research. Hence institutionalized incentives for maintaining some consensus matter.

Both pluralism and consensus are necessary. If the consensus is overwhelming, then radical innovation is stifled. Any dissent would be starved of effective critical dialogue, guidance, funding and attention. Kitcher (1993, ch. 8) thus established a notion of 'optimal' diversity in a scientific discipline. For scientific progress to be likely, there has to be a sufficient diversity of views and approaches for innovation, and adequate agreement to limit endless questioning and criticism. Neither diversity nor consensus should crowd out the other.[10]

Diversity applies not only to scientific ideas, but to individuals and to their motives as well. As Kitcher noted, there can be a diversity of motivations among researchers, from moral commitment to the advancement of knowledge, to self-interest, pursuit of status, esteem or monetary gain.[11] For Kitcher, motivational purity in science is neither necessary nor possible. Scientific advance depends on particular institutions and incentives that channel and combine varied individual incentives towards the general growth of knowledge.

Incentives are important. While curiosity of course is indispensable, a community of scientists cannot be motivated by inquisitiveness alone. Power, esteem and resources come in: they are needed to sustain and motivate a wider and heterogeneous body of researches over the *longue durée*. Any individual within a scientific community has to compromise with the consensus to access its power and resources.

In the social sciences, sociology may be a discipline that suffers from excessive diversity and insufficient consensus, at least since the 1970s and the end of its Parsonian dominance. Sociology exhibits a wide diversity of approaches and it continues to produce rich empirical research, but there is little agreement on its theoretical core, or even on its constitutive identity (Mouzelis, 1995).

By contrast, in a pioneering study of economics as a discipline, Richard Whitley (1986) noted a relatively high degree of agreement over core issues. This made the discipline more integrated and interdependent. Strategic task uncertainty was reduced by the common acceptance of core principles. Within a framework dominated by utility maximization, there is some diversity of theory, including varieties of game theory and of behavioural and experimental economics (Davis, 2006). This diversity has been a source of some theoretical innovation through cross-pollination, such as with behavioural game theory, or with behavioural

---

[10]   The simulation by Weisberg and Muldoon (2009) supports Kitcher's claim concerning optimal diversity. Weisberg and Muldoon (2009, p. 250) showed that 'mixed populations of mavericks and followers are valuable divisions of cognitive labor'. Their computer simulation is reminiscent of that by Allen and McGlade (1987), where 'fishing boats' were divided into maximizing 'Cartesians' who move to places that are believed most likely to yield fish on the basis of information available, and 'Stochasts' who take risks and search randomly. A fleet composed entirely of Cartesians would over-fish specific locations and be unlikely to find new ones without the help of some wandering Stochasts. A fleet composed entirely of Stochasts would under-exploit existing information. Allen and McGlade concluded that a mixture of Cartesians and Stochasts is overall more productive than a pure population.

[11]   Note the empirical study of scientific motivation by Lam (2011).

finance. But diversity is less evident within the core concepts and reigning protocols of mainstream economics. The sole pillar of Max U is enduringly dominant, the compulsion to use mathematics is supreme, and its adoption of ideas from outside the discipline is minimal.[12]

Elsewhere I have examined some limitations of Kitcher's framework to the diagnosis of problems within mainstream economics, including the problem of dominance of mathematical technique over theoretical and empirical substance, as alleged by Blaug (1997) and others (Lawson, 1997; Hodgson, 2013b). In this vein, Uskali Mäki (2005) has highlighted the importance and potential sub-optimality of positive feedback in the development of science. The peacock's tail positive feedbacks that reinforce mathematical formalism are an example. The case of economics suggests that Kitcher under-states the need to maintain an overarching concern for empirical or practical relevance. Some vital features of science are orthogonal to the questions of consensus and diversity.

As Steve Fuller (1988) pointed out, the establishment of consensus does not necessarily imply any revelation of truth. Nevertheless, that consensus is often the best guide we have. For example, without having been trained in climatology, many educated citizens accept that climate change is a problem because they are aware of the overwhelming consensus among experts in that area. Typically we trust in the institutions of science.

THE SCREENING OF SCIENTIFIC KNOWLEDGE

Any viable scientific community must employ rule-of-thumb criteria to consider whether a particular contribution by a researcher is to be taken seriously or ignored. At the root of the problem here is the need to process vast amounts of specialist information, and unavoidably to take short-cuts in doing so. Science is so specialized that no individual or committee can compare and assess multiple contributions by using their expert knowledge alone, even within a single discipline. We may not like institutionalized screening processes: we know that all of them are defective to a degree. But they are necessary, because of specialization,

---

[12]   Pieters and Baumgartner (2002, p. 504) examined inter-journal citation patterns in the mid-1990s and found that 'economics builds only slightly on knowledge from its sister disciplines' and lacks variety in terms of material from other social sciences. A major study by Fourcade et al. (2015) confirmed this insularity.

complexity, information overload, bounded rationality and the absence of omniscience.[13]

Because of the huge amounts of knowledge involved and the multiple specialist skills required to understand it, the scientific community often uses simple, rather than wide-ranging, multi-faceted or complex criteria. Hence the institutional affiliation of the scholar will matter, as will his or her count of publications in well-recognized journals. Today there are published global rankings of universities, departments and journals. We are all repeatedly measured.[14]

This is not a justification for any particular ranking scheme or criterion. Instead it is an argument that some such measures are indispensable. Consequently, criticism should not be directed at the *principle* of academic rankings of departments or journals, or of research assessments as such, but on the *details* of particular assessment or ranking schemes, in efforts to improve them. To be effective, this critical engagement should not be from outside, but within existing institutions of academic power.

Criticism of these criteria and rankings is easy: they all contain flaws. But once we understand the social nature of science, with its need for an interacting scientific community to process huge amounts of complex, specialist knowledge, and to establish some consensus over what is valuable and important, then some reliance on rough-and-ready measures is unavoidable. But problems arise when flawed measures become so ingrained that they are difficult to challenge or improve.

Consider some examples of possibly flawed screening criteria that have become established in some disciplines. The leading sociologist Niklas Luhmann (2005, p. 199) claimed that he deliberately kept his prose enigmatic to prevent it from being understood 'too quickly', which might produce simplistic misunderstandings. Decades earlier, C. Wright Mills (1959, p. 40) complained against deliberate obscurantism and over-elaborate language in sociology. He cited the work of Talcott Parsons as a prominent case. Parsons taught Luhmann at Harvard University. One may conjecture that the use of obscurantist language, to dress up relatively simple ideas, has emerged as a prominent screening

---

[13]   I use the term 'bounded rationality' in Simon's (1957) original sense of limited cognitive and computational capacity, in the face of large amounts of complex information. Prefiguring social epistemology, Simon (1957, p. 199) wrote: 'It is only because individual human beings are limited in knowledge, foresight, skill, and time that organizations are useful investments for the achievement of human purpose'.

[14]   Aistleitner et al. (2018) argued that the growth of scientometric techniques to measure and rank research in economics tends to reinforce the dominant paradigm.

criterion in sociology. Such obscurantism is a shibboleth: it demarcates a scientific community but impairs the development and proselytization of science.

After the formalist revolution in economics in the 1950s, when economists became afflicted by mathematics-envy, the capacity to use mathematics has become a foremost criterion (whether we like it or not) for deciding whether a researcher's contribution is to be taken seriously by mainstream economists. In addition, the type of mathematics must be sufficiently familiar to be understandable after postgraduate training, but sufficiently difficult to screen out the non-mathematical reader. There is strong path-dependence in the assumptions and type of mathematics used: different mathematical approaches or assumptions take a long time to become established.[15]

Because science is unavoidably a social process involving a screened social community, then some kind of selection criteria are used to determine entry into the elite. In economics, before the formalist revolution, these criteria were more wide-ranging. Then mathematics became compulsory. We may concur with Blaug (1997), Coase (1988), Friedman (1999, p. 137), Lawson (1997) and others that the over-emphasis on mathematical technique over real-world substance is a major cause for concern. It has crowded out other skills and forms of knowledge that are necessary to understand the real-world economy.[16] As Thomas Piketty (2014, p. 32) put it: 'To put it bluntly, the discipline of economics has yet to get over its childish passion for mathematics and for purely theoretical and often highly ideological speculation, at the expense of historical research and collaboration with the other social sciences.'

David Dequech (2017) has dug deeper, examining some of the norms and practices – additional to mathematical modelling – that researchers must seemingly adopt for their advancement in macroeconomics and financial economics. Any science builds up habits and norms that sustain it and limit critical challenges from outside. Would-be rebels must first conform and play the game.

In the face of a huge body of complex knowledge, some screening processes are necessary to maintain the boundaries of an expert scientific

---

[15]   Game theory was introduced into economics by von Neumann and Morgenstern (1944). It took about forty years for it to become widely adopted, and only after a major internal theoretical crisis in the prevailing general equilibrium paradigm (Rizvi, 1994b). Several prominent post-Keynesian economists use mathematics, but because different assumptions are used, their work does not guarantee entry into the mainstream citadel.

[16]   Mathematics is important but judgemental skills in economics are best enhanced by the addition of historical and comparative studies. But these have been pushed aside by mathematics, and judgemental capacities are thus limited (Yurko, 2018).

community with some degree of consensus. But the cases of both economics and sociology show that these boundary-maintaining mechanisms can have different degrees of effectiveness and can be distorting and partly dysfunctional. While some agreement is necessary, its particular nature and scope are crucial for the vitality of a science.

SCIENTIFIC REVOLUTIONS AND THE PECULIARITIES OF ECONOMICS

The difficulty of achieving a paradigm shift in economics that is centred on dethroning Max U has already been discussed in Chapter 3. In addition, changes in paradigm – where heterodoxy overturns and replaces the reigning orthodoxy – have not happened in economics in the manner suggested by accounts of paradigm shifts in other sciences.[17]

For example, the theory of continental drift was heterodox for centuries. Once global maps became available, it was noted as early as the late sixteenth century that some of the continents seem to fit together, like pieces in a jigsaw – particularly Africa and South America. But orthodoxy rejected the idea that they had once joined. In 1912 the dissident Alfred Wegener published a paper citing fossil and other evidence that was consistent with the idea that the continents were once joined and had drifted apart. But he was unable to provide a convincing explanation of the physical processes and causes of drift. The theory of continental drift remained heterodox until the 1960s.

But accumulating geological and other evidence suggested that the continents were once joined and had moved apart. But above all, continental drift became orthodox because the theory of plate tectonics, building on evidence from the ocean floor and elsewhere, revealed a mechanism to explain how the continents had moved. The provision of a better theory proved decisive, but it relied upon a large amount of corroborative evidence to become recognized as plausible.

Further examples of scientific paradigm shifts have been raised earlier in this book. Antoine-Laurent Lavoisier isolated what we now call oxygen, and an understanding of its role in combustion eventually provided a better explanation than the reigning phlogiston theory, which had difficulty explaining some of the evidence. Albert Einstein noted the failure of Newtonian physics to explain gravity, and he developed the

---

[17]   Kuhn himself admitted the looseness of his use of the term *paradigm*. My usage here is no less vague. The intention is simply to consider some major theoretical shifts in science and how they came about.

theory of general relativity to deal with the problem. This new theory was then supported by astronomical evidence.

These scientific revolutions were not achieved by evidence alone. But in most cases evidence played a major role, alongside the creation of a new theory. The new theory explained anomalous evidence where the old theory failed, and it provided a more plausible causal explanation.

Mainstream economics has gone through major phases of development. As the conventional history goes, the classical economists were eventually displaced by neoclassical marginalists, and so on. But unlike the scientific revolutions led by Lavoisier, Einstein and Wegener, empirical evidence in economics did not seem to play such a crucial part in these developments. There is no clear case of a paradigm shift in economics driven by empirical discovery.

Instead, what generally happened in economics were changes of vision, involving new concepts and underlying metaphors, which helped to open up new paths of enquiry. These shifts of vision were often prompted by developments in the socio-economic system, alongside the changing interests of economic actors and shifts in ideology or world-view.

In economics, primary assumptions often seem more important than the evidence. For example, James Duesenberry (1949) developed a model of consumer behaviour, inspired by the work of Veblen and based on habits and learning effects. In his model, as incomes rose, people acquired new habits of consumption that persisted, even if incomes later fell. Their tastes and preferences altered as they acquired new lifestyles. This model of aggregate consumer behaviour performed well in several econometric tests. But Duesenberry's model fell out of favour, not because it performed badly in statistical tests, but because it was not based on the orthodox idea of the rational, utility-maximizing consumer (Green, 1979).

There are several cases where evidence has empowered theoretical developments in economics. For example, as experimental economics became established in the 1980s, evidence accumulated to undermine the assumption that individuals tend to maximize their expected payoffs. This led in the 1990s to the mainstream adoption of the post-Simon version of behavioural economics. But, as established in Chapter 3, this did not mean the abandonment of the assumption that agents maximize their utility. The theoretical hard core remained intact.

As noted in Chapter 3, Max U in general is an empirically unfalsifiable proposition. This makes it difficult to remove. It was also buttressed by the consolidation of the economics profession in the late nineteenth century, which coincided with the installation of Max U and growing calls for the greater use of mathematics in economics.

Mainstream economics has changed in a number of important ways during the twentieth century. Partial equilibrium analysis gave way to general equilibrium theory, followed by the rise of game theory, experimental economics, behavioural economics, and so on. But as demonstrated in Chapter 3, underling these important shifts in theory and research programmes, there has been undying homage to Max U throughout.

Economics does not readily fit into the standard Kuhnian story, partly because it is difficult to determine what qualifies as a paradigm change. A.W. Coats proposed that the Keynesian Revolution in macroeconomics was the only major paradigm shift in economics after 1870. Coats (1969, p. 289) explained this in the following terms:

> With the exception of the Keynesian revolution of the 1930s, there have been no phases of paradigm change in economics quite like those in the natural sciences. This is due mainly to the nature of economic paradigms (or 'basic' theories) which are less precise and less liable to falsification. 'Critical anomalies' and 'crucial experiments' do not arise in economics, as in the natural sciences ...

But as Mark Blaug (1975) responded, even the Keynesian Revolution did not hinge on the resolution of empirical anomalies. Instead the Keynesian world-view builds on the belief that markets do not automatically bring themselves out of recession. It is difficult to contrive a convincing empirical test of this idea. Rather than adopting the Keynesian view that ongoing recession is an intrinsic problem with modern financial markets, the anti-Keynesians can always blame the failure of markets to return to full employment on other factors – such as misguided government policies, trade union militancy, and so on. Because it is impossible to isolate markets experimentally, other factors can always be accused for their malfunction.

The famous Duhem–Quine thesis notes that generally a bundle of hypotheses is tested: it is generally impossible to isolate and test one hypothesis alone (Quine, 1953; Harding, 1976; Cross, 1982). The complexity of socio-economic systems makes this problem particularly acute in the social sciences and helps to explain why there are relatively few empirically driven paradigm shifts.

REFORM VERSUS REVOLUTION

The preceding section shows that any heterodox strategy aimed at changing the dominant paradigm in economics must face up two major problems – the unfalsifiability of Max U at the core and the wider (Duhem–Quine) difficulty of using empirical evidence to substantiate or exclude particular causal explanations in complex socio-economic systems.

Some views of the nature of orthodoxy signal additional problems. For example, as noted in Chapter 2, Tony Lawson (2006, p. 492) claimed that 'the mainstream project of modern economics just is an insistence, as a discipline-wide principle, that economic phenomena be investigated using only certain mathematical–deductive forms of reasoning.' Consequently, a major paradigm shift along Lawsonian lines would involve a retraction of this insistence and a reduction in the (ontologically inappropriate) use of mathematics. Presumably, superior and non-mathematical explanations of empirical phenomena would have to be developed to empower this shift, otherwise it would not occur. But while we can point to many cases where the use of mathematics is redundant or ceremonial, it is hard to envisage how a major shift in the practices of economists could happen along these lines.

Frederic Lee's characterizations of orthodoxy and heterodoxy, and his overly politicized agenda for the latter, provide no more hope of a fundamental shift in scientific paradigm based on theory or evidence. As noted in Chapter 2, Lee (2008, 2009) characterized orthodoxy in terms of assumptions such as 'scarcity', 'rationality' and 'methodological individualism'. But he failed to define these terms or note their ambiguities. Neither did he point to crucial evidence supporting these theories that could convince a mainstream economist to shift position.

To look for possible forces for change in economics as a discipline, heterodox economists might consider the important but less-fundamental changes that have occurred in mainstream economics in the last fifty years, such as the rise of experimental and behavioural economics. What prompted these changes? How did they come about? What kind of problems in preceding theory did they claim to resolve? In this manner it may be possible to identify points of leverage, whereby heterodox approaches may be inserted.

But it is impossible to learn from the development of mainstream economics without becoming intimate with its details. A strategy of engagement is required. But for various reasons, and by inertia or design, much of heterodox economics has become disengaged. Many heterodox economists have moved out of economics departments into business schools and elsewhere, and placed themselves under different systems of academic interaction and power. The de facto widespread disengagement of heterodox economics from circles of power within mainstream economics restricts its capacity to mount a challenge to orthodoxy. Notably, some leading heterodox economists have abandoned this objective and championed a strategy of separation (Lee, 2008, 2012; Jo et al., 2017).

Could heterodox economics establish rival centres of academic power, while retaining a nominal attachment to economics, and demonstrate its superiority over conventional economics in a number of areas? Such rival centres of power would require a degree of consensus and a sustained research focus that are so far lacking in the theoretically diverse and fragmented heterodox community. Simply bringing people together under the *heterodox* label is not enough. A sense of belonging is insufficient. As shown in the following section, without attention to such problems, heterodox economics is likely to decline still further.

THE NEED FOR A FOCUSED RESEARCH COMMUNITY WITH INSTITUTIONALIZED POWER

An academic discipline or school requires not only a shared *raison d'être* but also some institutional mechanisms for sustaining conversation, channelling debate, appraising the importance and quality of arguments, screening out ungrounded claims, and so on. It has become a truism that science is a social process. But the full consequences of this for heterodox economics have yet to be taken on board. They are especially relevant for the issues of quality enhancement and the cumulative development of knowledge.

Here heterodox economics is in a difficult position. Precisely because it opposes the mainstream, its access to power and resources is limited. Dissent from the mainstream is an inadequate screening device within heterodoxy. Problems arise when deciding what work is to be taken seriously and establishing some adequate agreement over what is important. The contrasting theoretical positions with heterodoxy impair sufficient consensus. These difficulties are compounded by fundamental lack of agreement over what *orthodox* and *heterodox* mean.

The work of Polanyi, Collins, Hull, Kitcher and others on the workings of scientific communities carries some insights for heterodox economists. It highlights issues that may help to explain its limited cumulative advance and its waning influence within departments of economics.

Consider first the individual *incentives* to do research in heterodox economics. Of course, the intrinsic attraction of a particular heterodox theory, or a critical repulsion from a mainstream approach, may prompt heterodox curiosity. But intrinsic motivational factors are insufficient to sustain a scientific community. Even the most dedicated and honourable of scientists must eat, live, be clothed and pay the rent. Any viable scientific community must be able to bring different kinds of people on board and motivate them for long periods of time.

Lee (2009) and others have shown that the self-declared community of heterodox economists has diminished in global size and influence since the 1970s (Lee and Harley, 1997, 1998; Heise and Thieme, 2016). Whatever the reasons, any decline in the influence of heterodox economics, at least in departments of economics, obviously diminishes incentives – including career progression, status or remuneration – for researchers to devote their careers to this path. This affects the recruitment of younger economists to the area: heterodoxy then comes with manifest high career risks and apparently limited chances of success. This creates a vicious circle of decline.

The heterodox community is aware of this problem, but the strategic response has been limited. As Stephen Toulmin (1972) pointed out, most sciences gravitate toward their orthodox attractor. He identified established journals as tending to institutionalize mainstream views. He saw the founding of new journals as an important counterweight, and a source of variation. This is good advice. Heterodox economists have founded several journals, a few of which have been relatively successful, such as the *Cambridge Journal of Economics.*

So far so good. But there is also a frequent tendency by heterodox economists to disregard established rankings of journals or conventional citation impact data, on the grounds that they are flawed or biased (Lee and Harley, 1997, 1998). There have also been periodic, unsuccessful attempts to set up alternative 'heterodox' journal ranking systems (Lee, 2009; Lee and Elsner, 2010). As noted above, this adds the problem of getting alternative research *rankings* recognized and accepted, to the fundamental problem of getting alternative *research* recognized and accepted. Furthermore, the shunning of established rankings is much more likely to diminish rather than to enhance the repertoire of necessary incentives to attract and retain heterodox researchers.[18]

---

[18] Lee (2009, ch. 11) attempted to rank heterodox journals and UK heterodox departments. But it is more an endeavour to assess the degree of promotion of the community of heterodox economists, by putting weight on the export and import of

THE PROBLEM OF QUALITY CONTROL

Time and research budgets are limited. No researcher can go to every workshop or conference. The expected quality level affects the decision on whether to attend a particular academic event. Quality matters for worthwhile feedback on one's own presentation, and for expectations of learning something useful from other participants. Numbers attending heterodox events depend on expectations of quality. Perceptions of quality are also vital more generally for the reputation of 'heterodox economics'. The future of heterodoxy depends in part on assessments of quality.

The maintenance of high quality has become a particularly serious problem within the community of heterodox economists, for several reasons. The high level of internal theoretical diversity within heterodoxy, and the lack of a consensus on its nature and common core, reduces the proportion of well-informed experts in a particular heterodox area at any particular heterodox meeting, compared with more specialist and focused congregations. Hence the chances of good critical feedback are lower, simply as a consequence of the relatively high degree of diversity, and of the lack of consensus on several core issues.

Unrestricted tolerance of diversity within heterodoxy leads to a failure of quality control: anything goes. If things go too far, scholars in broad heterodox communities will lack sufficient rigorous criticism and scepticism to sharpen and improve their arguments, so that they can eventually be published in the higher quality journals, whether heterodox or mainstream.

Several of Polanyi's and Kitcher's points are appropriate here. In particular, the notion of a trade-off between diversity and consensus is highly relevant. Heterodox economics lacks agreement on issues as fundamental as its core assumptions and its nature and boundaries, thus thwarting possibilities for cumulative scientific development. Pluralism and diversity are welcome as potential sources of innovation, but new ideas need to be developed in a climate of intensely critical, expert scrutiny, based on teams of well-informed specialists.

Being in opposition to an orthodoxy (whatever that means) brings further problems, as with (relatively rare) parallel cases in different disciplines. The great heterodox economist Joan Robinson noticed one

---

citations (to and from other heterodox journals). The outcome is unconvincing as a measure of perceived quality, either within or beyond the heterodox community.

such problem. It is not well-known that Robinson's (1933a) first published paper was on the Shakespeare authorship controversy, where she saw merit in the argument that the plays and poems were probably not written by the William Shakspere (as his name was typically spelt in the original records) from Stratford-upon-Avon.[19]

Robinson pointed out that groups that oppose the consensus view that the Stratford man was the author have attracted dissidents who have invented fanciful theories and have opposed orthodoxy with weak arguments. Because the heretics are denied power in university departments of English and elsewhere, they cling together and allow weak or fanciful arguments to persist.

Robinson then noted the similarity within economics. Groups that define themselves in opposition to orthodoxy can attract people who misunderstand the mainstream, oppose it on faulty grounds or propose flaky alternative theories. Even if the opposition is right and orthodoxy is wrong, the opposition can be seriously impaired by low-quality allies in its ranks. In her honour, we may describe this as *the Joan Robinson problem* – it applies potentially to any academic heterodoxy.

Without using this label, the problem was also noted by Polanyi (1962, p. 61), who saw it as one of the reasons for consensus and authority within science:

> For scientific opinion may, of course, sometimes be mistaken, and as a result unorthodox work of high originality and merit may be discouraged or altogether suppressed for a time. But these risks have to be taken. Only the discipline imposed by an effective scientific opinion can prevent the adulteration of science by cranks and dabblers.

As long as pluralism is insufficiently balanced by consensus, focus and authority, the problem of quality control will persist in heterodox economics.

Heterodox economists also need to take pluralism even more seriously. To develop and sharpen their arguments, they should make stronger efforts to engage with advocates of orthodox positions, who tend to be outside their community. Such engagement is necessary to remove flaws and misunderstandings, and to strengthen the critical and constructive arguments. This is a major factor in favour of a strategy of engagement with orthodoxy, as advocated by several commentators and discussed in the following chapter (Colander, 2010; Colander et al., 2004; Davis,

---

[19]   There is no need to assess the merits or demerits of this heresy here: that would be beyond the point. But for a powerful argument see Poynton (2011).

2006, 2008; Fontana and Gerrard, 2006; Earl and Peng, 2012). But to forewarn the reader, the next chapter also explains why a strategy of engagement would also challenge the ultimate viability of the heterodox community.

CONCLUSION: THE IMPASSE OF HETERODOXY

The *heterodox* label means minority dissent. It is a negative definition, rather than one building on positive ground. It means being in opposition, not just for now – but indefinitely. For this reason, as Edward Fullbrook put it, 'it is a label for losers. In parliaments there is always the party or parties in opposition, but I do not know of any political party that has named itself such' (Mearman et al., 2019, p. 256).

The use of the 'heterodox economics' label to organize, incentivize and empower criticism of the mainstream has several major problems, especially when we consider the social mechanisms of scientific scrutiny and development. We have to consider that organizing under the *hetero-dox* label is severely problematic and, at least in terms of establishing power in the most influential parts of academic economics, it has been mostly a failure.

The *post-Keynesian* label obviously refers to a set of approaches that build on the contribution of Keynes. This is more definite than 'hetero-dox' but severe differences exist over what defines 'post-Keynesianism' and what should be included within it. These differences remain unresolved, impairing the use of this label as well.

After several decades, with an evident decline of influence of self-described *heterodox* and *post-Keynesian* approaches in departments of economics (Lee and Harley, 1997, 1998), it is time for a serious re-evaluation of current strategy. That urgency is compounded by the realization that mainstream economics has changed relatively little after the Great Crash of 2008.

6. Some possible ways forward

Others apart sat on a hill retired,
In thoughts more elevate, and reasoned high
Of Providence, Foreknowledge, Will, and Fate –
Fixed fate, free will, foreknowledge absolute –
And found no end, in wandering mazes lost.

John Milton, *Paradise Lost*

Given the evidence and arguments produced in previous chapters, a viable strategy for any enduringly productive community of dissenting economists (or other scientists) must address the following five issues:

1. ***Raison d'être***. The community must have an adequate and sufficiently focused *raison d'être*. This should be specified in terms of a real-world zone of enquiry, or the promotion or development of a particular theoretical approach, or the promotion or development of a particular set of analytical techniques, or the promotion or development of policies in some problem area, or some combination of these.
2. **Arena of engagement**. The answer to (1) above helps to determine an *institutional arena of engagement* with existing segments of organized science. For example, if the aim and *raison d'être* of the community is to criticize policies of economic austerity, then its arena of engagement would be groups of economists and other social scientists that are concerned with the development, promotion, critique or evaluation of austerity policies.
3. **Incentives**. There must be *incentives* for high-quality researchers to join the community and to remain active in it for sustained periods of time. Another important reason for incentives is to induce researchers to abide by some consensus positions in the field, as noted in (5) below, as long as the overall effect is not to stifle pluralism and innovation. As well as scientific curiosity and intrinsic interest in the research itself, these incentives would include money, status and other inducements.
4. **Quality control**. There must be institutionalized mechanisms in the community to sustain quality control and for *quality enhancement*.

This in turn requires concentrations of sustained and focused expertise in particular areas.

5. **A degree of consensus**. While maintaining a necessary degree of structured or limited pluralism, there must be a *degree of consensus* in the field to avoid endless dispute over fundamentals, to help build cumulative knowledge, and in turn to reinforce (3) and (4). Given that (3) also helps to sustain (5), these two attributes create a positive feedback loop.

These five requirements may be satisfied by multiple strategies. Some possibilities are discussed below. The eight strategies discussed here do not fare equally under critical scrutiny, especially when taking these five requirements into consideration, but they are all laid out here for wider discussion and possible experimentation. The aim here is to start a wider conversation about possibilities, not to lay down a particular line at this stage.

It should already be clear that existing heterodox economics has current major deficiencies in all five of these areas. There is little agreement on its *raison d'être*. Because of historical inertia, there seems to be an often-unquestioned default assumption that its *institutional arena of engagement* is within university departments of economics. But this is not always necessarily the case, as the illustrative example of focusing on anti-austerity policies in (2) above illustrates. As noted in Chapter 4 above, evolutionary economics has already largely migrated out of university departments of economics.

Little strategic attention has been given by heterodoxy to incentives, except for observations that opportunities for heterodox economists have been rapidly diminishing (Lee and Harley, 1997, 1998; Heise and Thieme, 2016). Although outstanding work has been produced by several heterodox economists (for example in macroeconomics and in economic methodology), failures elsewhere of quality control create serious problems for the sustainability of heterodox economics and its community. Finally, while most heterodox economists accept and promote pluralism, there is little recognition that excessive pluralism means endless debate over everything, which greatly inhibits cumulative progress. There must be some (adaptable) consensus to serve as a foundation upon which to build.

A further problem is that the academic power base of mainstream economics has narrowed to a small number of US universities and US-based academic journals. One study found that the most highly-cited journals in economics were edited by people from a narrow range of (principally US) academic institutions and published works by authors from a similarly restricted set of universities (Hodgson and Rothman, 1999). Analysing the job histories of tenure-track economists hired by the top 35 US economics departments, James Heckman and Sidharth Moktan (2018) found that publications in the deemed top five journals had a powerful influence on tenure decisions and rates of transition to tenure. Economics is now controlled and guided by a few US institutions and journals.

Whatever the difficulties, any strategy must choose an institutional arena of engagement, connect with its established, consensus positions in that arena, and open a conversation with those defending them. In regard to economics, this is becoming increasingly difficult. But there are now substantial international networks of economists *outside departments of economics*, in business schools, innovation studies, sociology, philosophy, political science and elsewhere. Many of these institutions admit wide-ranging dialogue. The broader project of changing social science is still possible. But we must give much more thought to the strategic question of how this can be achieved.

STRATEGY 1: SPLITTING ECONOMICS

Some heterodox economists argue against a strategy of engagement with orthodoxy. Instead they propose that heterodoxy prioritizes the development of its own integrated community (Lee, 2008, 2009, 2012; Lee and Lavoie, 2013; Lavoie, 2012; Jo et al., 2017). Lee (2012, p. 342) was forthright on this point: 'Since the entire theoretical corpus of neo-classical economics is false knowledge, it is not clear why heterodox economists should pay attention to the mainstream frontier advances.' In response, for the benefit of science, engagement is necessary to counter false knowledge and to replace it by valid knowledge. While Lee argued that heterodox economists should disregard much of mainstream economics, he did not argue that economics departments should be split (Dow, 2011b). But disengagement would suggest separation.

A formal separation of departmental structures – with heterodox 'Political Economy' alongside mainstream 'Economics' – has been tried at the University of Sydney in Australia. The struggle in that university for an alternative teaching programme in political economy began in the 1960s. The dispute erupted in the 1970s and 1980s and lingered on afterwards. An opportunity arose when economics at Sydney moved in the direction of finance and business. This led to the creation of a Department of Political Economy in the Faculty of Arts and Social Sciences in 2008.

These developments are summarized in an article by Evan Jones and Frank Stilwell (1986) and a book by Gavan Butler, Jones and Stilwell (2009). These authors were involved in the agitation for heterodox economics in Sydney. Their publications show that the dispute was highly politicized, with supporters of neoclassical courses described as 'right' and supporters of heterodoxy as 'left'. Butler et al. (2009, p. ix) made it clear in their introduction that in part it was a conflict over political ideology, where the supporters of 'political economy' promoted 'a less benign view of capitalism and its capacity to deliver economic outcomes that are efficient, equitable and sustainable'. It was as much a dispute about normative attitudes to capitalism as over what theories are more useful to understand capitalism. It 'generated extreme bitterness of feeling' (Jones and Stilwell, 1986, p. 29).

Jones and Stilwell (1986, p. 26) attempted to define the neoclassical paradigm. There are a number of flaws in their effort. Among the neoclassical axioms, according to Jones and Stilwell, is 'a psychological motivation postulate that the individual is a rational calculating machine in pursuit of maximum material gain'. Not exactly. Neoclassical economics does not assume that agents are calculating machines, but that they act 'as if' they were. Furthermore, neoclassical economics does not generally assume that agents maximize 'material gain', it more typically assumes they maximize expected utility. These are relatively small but symptomatic errors.

Other mistakes are more consequential. Jones and Stilwell (1986, p. 26) made the claim that neoclassical economics upholds 'an economic sphere comprising an all-pervasive competitive market mechanism ... and a political sphere containing a government structure whose role is to support the appropriate economic environment'. Although this might bear a vague resemblance to some versions of neoclassical theory, it is unrepresentative of neoclassical economics as a whole. At least since the 1960s there has been a burgeoning mainstream literature – in 'public choice' and elsewhere (Buchanan and Tullock, 1962; Mueller, 1979) – that tries to explain the political sphere using neoclassical assumptions, including utility-maximizing individuals. Instead of dividing the economic and political spheres from one another, neoclassical economics has progressively attempted to conflate them under the same explanatory logic. The idea that modern neoclassical economics separates the economic from the political spheres is false. Instead, neoclassical economics claims to be the science of choice, applicable in any sphere where (human or non-human) choices are made.

Jones and Stilwell thus created a fiction to delineate the neoclassical approach (which is wrongly alleged to separate the economic from the political sphere) from what is called '*the* political economy approach' (which is said to bring politics and economics together). Roger Backhouse (2004, p. 268) noted the tendency of dissenters to create mythological histories of their ideas: 'current heterodoxies are read back into the past to create traditions on which the dominant majority turned its back. All such accounts contain a large element of myth.' In Sydney a historical myth was created to force a distinction between economics and political economy.

As well as being false in its description of neoclassical economics, this is a substandard intellectual history of the use of the term *political economy*. As H.W. Arndt (1984) and Peter Groenewegen (1985, 1987) pointed out, there is no historical basis to assume that *political economy* has a meaning that is fundamentally distinct from *economics*. Although Alfred Marshall (1920, p. 1) was one of the first promoters of the term *economics*, he regarded it as essentially synonymous with *political economy*. *Political economy* was the original term but eventually *economics* became more widely preferred. Some mainstream journals, notably the Chicago-based and largely neoclassical *Journal of Political Economy*, have kept the older term. It does not signify any difference from mainstream views.

After attempting to contrast neoclassical economics with political economy, Jones and Stilwell (1986, p. 27) again made the link with ideology. Neoclassical economists were said to be committed to 'a pervasive and all-powerful market mechanism'. Jones and Stilwell then drew the following conclusion:

> Thus the conventional paradigm serves to support the status quo of the contemporary politico-economic structure, yet it does so not by defending it explicitly but by obfuscation. The defence of the status quo involves an incoherent mixture of a reification of the ideal market economy with a pragmatic acknowledgement of certain contemporary institutional realities, overlaid with an unarticulated class prejudice.

This ideological characterization might correspond with the attitudes of a great number of neoclassical economists. But Jones and Stilwell did not demonstrate that these pro-market views flow logically from neoclassical theory. Furthermore, numerous prominent *neoclassical* economists are critical of the 'market fundamentalist' view that markets are the solution to every problem. Among them are the Nobel Laureates Kenneth Arrow, Paul Krugman and Joseph Stiglitz. The history of the socialist calculation debate is once again ignored, when socialists such as Oskar Lange and Abba Lerner used neoclassical theory to argue for the plausibility of socialism. All these inconvenient truths get in the way of the separatist mythology that is required to draw a line between *economics* and *political economy*.

When the narrative switched from critique of neoclassical theory to the contrasting nature of *political economy*, Jones and Stilwell (1986, p. 28) wrote: 'the method of the political economists has been historically based, drawing on the conceptual frameworks of Marxism, institutional economics, post-Keynesian economics, and feminist studies'. Note the use of the definite article at the beginning of the quote: '*the* method'. But there is no adequate account of the core set of methodological ideas that is common to these approaches.

Note also the same-old omissions from the list. There was no mention of the original behavioural economics of Herbert Simon, of critics of Max U from Adam Smith to Amartya Sen, of the evolutionary economics of Richard Nelson and Sidney Winter, or of the Austrian School's critique of neoclassical theory. Mention of these particular dissenters would not have served their leftist ideological purposes and their attempt to establish that neoclassical theory is 'right-wing'.

Unlike Cambridge, the Sydney dissenters eventually pursued a strategy of division, and were ultimately successful in making the split, partly because economics at Sydney became more oriented to business and finance. I do not doubt that some excellent teaching and discussion go on in the Department of Political Economy, which I am told is very successful in its recruitment of students. The struggle at the University of Sydney to broaden the economics curriculum and to bring in other perspectives outside neoclassical theory is a noble effort. Economics suffers globally from insufficient theoretical pluralism. But there is not much evidence of ideological pluralism or viewpoint diversity in the Department of Political Economy.

Marxism and left politics are dominant. In 2018 the Department of Political Economy boasted four Honorary Professors, namely Terrence McDonough, James Stanford, Yanis Varoufakis and Erik Olin Wright. All four have taken a strong left political stance, and three of them are declared Marxists.[1] The department website also announced numerous critiques of an ill-defined ideology of *neoliberalism*.[2] There are also quaint retro-1970s seminars on Marxian value theory. Pluralism in the

---

[1] Erik Olin Wright died in January 2019.

[2] The extensive literature on the term shows little agreement on what *neoliberalism* means. As Philip Mirowski and Dieter Plehwe (2009, p. xvii) put it, *neoliberalism* for some has become 'a brainless synonym for modern capitalism'. See also Boas and Gans-Morse (2009), Burgin (2012, pp. 57, 82), Venugopal (2015) and Hodgson (2019c, 2019d).

Sydney department does not seem to stretch very far beyond Marxism and its fellow travellers.

Of course, the circumstances in the University of Sidney were unique. But there are common features with other heterodox struggles elsewhere. With the failure to establish a clear *theoretical* identity for heterodoxy, it is all too tempting to use leftist ideology as the alternative glue to bind people together. But to achieve this, a false theoretical narrative has to be manufactured, where *neoclassical economics* is deemed to be necessarily 'right wing'. This misunderstands neoclassical theory and undermines the goal of scientific advance.

While student interest and recruitment may be high, the Department of Political Economy at the University of Sydney is not yet visible in the research rankings. By contrast, the School of Economics, also within the Faculty of Arts and Social Sciences at the same university, has achieved relatively high international rankings (Repec, 2018). This is not a very comfortable position for Political Economy in Sydney. It would be tempting for an administrator to fuse the two together under mainstream control.

The Sydney experience illustrates some of the major potential problems with a strategy of separation. Without a sufficiently clear *raison d'être* for the breakaway department, and with a flawed understanding of the nature and ideological implications of neoclassical theory, a department of political economy can end up as a largely ideological grouping, with an excessively constrained pluralism in theory, and an even more limited pluralism of political viewpoints.

Could this separation strategy work elsewhere? The creation of new, separate departments brings funding and new academic positions. It thereby creates new incentives, but these are limited by the number and funding of Departments of Political Economy that can be created alongside mainstream Departments of Economics. Few universities can afford the luxury of both. There is still the problem of a positive *raison d'être* – other than (leftist) ideology or the negative definition of opposition to the mainstream. Without a *raison d'être* the building of sufficient consensus is also difficult. The strategy of separation does not seem to hold out much hope for the transformation of economics as a discipline. It might hold some hope for the preservation of the heterodox community. But separation can mean isolation, particularly as an ideological enclave. And there is relatively little evidence of cumulative theoretical advance or of an escape from the dominance within heterodoxy of Marxism.

STRATEGY 2: ENGAGEMENT WITH MAINSTREAM ECONOMICS

Arguably, any strategy that chooses economics as its broader institutional arena of engagement must engage with orthodox economics. Such an engagement strategy has been advocated by several commentators (Colander, 2010; Colander et al., 2004; Davis, 2006, 2008; Fontana and Gerrard, 2006; Earl and Peng, 2012).

The Institute for New Economic Thinking (INET), which was funded by George Soros, might be following an engagement strategy, although this is not clearly articulated, as far as I am aware. INET has kept some distance from long-established heterodox groups and has instead co-opted innovative economists who are closer to, or more integrated within, the mainstream. Is it possible to engage with mainstream economics while also maintaining links with heterodoxy? Perhaps INET believes that heterodox engagement would undermine mainstream engagement. This is one of several dilemmas of an engagement strategy.

The tactical preference for innovative mainstream thinkers over long-lasting or more radical heterodox groups ends up ducking debate over some serious limitations of core mainstream theory. It may seem that INET has become a grant-awarding body situated largely within the mainstream. Its capacity to change economics is thereby limited.

But some advantages of an engagement strategy are clear. Dialogue with expert outsiders is needed to obtain critical feedback and to refute, sharpen or reinforce dissenting positions. Dealing with orthodoxy directly provides incentives for scholars to make their criticisms and alternative arguments as robust as possible, to avoid outright dismissal or even ridicule. A strategy of engagement might help to overcome the Joan Robinson problem of quality control.

Engagement means opening up a constructive and sustained dialogue with mainstream, including behavioural, evolutionary, new-institutional and other economists. The scope would be much broader than Lee's (2009) listing of the elements of 'heterodox economics', and it would be in strong contrast to his declaration of disengagement from the mainstream. It would require critical engagement with modellers and econometricians, whether to question the overall value of a concentration on technique, or to develop different and more suitable techniques.

But some proponents of an engagement strategy seem to take a number of things for granted. These deficiencies become more obvious when we consider the way science works in interactive communities, as discussed in Chapter 5. What is the *community* that must engage with orthodoxy? Is it the current community of self-described heterodox economists? If so, what is its focus? Again, what is its *raison d'être?* There is little traction in promoting a strategy of engagement between one scientific community and another, where the community that is engaging with the mainstream has not yet agreed on its core assumptions, focus and *raison d'être.* Diverse and disjointed criticism from a heterodox camp would not encourage a mainstream audience to take heterodoxy seriously.

The lack of focus and of *raison d'être* threatens the cohesiveness of the heterodox community in these circumstances. At least as it exists at present, mainstream scholars have limited incentives to engage with heterodox scholars. A broad strategy of engagement by existing heterodoxy would cover a large number of topics and specialisms and would be likely to lead to the partial assimilation of some of the heterodox within orthodoxy, as well as to the fragmentation of the heterodox community as a whole. This is not necessarily a bad thing, especially if heterodox engagement led to significant improvements in the discipline. But it would not be conducive to the survival of heterodoxy as a community. A strategy of engagement could become a strategy for the dissolution of heterodoxy itself.

An ambitious engagement strategy may lack feasibility. Mario Cedrini and Magda Fontana (2018) have established that mainstream economics is itself fragmenting into diverse specialisms. This means that the building of bridges must cross into multiple islands, not one. Specialization makes it more difficult to establish extensive and synergetic dialogue with the economics mainstream.

A further problem is that an engagement strategy is very difficult to pursue when mainstream economists habitually ignore topics where the heterodox community has insight and intellectual strength. Consider the history and methodology of economic thought, for example. Would impactful conversation in such areas be possible? As Sheila Dow (2011b, p. 1161) pointed out: 'the refusal by most mainstream economists to address methodological issues ... has been a very significant stumbling block in such attempts at communication'.

In sum, an engagement strategy has problems as well as potential benefits. Most crucially, any engagement strategy threatens the integrity and future of any engaging heterodoxy, by forcing its dissolution or its integration into the mainstream community. Furthermore, engagement across a wide range of specialisms is difficult and arguably over-ambitious. Because an engagement strategy could end with the dissolution of the heterodox community, it is unlikely to be popular among its members.

Ironically, the opposite strategies of separation and engagement are both deeply problematic for heterodoxy. It is important to consider other suggestions.

STRATEGY 3: UNIFYING THE SOCIAL SCIENCES

Another interesting and creative strategy has been proposed by David Colander (2014) and others (Colander et al., 2010; Colander and Kupers, 2014). They suggest an ambitious 'transdisciplinary' strategy that prioritizes engagement across the range of social sciences, focusing on greater pluralism in that broader arena rather than in economics alone. Colander (2014, p. 517) proposed 'that heterodox economists should support administratively combining all the social sciences into a single social science department at the graduate level, or at a minimum providing a one-year shared core training for all social scientists'.

But Colander (2014, p. 523) acknowledged the goal as unrealistic, at least for a while: 'the proposals are controversial and stand little chance of being implemented'. Nevertheless, this trans-disciplinary orientation might be more feasible than changing economics directly, and it would be 'far more likely to advance heterodox economists' pluralist agenda than an agenda of pushing for more pluralism within economics'. Colander and his colleagues offered useful detailed indications of what may be involved in this strategy, including outlines of core trans-disciplinary courses.

This is a very attractive proposal. It promises to break down the obsolete and decaying barriers between the social sciences. Both sociologists and economists study society: both sociologists and economists study the economy. There is 'economics of the family' alongside 'economic sociology'. Economists, sociologists and political scientists study the polity. Numerous economists, sociologists and political scientists have been smitten by rational choice theory. They have lost much of their previous ability to define themselves as separate disciplines, yet they carry on as if this problem did not exist. This trans-disciplinary strategy is a promising way out of this impasse.

But other than being advantaged by a myriad of possible connections, does this trans-disciplinary strategy adequately address the problems of identity, strategy and survival for heterodox economics? It does not.

Colander considered why his trans-disciplinary strategy 'makes sense for heterodox economics'. Colander (2014, p. 523) wrote: 'pushing for these proposals is far more likely to advance heterodox economists' pluralist agenda than an agenda of pushing for more pluralism within economics'. Probably true. But adding a team with more muscle to the push does little to address the problems of how the team stays together, how it defines its mission, where it goes, how it deals with internal quality control, and so on.

A trans-disciplinary strategy would have to be adopted by the university administration. Colander points out that this would put pressure from above on economics departments to become more pluralistic. For instance, 'heterodox economists can get administrative support for joint hires, and to put pressure on mainstream economics department to be less methodologically narrow than they currently are' (Colander, 2014, p. 523). Colander also surmised that journal rankings may improve by rewarding multi-disciplinary research.

For heterodox economics, the biggest advantage of the trans-disciplinary strategy is that it would offer individual heterodox economists enhanced opportunities to influence economics and other social sciences. But the problems of the development of heterodox economics *as a scientific community* are not addressed. The trans-disciplinary strategy does not really resolve the problems concerning identity, *raison d'être*, research focus and quality control in the heterodox community as a whole.

Something resembling the trans-disciplinary strategy has already been tried. The sociologist Amitai Etzioni (1988) published *The Moral Dimension: Toward a New Economics*. Basically, Etzioni's argument was to preserve Max U for the 'economic' aspect of behaviour and add a 'moral dimension' to it. As Michael Piore (2003, p. 120) argued, the thrust of Etzioni's approach 'is to preserve the core of the neoclassical paradigm and to add on to it, or to modify it, at several key points'.

Etzioni helped found the Society for the Advancement of Socio-Economics (SASE). But while this organization grew quickly, it soon abandoned the aim to build 'new economics' as a distinctive paradigm, and instead became a multi-disciplinary forum for sociologists, economists and political scientists. In this latter incarnation it is closer to the trans-disciplinary proposal of Colander and others.

But it has not worked out in the manner that Colander and others envisaged. Furthermore, SASE made little attempt to join forces with established groups of heterodox economists. The differences between socio-economics and other movements with similar names are not made clear (Hodgson, 2008). These include economic sociology (now a division within the American Sociological Association) and social economics (long organized in the Association for Social Economics).

SASE has not served as a crucible for further theoretical advance along the lines of Etzioni's (1988) book. Its impact on mainstream economics has been minimal. In mainstream economics the 'moral dimension' is smothered by Max U. SASE has not led to the breaking down of disciplinary barriers in academic institutions. The experience with SASE suggests that while there is a large audience for multi-disciplinary gatherings, without a viable and sustained strategy to break down academic barriers the impact on the separate disciplines – including economics – will be limited.[3]

STRATEGY 4: GOING INTO BUSINESS

Another strategy is to enter other departments, outside economics, where economists of various kinds can find a home. Foremost among these refugee camps are business schools. Many mainstream and non-mainstream economists have migrated to business schools since the 1980s. This option has allowed heterodox approaches to survive: but other pressures and concerns have come into play. Organizing and strategizing heterodoxy in this fragmented business school environment of multiple disciplines and specialisms creates new challenges.

Business schools in the US have tended to compartmentalize themselves into disciplines and have been less conducive to heterodox economics and to inter-disciplinary conversation. By contrast, a greater number of heterodox economists are in UK business schools, and at least nominally there has been a greater commitment to inter-disciplinarity. There are increasing numbers of business schools in Continental Europe, but as yet they have not received a large influx of heterodox economists.

All business schools are on the international market for students and faculty, and most enter into international quality rankings. These rankings are largely (but not entirely) dominated by business schools in the US. Consequently, there is ongoing pressure to conform to US norms.

Competition between business schools pushes them to fight for positions in different rankings, several of which are global. If you are labelled as an 'economist' of any kind, then you are obliged to take the rankings seriously, including those of journals in mainstream economics. Anyone in a business school is competing with colleagues over promotion, funding, and so on. The heterodox economist in a business school is thus obliged to demonstrate the quality of his or her research by referring

---

[3]   Boettke (2019) proposed an interesting strategy for the Austrian School. Building on the analyses of M. Polanyi (1962) and Collins (1998), Boettke notes the marginalized position of the Austrian School within economics and recommends that horizontal relationships are built with 'political economy' groupings within political science.

to mainstream criteria. While the retreat of heterodox economists into business schools has served as a means of survival for many, it has done little to solve the problems of dissenting identity and *raison d'être*.

Consider the 'outsider heterodoxy' of evolutionary economics, as discussed in Chapter 4. Among all the strains of heterodoxy, evolutionary economics is one of the most suited for the business school environment. It has influenced strategic management, innovation studies, organization studies, entrepreneurship and business economics. Some but not all evolutionary economists are located in business schools. But as yet there is no strong and well-known cluster of researchers explicitly around 'evolutionary economics' in any leading business school. The failure of evolutionary economics to establish a distinctive and cohesive presence in leading business schools, which in some respects is their natural home, does not bode well for the 'going into business' strategy for heterodoxy as a whole.

STRATEGY 5: SPECIALIST REGROUPMENT

Another possible strategy is for a subset (or subsets) of heterodox economists to abandon a generalist mission within economics and organize around a particular approach that has evident success and future potential.

A notable area of advance by some post-Keynesian economists, which achieved some recognition during and after the 2008 Great Crash, was the work on financial fragility by Hyman Minsky and his followers. To this may be added the related and impressive body of 'modern monetary theory'.[4] This work has a huge potential impact on monetary policy, financial regulation and the development of a new world financial order. This makes it potentially viable as a school – working toward a future community and global network of scholars, with funding, incentives, consensus and cumulative research.

This fifth strategy answers the problem of a *raison d'être* by establishing an identity over points (a) and (b) in the conclusion of Chapter 2 above. The objects of study under (a) would become money and the financial system in modern economies. The defining theoretical approach under (b) would be Keynesian, with assumptions about uncertainty, the nature of money, the role of finance and so on.

---

[4] See, for example, Minsky (1986), Dymski and Pollin (1994), Wray (1998, 2012, 2016).

But if it is to develop further and have an impact, this school requires much more concentrated focus than the broader 'post-Keynesian' movement had previously adopted. Such concentration and consensus are necessary to focus on ongoing, empirically-grounded research that repeatedly demonstrates to others the superiority of the core principles and ideas of this school. At the same time, promoters of modern monetary theory should be more open about the policy problems, including difficulties and adverse outcomes, such as with deficit spending and allied job-guarantee programmes. In complex, real-world economic policy, there are no silver bullets.

This fifth strategy will take off only if its practitioners publish in existing major journals, or they quickly establish high profile and influential journals of their own, using all the necessary tricks to seek attention and citations. The mainstream must be persuaded to pay some attention, or this strategy will fail.

So far in this area, despite widespread complaint in the media and elsewhere about the failures of mainstream approaches, they have endured and proved difficult to push aside (Hodgson, 2009). In response, the temptation of these modern monetary theorists might be to withdraw from dialogue, and to focus on doctrinal incantation rather than empirically grounded demonstration. Such a retreat could be fatal.

Other important topics do not offer heterodox economists a specialist rescue strategy. Consider the global problem of economic inequality. The best research in this area has been carried out by economists situated in the mainstream, including Anthony Atkinson (2015), Branko Milanovic (2005) and Thomas Piketty (2014). Unless heterodoxy can offer a distinctive approach, inequality research offers it no salvation. Concerned heterodox scholars would be better off working with mainstream economists in the area.

The mistaken belief that inequality research somehow signals a route for heterodox advance derives from the false assumption that the mainstream theoretical core is intrinsically pro-inequality. Of course, the Paretian welfare criterion is intrinsically conservative and it highly limits redistribution. But the deeper utilitarian foundations of economics have a more egalitarian history, going back to Bentham and the idea of maximizing overall happiness. In this approach, redistribution may thus be acceptable if the marginal utility of a payment to the poor is greater than it would be for the rich.

STRATEGY 6: DEVELOPING ALTERNATIVES TO MAX U

In Chapters 2 and 3 it was argued that the persistent, core, defining characteristic of orthodox economics is the assumption of utility-maximizing agents. Consequently, the most coherent defining feature of heterodoxy is the rejection of Max U. Its principal *raison d'être* would be to develop an alternative theory of human motivation.

Imagine that such a heterodox project to criticize Max U could get off the ground and attract a critical mass of heterodox economists. This group would face the central problem that in general terms Max U is unfalsifiable. Consequently, it cannot be refuted by empirical evidence alone. It would be a major strategic, as well as a theoretical error, to propose otherwise. Claims that Max U has been refuted by evidence will simply be met by the construction of ever-more glamorous Max U functions that can accommodate that evidence within reasonable tolerances. The circuit of Max U criticism, adjustment and rebuttal has been repeated endlessly in the past. The ultimate result has been the regeneration of Max U, not his demise.

Consequently, the challenge for these heterodox economists is to develop alternative strategies to persuade others of the limitations of Max U. An up-front admission of the unfalsifiability of Max U is necessary to get this strategy off the ground and to focus the attention of critics and defenders on alternative criteria of appraisal.

Importantly, Max U leads to misguided policies. Fitting Max U functions to data on past behaviour is necessarily backward-looking. But using Max U to design policy is forward-looking and must be subject to different criteria of assessment. The forward-looking use of an estimated Max U policy assumes that all motivations can be reduced to the single metric of utility. It assumes widespread substitutability between alternative motivations or behaviours. It attempts to force all the springs of understanding and motivation into preference functions, overlooking the possibility that relations or structures may also play a part in the determination of behaviour.

The use of Max U for policy purposes has major implications. For example, the motivations of healthcare professionals are reduced to Max U terms, subsuming ethical and emotional commitments to caring for the sick. Within utility functions a substitutability between monetary rewards and ethical motivation is assumed. Consequently, the vital ethical and professional commitment to the care of others is undermined by Max U (Hodgson, 2013a, ch. 8; Davis and McMaster, 2017).

Similar arguments concerning the importance of cultivating moral as well as pecuniary motivations apply to the design of policies to deal with organizational corruption, to enhance obedience to the law, to mitigate climate change, to caring activities generally, and to the management of business employees (Tyler, 1990; J. Nelson, 1995; Jochimsen, 2003; Minkler, 2008; Hodgson, 2013a).

With this forward-looking, policy-oriented agenda, a strategy should be developed to appraise these arguments via real-world case studies, surveys, laboratory experiments and other empirical methods. This strategy could recruit support from leading experimental economists, including Nobel Laureate Vernon Smith and Bart Wilson. They have argued that fitting everything into individual preference functions is unconvincing, and for attention to be given to social relations and morality. They have drawn on Adam Smith's *Theory of Moral Sentiments* (1759) for inspiration and found Smith's arguments to be superior to the utilitarianism of Max U (Wilson, 2010; Smith, 2013; Smith and Wilson, 2019).

Another major part of this project to replace Max U would be to build on the modern theory of genetic and cultural evolution. This would follow the lead of Charles Darwin (1871) and demonstrate clearly that our capacities for moral evaluation have evolved over thousands or millions of years through group selection (Sober and Wilson, 1998; De Waal, 2006; Joyce, 2006; Kitcher, 2011; Boehm, 2012; Hodgson, 2013a, 2014a).

By contrast, Max U has difficulty coping with evolutionary arguments (Veblen, 1898b, p. 188; Hodgson, 2015a). Were his ready-for-anything preferences present at his birth? If so, how is the miraculous emergence of the capacity to compare and decide over a multitude of possible future alternatives explained? If not, what is the explanation for the development of his preferences through time? Max U theory provides no convincing explanation here. Evolutionary theory is a powerful weapon against Max U.

Neurological research is also another possible area for the critique of Max U and for the development of alternatives. Studies show that oxytocin levels in the brain are related to levels of trust (Zak, 2004, 2011a, 2011b). Research has also identified the neural processes associated with pro-social dispositions (Fehr and Camerer, 2007; Vercoe and Zak, 2010). There is also evidence that human decision-making in social dilemmas relies on areas of the brain connected with emotions, as well as in the pre-frontal cortex. Moral judgements are not exclusive to the deliberative pre-frontal cortex but relate also to several other brain areas, some of early evolutionary origin (Greene and Haidt, 2002; Tancredi,

2005; Zak, 2011a, 2011b). This research can help to inspire a richer theory of human motivation.

The development of alternatives to Max U would have to draw heavily from psychology, as well as from philosophy and other disciplines. It would need a theory of agency that accepts the modular nature of the brain and the habitual or instinctive basis of much behaviour. In this respect it may build on the legacies of William James, Thorstein Veblen and John Dewey, among others (James, 1890; Veblen, 1914; Dewey, 1922; Plotkin, 1994; Hodgson, 2004a, 2010).

This strategy to confront Max U within economics and to develop alternatives has strong academic credibility, from both within and outside economics. The radical nature of its critique, involving the attack on a core assumption within economics, would involve risks for both mature and younger researchers. But if sustained and done well, it could reap rewards.

A key problem would be to establish and develop highly regarded journals that were devoted to this research. At least for the foreseeable future it is difficult to get attacks on Max U published in the leading journals of economics. Many of the heterodox journals would accept this material, but currently they do not perform well on the rankings and hence do not provide sufficient incentives for those working in this area. But it might be worth trying to transform an existing journal that shares these concerns and would benefit from greater focus and sense of direction. The *Review of Social Economy* is an obvious nominee.

Another option would be to create a new journal focused on the question of motivation. It could be called the *Journal for the Analysis of Economic Motivation*, or something like that. Such a new journal would be required to pursue a sustained strategy to rise up the rankings.

But overall, the key problem for this strategy is its arena of engagement. It faces the dilemma of hanging on within economics, and trying to gain influence from inside, or of setting up shop outside. The outside options could include a sub-department within (say) sociology or psychology, or of going it alone. All these alternatives are unproven, and face obvious difficulties in gathering support and funding.

STRATEGY 7: FOCUSING ON INSTITUTIONS – FROM INSIDE ECONOMICS

Two final suggestions are different from the others in a crucial respect: they focus on real confined objects of analysis rather than the whole economy. Reflecting the growing global recognition of the importance of institutions, the object of study (*raison d'être* (a) in Chapter 2) in these cases would be the institutions (and organizations) of the economy.

Should this institution-oriented strategy be oriented principally toward economics or be broader and multi-disciplinary? Consider the economics-oriented version first. This narrower strategy is adopted by the Society for Institutional and Organizational Economics (SIOE – formerly the International Society for New Institutional Economics (ISNIE), founded in 1996). Describing themselves as 'new institutional economists', they aim to establish this kind of institutional research within leading journals and departments of economics.

As noted previously, according to the different criteria suggested by Roger Backhouse (2000) and Fred Lee (2008, 2009), the new institutional economics would not qualify as heterodox. But Tony Lawson's (1997, 2003, 2004) criteria – which concern mathematical formalism – would make at least the work of Ronald Coase, Douglass North, Elinor Ostrom and Oliver Williamson heterodox.

In addition to focusing on the objects of analysis of institutions (including organizations) under *raison d'être* (a), this SIOE/ISNIE strategy involves applying techniques and approaches that are prominent in mainstream economics. Hence it has an additional stipulation under *raison d'être* (b) – it uses mainstream techniques and approaches. Whether it is designated as heterodox or orthodox, it is useful to evaluate this strategy.

At first sight this strategy seems remarkably successful. No less than four Nobel Laureates have been closely associated with ISNIE or SIOE, namely Coase, North, Ostrom and Williamson. On the other hand, it seems that as many institutional economists in this genre are situated outside as well as inside departments of economics. Consequently, it seems only a partial conquest of economics itself.

Consider the impressive work in new institutional economics by Daron Acemoglu and his colleagues. They have published in several leading economics journals, while demonstrating their mastery of cutting-edge econometric techniques (Acemoglu et al., 2001, 2002, 2005a, 2005b, 2011; Acemoglu and Johnson, 2005). Otherwise, the discursive style of much research in new institutional economics makes it difficult to get it published in the more prestigious, mathematically oriented journals in economics. Here Lawson's discussion of formalism comes into play.

While new institutional economics can get published in top economics journals by using econometrics, their modelling options are limited. Game theory is an established possibility (Aoki, 2001; Young, 1998), but this is often less suitable for complex institutions and practically oriented analysis. Claude Ménard and Mary Shirley noted the difficulties that new institutional economists face to get their work accepted in mainstream journals. Ménard and Shirley (2014, pp. 558–60) identified 'the dominance of formalism as it exists today' as an obstacle to the greater dissemination of new institutional ideas, because 'complexities and nuances ... greatly burden the modeling exercise'. Consequently, other ways forward must be addressed, such as fieldwork and case studies.

Faced with these barriers to mainstream acceptance, new institutional economists have to some degree been economical with the truth of its own history. When its students and followers are urged to adopt the standard methods of economics, it is often overlooked, for example, that Coase was a strong critic of Max U and North addressed 'neoclassical' assumptions with increasing disapproval (Coase, 1977, 1988; North, 1990, 1994).

This strategy may also run into internal theoretical difficulties. It is arguable that institutions cannot be adequately understood within a Max U framework. If this were true, then this strategy and project might run into the sand, requiring a different approach. Such arguments led Eirik Furubotn (1997, pp. 454–8) to propose that *the orthodox neoclassical model has proved to be an essentially misleading guide for modern institutional economics*', hence the new institutional economics 'must lose its connections with neoclassicism'. He is not alone in reaching this conclusion: the points made by Coase and North have been noted already.

If in some cases people obey rules because of moral or other non-instrumental motives, then it is challengeable whether Max U can capture these motivations adequately. This is illustrated by the problem of law enforcement. Contrary to the Max U arguments of Gary Becker (1968, p. 176) and others, where 'a person commits an offense if the expected utility to him exceeds the utility he could get from using his time and other resources on other activities', morally-motivated agents may obey the law principally because they believe it is the right and moral thing to do. There is strong evidence for the prevalence of such moral motivation in this sphere (Tyler, 1990). If Max U proves inadequate to understand rule-following behaviour, then that challenges a strategy of orientation toward orthodox economics.

STRATEGY 8: FOCUSING ON INSTITUTIONS – FROM MULTIPLE DISCIPLINES

This leads to a strategy that adopts the same *raison d'être* (a) – the real-world zone of enquiry is the study of institutions – but does not define its approach in terms of a particular discipline or set of methods. Instead, the approach is to draw from multiple disciplines, including anthropology, biology, geography, history, law, politics, psychology, philosophy, social theory and sociology, as well as from economics itself. Researchers from these disciplines are called upon to collaborate in the study of the institutions (and organizations) of economic life, and to create some consensus over core concepts.

This more inclusive strategy draws from disciplines such as law, without necessarily requiring that they should be framed using the concepts and methods of mainstream economics (as in much of the *law and economics* literature). It draws from philosophy and social theory because these disciplines are essential to understand the ontology of institutions. It draws from organization science because that has much to teach about the nature of organizations. And so on.

This inclusive strategy is adopted by the World Interdisciplinary Network for Institutional Research (WINIR), which was founded in 2013 and is now as large as several heterodox associations. WINIR is the major shareholder in the *Journal of Institutional Economics*, which describes itself as 'a multi-disciplinary forum for research on economic institutions'. The *Journal of Institutional Economics* has risen up the rankings and has achieved Clarivate Analytics (formerly Thomson-Reuters) citation impact factors that are higher than those for long-established heterodox journals.

The broader version of this strategy-focused institutional research, with inputs from multiple disciplines, would dovetail with the aforementioned trans-disciplinary strategy proposed by Colander and his co-workers. It would help to prepare the networks and foundations for greater unification across the social sciences. It could also dovetail with the aforementioned strategy to develop alternatives to Max U.

Although this is going to be a long haul, and the building of an academic community in this area will be difficult, there are some grounds for optimism with this strategy. There is a similar and highly successful precedent. The inter-disciplinary field of innovation studies cohered and took off in the 1980s, and it now sports its own institutes, academic positions, journals and degrees (Martin, 2012). The field of institutional research can appeal to the fact that institutional innovation is just as important as technological innovation, and the social technology of institutions is just as important as the technology of materials. They all need substantial attention.

On the downside, inter-disciplinary research is much less prominent in the US, which is the major powerhouse of much scientific research within universities. Units of innovation studies are stronger in Europe than North America. This eighth strategy may work much more effectively in Europe than elsewhere.

CONCLUSION: HAS HETERODOX ECONOMICS A FUTURE?

It is no longer viable for heterodox economists to work on as they have been doing, simply in the faith that someday, somewhere and somehow, more and more people will be persuaded of their veracity. This faith rests on a remarkably individualistic and de-institutionalized view of science. It is refuted by better understandings of science works, and also rubs against the anti-individualist pronouncements of many heterodox economists.

The self-described heterodox community needs to consider its future strategic options, especially in the light of research on the sociology of scientific communities, their social epistemology, and the drivers of scientific advance. One thing is sure, the strategy of using 'heterodox economics' as a banner to organize dissent from the mainstream has been at best of limited success, and this is not simply because of mainstream or rightist ideological resurgence.

Part of the problem in the past is that heterodoxy has been united more by (leftist) ideology than by analysis. This ideological orientation is ultimately damaging for the development of heterodoxy. It creates leftist ghettos that become ill-prepared to engage adequately with other communities outside. There may be many older heterodox economists that wish to continue along the road of 'left-wing economics', where ideology is at least as important as theoretical substance in the processes of academic evaluation.

Among the problems with the over-politicization of communities of heterodox or orthodox economists is the tendency toward conformation bias – to search for evidence to confirm a view, rather than to challenge it. This inclination can be countered by viewpoint diversity within academic communities. We should be wary of communities of social scientists that congregate around a narrow range of political views. Such circumstances encourage groupthink rather than genuine pluralism and open debate. Analytical positions are dismissed simply because they are said to be 'right wing', rather than through critique of the analysis involved.

Eight strategies for heterodoxy have been discussed in this chapter, including the pros and cons in each case. Science, like the economy, is a complex system, and we cannot predict the outcomes. There is a need for experimentation. But with the arguments and evidence we have to hand, it is clear that 'heterodox economics' as an organizing label has major problems.

My current personal assessment would put Strategy 3 (unifying the social sciences), Strategy 5 (specialist regroupment), Strategy 6 (developing alternatives to Max U), and Strategy 8 (focusing on economic institutions from multiple disciplines) above the others as current priorities for experimentation. These four preferred strategies are complementary rather than mutually exclusive.

This book has shown how heterodox economics has been affected in several ways by the circumstances and preconceptions of its founders. Some attributes have been self-reinforcing through time. But we are no longer living in the Cambridge of the 1950s or 1960s. The world has changed dramatically and so too have universities and disciplines. The luxury of heterodoxy has increased in price and its extrinsic rewards have declined. It needs to consider different strategies to survive. We need to offer something better to the scholars of the future.

References

Acemoglu, Daron and Johnson, Simon (2005) 'Unbundling Institutions', *Journal of Political Economy*, **113**(5), October, pp. 949–95.

Acemoglu, Daron, Johnson, Simon and Robinson, James A. (2001) 'The Colonial Origins of Comparative Development: An Empirical Investigation', *American Economic Review*, **91**(5), December, pp. 1369–401.

Acemoglu, Daron, Johnson, Simon and Robinson, James A. (2002) 'Reversal of Fortune: Geography and Institutions in the Making of the Modern Income Distribution', *Quarterly Journal of Economics*, **117**(4), November, pp. 1231–94.

Acemoglu, Daron, Johnson, Simon and Robinson, James A. (2005a) 'Institutions as a Fundamental Cause of Long-Run Growth', in Aghion, Philippe and Durlauf, Steven N. (eds) *Handbook of Economic Growth: Volume 1A* (North Holland: Elsevier), pp. 385–472.

Acemoglu, Daron, Johnson, Simon and Robinson, James A. (2005b) 'The Rise of Europe: Atlantic Trade, Institutional Change and Economic Growth', *American Economic Review*, **95**(3), June, pp. 546–79.

Acemoglu, Daron, Cantoni, Davide, Johnson, Simon and Robinson, James A. (2011) 'The Consequences of Radical Reform: The French Revolution', *American Economic Review*, **101**(7), December, pp. 3286–307.

Ackerman, Robert (1976) *The Philosophy of Karl Popper* (Amherst, MA: University of Massachusetts Press).

Adaman, Fikret and Devine, Patrick (1996) 'The Economic Calculation Debate: Lessons for Socialists', *Cambridge Journal of Economics*, **20**(5), September, pp. 523–37.

Aglietta, Michel (1979) *A Theory of Capitalist Regulation: The US Experience*, trans. by David Fernbach from the French edn of 1976 (London: NLB).

Aistleitner, Matthias, Kapeller, Jakob and Steinerberger, Stefan (2018) 'The Power of Scientometrics and the Development of Economics', *Journal of Economic Issues*, **52**(3), September, pp. 816–34.

Akerlof, George A. and Kranton, Rachel E. (2010) *Identity Economics* (Princeton, NJ: Princeton University Press).

Albert, Michael (2004) 'Market Madness', *Znet*. Available at http://zcomm.org/znetarticle/market-madness-by-michael-albert-1/. (Retrieved 1 October 2014.)

Alchian, Armen A. (1950) 'Uncertainty, Evolution, and Economic Theory', *Journal of Political Economy*, **58**(2), June, pp. 211–22.

Aldrich, Howard E. (1999) *Organizations Evolving* (London: Sage).

Aldrich, Howard E. and Ruef, Martin (2006) *Organizations Evolving*, 2nd edn (London: Sage).

Aldrich, Howard E., Hodgson, Geoffrey M., Hull, David L., Knudsen, Thorbjørn, Mokyr, Joel and Vanberg, Viktor J. (2008) 'In Defence of Generalized Darwinism', *Journal of Evolutionary Economics*, **18**(5), October, pp. 577–96.

Allen, Peter M. and McGlade, J.M. (1987) 'Modelling Complex Human Systems: A Fisheries Example', *European Journal of Operational Research*, **30**(2), pp. 147–67.

Allen, R.T. (1998) *Beyond Liberalism: The Political Thought of F.A. Hayek and Michael Polanyi* (New Brunswick, NJ: Transaction).

Aoki, Masahiko (2001) *Toward a Comparative Institutional Analysis* (Cambridge, MA: MIT Press).

Arndt, H.W. (1984) 'Political Economy', *Economic Record*, **60**(3), September, pp. 266–73.

Arrow, Kenneth J. (1978) 'A Cautious Case for Socialism', *Dissent*, **25**, Fall, pp. 472–80.

Arrow, Kenneth J. (1994) 'Methodological Individualism and Social Knowledge', *American Economic Review (Papers and Proceedings)*, **84**(2), May, pp. 1–9.

Arrow, Kenneth J. and Hahn, Frank H. (1971) *General Competitive Analysis* (Edinburgh: Oliver and Boyd).

Arthur, W. Brian, Durlauf, Steven N. and Lane, David A. (eds) (1997) *The Economy as an Evolving Complex System II* (Redwood City, CA: Addison-Wesley).

Aspromourgos, Tony (1986) 'On the Origins of the term "Neoclassical"', *Cambridge Journal of Economics*, **10**(3), September, pp. 265–70.

Atkinson, Anthony B. (2015) *Inequality: What Can Be Done?* (Cambridge, MA: Harvard University Press).

Axelrod, Robert M. (1984) *The Evolution of Cooperation* (New York: Basic Books).

Ayres, Clarence E. (1944) *The Theory of Economic Progress* (Chapel Hill, NC: University of North Carolina Press).

Backhouse, Roger E. (1996) 'The Changing Character of British Economics', *History of Political Economy, Annual Supplement to Volume 28*, pp. 33–60.

Backhouse, Roger E. (1998) 'The Transformation of U.S. Economics, 1920–1960, Viewed through a Survey of Journal Articles', in Morgan, Mary S. and Rutherford, Malcolm H. (eds) *The Transformation of*

American Economics: From Interwar Pluralism to Postwar Neoclassicism, Annual Supplement to Volume 30 of History of Political Economy (Durham, NC: Duke University Press), pp. 85–107.

Backhouse, Roger E. (2000), 'Progress in Heterodox Economics', *Journal of the History of Economic Thought*, **22**(2), 149–57.

Backhouse, Roger E. (2004), 'A Suggestion for Clarifying the Study of Dissent in Economics', *Journal of the History of Economic Thought*, **26**(2), 261–71.

Backhouse, Roger E. and Cherrier, Béatrice (2017) 'The Age of the Applied Economist: The Transformation of Economics since the 1970s', *History of Political Economy*, 49 (Supplement), pp. 1–33.

Bannister, Robert C. (1988) *Social Darwinism: Science and Myth*, 2nd edn, with a new preface (Philadelphia, PA: Temple University Press).

BBC News (2011) 'Chile Recognises 9,800 more Victims of Pinochet's Rule', *BBC News*, 18 August. Available at https://www.bbc.co.uk/news/world-latin-america-14584095. (Retrieved 6 December 2018.)

Becker, Gary S. (1968) 'Crime and Punishment: An Economic Approach', *Journal of Political Economy*, **76**(2), March–April, pp. 169–217.

Becker, Gary S. (1976a) *The Economic Approach to Human Behavior* (Chicago, IL: University of Chicago Press).

Becker, Gary S. (1976b) 'Altruism, Egoism, and Genetic Fitness: Economics and Sociobiology', *Journal of Economic Literature*, **14**(2), December, pp. 817–26.

Becker, Gary S. (1991) *A Treatise on the Family*, 2nd edn (Cambridge, MA: Harvard University Press).

Berg, Nathan and Gigerenzer, Gerd (2010) 'As-if Behavioral Economics: Neoclassical Economics in Disguise?', *History of Economic Ideas*, **18**(1), pp. 133–66.

Berger, Sebastian (2017) *The Social Costs of Neoliberalism: Essays on the Economics of K. William Kapp* (Nottingham: Spokesman).

Bertalanffy, Ludwig (1950) 'The Theory of Open Systems in Physics and Biology', *Science*, **111**, pp. 23–9.

Besley, Timothy and Hennessy, Peter (2009) 'Letter to Her Majesty the Queen', 22 July. Available at http://wwwf.imperial.ac.uk/~bin06/M3A22/queen-lse.pdf. (Retrieved 7 December 2018.)

Bhaskar, Roy (1975) *A Realist Theory of Science* (Leeds: Leeds Books).

Bhaskar, Roy (1986) *Scientific Realism and Human Emancipation* (London: Verso).

Bhaskar, Roy (1989) *Reclaiming Reality: A Critical Introduction to Contemporary Philosophy* (London: Verso).

Bhaskar, Roy and Collier, Andrew (1998) 'Introduction: Explanatory Critiques', in Archer, Margaret S., Bhaskar, Roy, Collier, Andrew, Lawson, Tony and Norrie, Alan (eds) *Critical Realism: Essential Readings* (London: Routledge), pp. 385–94.

Bhupatiraju, Samyukta, Nomaler, Önder, Triulzi, Giorgio and Verspagen, Bart (2012) 'Knowledge Flows – Analyzing the Core Literature of Innovation, Entrepreneurship and Science and Technology Studies', *Research Policy*, **41**(7), pp. 1205–18.

Bladel, John P. (2005) 'Against Polanyi-Centrism: Hayek and the Re-emergence of "Spontaneous Order"', *Quarterly Journal of Austrian Economics*, **8**(4), Winter, pp. 15–30.

Blau, Peter J. (1994) *The Organization of Academic Work* (New Brunswick, NJ: Transaction).

Blaug, Mark (1974) *The Cambridge Revolution: Success or Failure?* (London: Institute of Economic Affairs).

Blaug, Mark (1975) 'Kuhn versus Lakatos, or Paradigms versus Research Programmes in the History of Economics', *History of Political Economy*, **7**(4), Winter, pp. 399–433.

Blaug, Mark (1990) *Economic Theories: True or False? Essays on the History and Methodology of Economics* (Aldershot, UK and Brookfield, VT, USA: Edward Elgar Publishing).

Blaug, Mark (1992) *The Methodology of Economics: Or How Economists Explain*, 2nd edn (Cambridge: Cambridge University Press).

Blaug, Mark (1993) Review of D.R. Steele *From Marx to Mises*, *Economic Journal*, **103**(6), November, pp. 1570–71.

Blaug, Mark (1997) 'Ugly Currents in Modern Economics', *Options Politiques*, **18**(17), September, pp. 3–8. Extended and revised in Mäki, Uskali (ed.) (2002) *Fact and Fiction in Economics: Models, Realism and Social Construction* (Cambridge, UK and New York, NY, USA: Cambridge University Press), pp. 35–56.

Blaug, Mark (1999) 'The Formalist Revolution or What Happened to Orthodox Economics After World War II?' in Backhouse, Roger E. and Creedy, John (eds) *From Classical Economics to the Theory of the Firm: Essays in Honour of D.P. O'Brien* (Cheltenham, UK and Northampton, MA, USA: Edward Elgar Publishing), pp. 257–80.

Blaug, Mark (2003) 'The Formalist Revolution of the 1950s', in Samuels, Warren J., Biddle, Jeff E. and Davis, John B. (eds) *A Companion to the History of Economic Thought* (Malden, MA, USA and Oxford, UK: Blackwell), pp. 395–410.

Blinov, Evgeny (2016) 'The New Scientific Policy: The Early Soviet Project of "State-Sponsored Evolutionism"', *Social Epistemology*, **31**(1).

Bliss, Christopher (2010) 'The Cambridge Post-Keynesians: An Outsider's Insider View', *History of Political Economy*, **42**(4), Winter, pp. 631–52.

Boas, Taylor C. and Gans-Morse, Jordan (2009) 'Neoliberalism: From New Liberal Philosophy to Anti-Liberal Slogan', *Studies in Comparative International Development*, **44**(2), June, pp. 137–61.

Boehm, Christopher (2012) *Moral Origins: The Evolution of Virtue, Altruism and Shame* (New York: Basic Books).

Boettke, Peter J. (ed.) (2000) *Socialism and the Market: The Calculation Debate Revisited* (London, UK and New York, NY, USA: Routledge).

Boettke, Peter J. (2001) *Calculation and Coordination: Essays on Socialism and Transitional Political Economy* (London, UK and New York, NY, USA: Routledge).

Boettke, Peter J. (2019) 'What is Still Wrong with the Austrian School of Economics?', *Review of Austrian Economics*, forthcoming.

Boland, Lawrence A. (1981) 'On the Futility of Criticizing the Neoclassical Maximization Hypothesis', *American Economic Review*, **71**(5), December, pp. 1031–36.

Borgatti, Stephen P., Everett, Martin G. and Freeman, L.C. (2002) *UCINET 6.0 Version 1.00* (Natick, MA: Analytic Technologies).

Boulding, Kenneth E. (1981) *Evolutionary Economics* (Beverly Hills, CA: Sage Publications).

Bowler, Peter J. (1997) *Life's Splendid Drama: Evolutionary Biology and the Reconstruction of Life's Ancestry, 1860–1940* (Chicago, IL: University of Chicago Press).

Bowles, Samuel (2004) *Microeconomics: Behavior, Institutions, and Evolution* (Princeton, NJ: Princeton University Press and New York, NY: Russell Sage Foundation).

Bowles, Samuel and Gintis, Herbert (2011) *A Cooperative Species: Human Reciprocity and its Evolution* (Princeton, NJ: Princeton University Press).

Boyd, Robert and Richerson, Peter J. (1985) *Culture and the Evolutionary Process* (Chicago, IL: University of Chicago Press).

Boyer, Robert and Mistral, Jacques (1978) *Accumulation, Inflation et Crises* (Paris: Universitaire de France).

Boyer, Robert and Yamada, Toshio (eds) (2000) *Japanese Capitalism in Crisis: A Regulationist Interpretation* (London, UK and New York, NY, USA: Routledge).

Brady, Michael Emmett and Arthmar, Rogério (2012) 'Keynes, Boole and the Interval Approach to Probability', *History of Economic Ideas*, **20**(3), pp. 65–84.

Braun, Eduard (2015) 'Carl Menger's Contribution to Capital Theory', *History of Economic Ideas*, **23**(1), pp. 77–99.

Breslin, Dermot (2011) 'Reviewing a Generalized Darwinist Approach to Studying Socio-Economic Change', *International Journal of Management Reviews*, **13**(2), pp. 218–35.

Buchanan, James M. and Tullock, Gordon (1962) *The Calculus of Consent: Logical Foundations of Constitutional Democracy* (Ann Arbor, MI: University of Michigan Press).

Bunge, Mario A. (1979) *Treatise on Basic Philosophy*, vol. 4, *Ontology II: A World of Systems* (Dordrecht: Reidel).

Burczak, Theodore (2006) *Socialism after Hayek* (Ann Arbor, MI: University of Michigan Press).

Burgin, Angus (2012) *The Great Persuasion: Reinventing Free Markets since the Depression* (Cambridge, MA: Harvard University Press).

Busenitz, Lowell W., West, G. Page, Shepherd, Dean, Nelson, Teresa, Chandler, Gaylen N. and Zacharakis, Andrew (2003) 'Entrepreneurship Research in Emergence: Past Trends and Future Directions', *Journal of Management*, **29**(3), pp. 285–308.

Buss, David M. (1999) *Evolutionary Psychology: The New Science of the Mind* (Needham Heights, MA: Allyn and Bacon).

Butler, Gavan, Jones, Evan and Stilwell, Frank (2009) *Political Economy Now! The Struggle for Alternative Economics at the University of Sydney* (Sydney: Darlington Press).

Cahlik, Tomas (2000) 'Search for Fundamental Articles in Economics', *Scientometrics*, **49**(3), pp. 389–402.

Camerer, Colin F. (2003) *Behavioral Game Theory: Experiments in Strategic Interaction* (Princeton, NJ: Princeton University Press).

Camerer, Colin F., Loewenstein, George and Prelec, Drazen (2005) 'Neuroeconomics: How Neuroscience Can Inform Economics', *Journal of Economic Literature*, **43**(1), March, pp. 9–64.

Camerer, Colin F., Loewenstein, George and Rabin, Matthew (eds) (2004) *Advances in Behavioral Economics* (New York, NY: Russell Sage Foundation and Princeton, NJ: Princeton University Press).

Camic, Charles and Hodgson, Geoffrey M. (eds) (2011) *Essential Writings of Thorstein Veblen* (London, UK and New York, NY, USA: Routledge).

Campbell, Donald T. (1965) 'Variation, Selection and Retention in Sociocultural Evolution', in Barringer, H.R., Blanksten, G.I. and Mack, R.W. (eds) *Social Change in Developing Areas: A Reinterpretation of Evolutionary Theory* (Cambridge, MA: Schenkman), pp. 19–49.

Canterbery, E. Ray (2010) *The Making of Economics, Volume III: The Radical Assault* (Singapore: World Scientific).

Case, Donald O. and Higgins, Georgeann M. (2000) 'How Can we Investigate Citation Behavior? A Study of Reasons for Citing Literature in Communication', *Journal of the American Society for Information Science and Technology*, **51**(7), pp. 635–45.

Cawkell, A.E. (1976) 'Understanding Science by Analysing its Literature', *The Information Scientist*, **10**(1), pp. 3–10.

Cedrini, Mario and Fontana, Magda (2018) 'Just another Niche in the Wall: How Specialization is Changing the Face of Mainstream Economics', *Cambridge Journal of Economics*, **42**(2), February, pp. 427–51.

Charness, Gary and Rabin, Matthew (2002) 'Understanding Social Preferences with Simple Tests', *Quarterly Journal of Economics*, **117**(3), August, pp. 817–69.

Chick, Victoria and Dow, Sheila C. (2005) 'The Meaning of Open Systems', *Journal of Economic Methodology*, **13**(3), September, pp. 363–81.

Chung, Joseph Sang-Hoon (1972) 'North Korea's "Seven Year Plan" (1961–70): Economic Performance and Reforms', *Asian Survey*, **12**(6), June, pp. 527–45.

Clark, John Bates (1899) *The Distribution of Wealth: A Theory of Wages, Interest and Profits* (New York: Macmillan).

Cliff, Tony (1955) *Stalinist Russia: A Marxist Analysis* (London: Michael Kidron).

Coase, Ronald H. (1937) 'The Nature of the Firm', *Economica*, **4**, New Series, November, pp. 386–405.

Coase, Ronald H. (1960) 'The Problem of Social Cost', *Journal of Law and Economics*, **3**(1), October, pp. 1–44.

Coase, Ronald H. (1974) 'The Market for Goods and the Market for Ideas', *American Economic Review (Papers and Proceedings)*, **64**(2), May, pp. 384–91.

Coase, Ronald H. (1977) 'Economics and Contiguous Disciplines', in Mark Perlman (ed.) *The Organization and Retrieval of Economic Knowledge* (Boulder, CO: Westview Press), pp. 481–91.

Coase, Ronald H. (1988) *The Firm, the Market, and the Law* (Chicago, IL: University of Chicago Press).

Coats, A.W. (1969) 'Is There a "Structure of Scientific Revolutions" in Economics?', *Kyklos*, **22**(2), May, pp. 289–96.

Coats, A.W. (1993) *The Sociology and Professionalization of Economics: British and American Economic Essays, Volume II* (London: Routledge).

Coats, A.W. (2001) 'Reflections on the Progress of Heterodox Economics', in Garrouste, Pierre and Ioannides, Stavros (eds) *Evolution and Path Dependence in Economic Ideas: Past and Present* (Cheltenham, UK and Northampton, MA, USA: Edward Elgar Publishing), pp. 225–38.

Cohen, Avi J. (2014) 'Veblen *Contra* Clark and Fisher: Veblen–Robinson–Harcourt Lineages in Capital Controversies and Beyond', *Cambridge Journal of Economics*, **38**(6), November, pp. 1493–515.

Cohen, Avi J. and Harcourt, Geoffrey C. (2003) 'Whatever Happened to the Cambridge Capital Theory Controversies?', *Journal of Economic Perspectives*, **17**(1), Winter, pp. 199–214.

Cohen, Wesley M. and Levinthal, Daniel A. (1990) 'Absorptive Capacity: A New Perspective on Learning and Innovation', *Administrative Science Quarterly*, **35**(1), pp. 128–52.

Colander, David C. (2000a) 'The Death of Neoclassical Economics', *Journal of the History of Economic Thought*, **22**(2), June, pp. 127–43.

Colander, David C. (2000b) 'New Millennium Economics: How Did it Get this Way, and What Way is it?', *Journal of Economic Perspectives*, **14**(1), Winter, pp. 121–32.

Colander, David C. (ed.) (2000c) *The Complexity Vision and the Teaching of Economics* (Cheltenham, UK and Northampton, MA, USA: Edward Elgar Publishing).

Colander, David C. (2000d) *Complexity and the History of Economic Thought* (London, UK and New York, NY, USA: Routledge).

Colander, David C. (2005a) 'The Making of an Economist Redux', *Journal of Economic Perspectives*, **19**(1), Winter, pp. 175–98.

Colander, David C. (2005b) 'The Future of Economics: The Appropriately Educated in Pursuit of the Knowable', *Cambridge Journal of Economics*, **29**(6), November, pp. 927–41.

Colander, David C. (2010) 'Moving beyond the Rhetoric of Pluralism: Suggestions for an "Inside-the-Mainstream" Heterodoxy', in William Garnett, Erik Olsen and Martha Starr (eds) *Economic Pluralism* (London, UK and New York, NY, USA: Routledge), pp. 36–47.

Colander, David C. (2014) 'The Wrong Type of Pluralism: Toward a Transdisciplinary Social Science', *Review of Political Economy*, **26**(4), October, pp. 516–25.

Colander, David C. and Freedman, Craig (2019) *Where Economics Went Wrong: Chicago's Abandonment of Classical Liberalism* (Princeton, NJ, USA and Oxford, UK: Princeton University Press).

Colander, David C. and Kupers, Roland (2014) *Complexity and the Art of Public Policy* (Princeton, NJ: Princeton University Press).

Colander, David C., Holt, Richard P.F. and Rosser, J. Barkley, Jr (2004) 'The Changing Face of Economics', *Review of Political Economy*, **16**(4), October, pp. 485–99.

Colander, David C., Kupers, Roland, Lux, Thomas and Rothschild, Casey (2010) 'Reintegrating the Social Sciences: The Dahlem Group', Middlebury College Economics Discussion Paper No. 10-33. Available at http://sandcat.middlebury.edu/econ/repec/mdl/ancoec/1033.pdf. (Retrieved 17 June 2018.)

Coldicutt, Samuel (2010) 'Post-war Heterodoxy and its Decline at the Cambridge Faculty of Economics, 1986–1998', University of Cambridge, unpublished undergraduate dissertation.

Collier, Andrew (1994) *Critical Realism: An Introduction to Roy Bhaskar's Philosophy* (London: Verso).

Collins, Randall (1998) *The Sociology of Philosophies: A Global Theory of Intellectual Change* (Cambridge, MA: Harvard University Press).

Cosmides, L. and Tooby, J. (1994) 'Better than Rational: Evolutionary Psychology and the Invisible Hand', *American Economic Review (Papers and Proceedings)*, **84**(2), May, pp. 327–32.

Courtois, Stéphane, Werth, Nicolas, Panné, Jean-Louis, Packowski, Andrzej, Bartošek, Karel and Margolin, Jean-Louis (1999) *The Black Book of Communism: Crimes, Terror, Repression* (Cambridge, MA: Harvard University Press).

Crane, Diana (1972) *Invisible Colleges: Diffusion of Knowledge in Scientific Communities* (Chicago, IL: University of Chicago Press).

Crespo, Ricardo F. (2013) 'Two conceptions of Economics and Maximisation', *Cambridge Journal of Economics*, **37**(4), July, pp. 759–74.

Cross, Rod (1982) 'The Duhem–Quine Thesis, Lakatos and the Appraisal of Theories in Macroeconomics', *Economic Journal*, **92**(2), June, pp. 320–40.

Culnan, Mary J. (1986) 'The Intellectual Development of Management Information Systems, 1972–1982: A Co-Citation Analysis', *Management Science*, **32**(2), pp. 156–72.

Culnan, Mary J. (1987) 'Mapping the Intellectual Structure of MIS, 1980–1985: A Co-Citation Analysis', *MIS Quarterly*, **11**(3), pp. 341–53.

Cyert, Richard M. and March, James G. (1963) *A Behavioral Theory of the Firm* (Englewood Cliffs, NJ: Prentice-Hall).

D'Amico, Daniel J. (2015) 'Spontaneous Order', in Boettke, Peter J. and Coyne, Christopher (eds), *The Oxford Handbook of Austrian Economics* (Oxford, UK and New York, NY, USA: Oxford University Press), pp. 115–42.

Dachs, Bernhard, Roediger-Schluga, Thomas, Widhalm, Clemens and Zartl, Angelika (2001) 'Mapping Evolutionary Economics: A Bibliometric Analysis', paper presented at EMAEE 2001 Conference. Austria, 13–15 September.

Daly, Herman E. (1974) 'The Economics of the Steady State', *American Economic Review (Papers and Proceedings)*, **64**(2), May, 15–21.

Darwin, Charles R. (1859) *On the Origin of Species by Means of Natural Selection, or the Preservation of Favoured Races in the Struggle for Life*, 1st edn (London: Murray).

Darwin, Charles R. (1871) *The Descent of Man, and Selection in Relation to Sex*, 2 vols (London, UK: Murray and New York, NY, USA: Hill).

Davidson, Paul (1980) 'Post Keynesian Economics', *Public Interest*, Special edn, pp. 151–73.

Davis, John B. (1995) 'Personal Identity and Standard Economic Theory', *Journal of Economic Methodology*, **2**(1), June, pp. 35–52.

Davis, John B. (2003) *The Theory of the Individual in Economics: Identity and Value* (London, UK and New York, NY, USA: Routledge).

Davis, John B. (2005) 'Heterodox Economics, the Fragmentation of the Mainstream and Embedded Individual Analysis', in Robert Garnett and John Harvey (eds) *The Future of Heterodox Economics* (Ann Arbor, MI: University of Michigan Press), pp. 53–72.

Davis, John B. (2006) 'The Turn in Economics: Neoclassical Dominance to Mainstream Pluralism?', *Journal of Institutional Economics*, **2**(1), April, pp. 1–20.

Davis, John B. (2007) 'Akerlof and Kranton on Identity in Economics: Inverting the Analysis', *Cambridge Journal of Economics*, **31**(3), May, pp. 349–62.

Davis, John B. (2008) 'The Turn in Recent Economics and Return of Orthodoxy', *Cambridge Journal of Economics*, **32**(3), May, pp. 349–66.

Davis, John B. and McMaster, Robert (2017) *Health Care Economics* (London, UK and New York, NY, USA: Routledge).

Dawkins, Richard (1976) *The Selfish Gene* (Oxford: Oxford University Press).

De Soto, Hernando (2000) *The Mystery of Capital: Why Capitalism Triumphs in the West and Fails Everywhere Else* (New York: Basic Books).

De Waal, Frans B.M. (2006) *Primates and Philosophers: How Morality Evolved* (Princeton, NJ: Princeton University Press).

Dequech, David (2007) 'Neoclassical, Mainstream, Orthodox, and Heterodox Economics', *Journal of Post Keynesian Economics*, **30**(2), Winter, pp. 279–302.

Dequech, David (2017) 'Some Institutions (Social Norms and Conventions) of Contemporary Mainstream Economics, Macroeconomics and Financial Economics', *Cambridge Journal of Economics*, **41**(6), November, pp. 1627–52.

Devine, Patrick (1988) *Democracy and Economic Planning: The Political Economy of a Self-Governing Society* (Cambridge: Polity Press).

Dewey, John (1922) *Human Nature and Conduct: An Introduction to Social Psychology*, 1st edn (New York: Holt).

Dhami, Sanjit (2016) *The Foundations of Behavioral Economic Analysis* (Oxford, UK and New York, NY, USA: Oxford University Press).

Di Tella, Rafael and MacCulloch, Robert (2006) 'Some Uses of Happiness Data in Economics', *Journal of Economic Perspectives*, **20**(1), Winter, pp. 25–46.

Dickinson, Henry D. (1933) 'Price Formation in a Socialist Community', *Economic Journal*, **43**, pp. 237–50.

Dickinson, Henry D. (1939) *Economics of Socialism* (Oxford: Oxford University Press).

Dikötter, Frank (2010) *Mao's Great Famine: The History of China's Most Devastating Catastrophe, 1958–62* (London: Bloomsbury).

Dikötter, Frank (2016) *The Cultural Revolution: A People's History 1962–1976* (London: Bloomsbury).

Dobb, Maurice (1929) *Capitalist Enterprise and Social Progress* (London: Routledge and Kegan Paul).

Dobb, Maurice (1937) *Political Economy and Capitalism* (London: Routledge and Kegan Paul).

Dobb, Maurice (1949) *Soviet Economic Development since 1917* (London: Routledge and Kegan Paul).

Dobb, Maurice (1955) *On Economic Theory and Socialism: Collected Papers* (London: Routledge and Kegan Paul).

Dobb, Maurice (1960) *An Essay on Economic Growth and Planning* (London: Routledge and Kegan Paul).

Dobb, Maurice (1969) *Welfare Economics and the Economics of Socialism: Towards a Commonsense Critique* (Cambridge: Cambridge University Press).

Dobb, Maurice (1970) 'The Sraffa System and Critique of the Neo-Classical Theory of Distribution', *De Economist*, **118**, pp. 347–62.

Dolfsma, Wilfred and Leydesdorff, Loe (2010) 'The Citation Field of Evolutionary Economics', *Journal of Evolutionary Economics*, **20**(5), October, pp. 645–64.

Dollimore, Denise and Hodgson, Geoffrey M. (2014) 'Four Essays on Economic Evolution: An Introduction', *Journal of Evolutionary Economics*, **24**(1), January, pp. 1–10.

Dopfer, Kurt and Nelson, Richard R. (2018) 'The Evolution of Evolutionary Economics', in Nelson, Richard R., Dosi, Giovanni, Helfat, Constance, Pyka, Andreas, Saviotti, Pier Paolo, Lee, Keun, Dopfer, Kurt et al. (eds) *Modern Evolutionary Economics: An Overview* (Cambridge, UK and New York, NY, USA: Cambridge University Press), pp. 208–229.

Dosi, Giovanni (1982), 'Technological Paradigms and Technological Trajectories: A Suggested Interpretation of the Determinants and Directions of Technical Change', *Research Policy*, **11**(3), pp. 147–62.

Dosi, Giovanni, Freeman, Christopher, Nelson, Richard, Silverberg, Gerald and Soete, Luc L.G. (eds) (1988) *Technical Change and Economic Theory* (London: Pinter).

Dow, Sheila C. (1990) 'Beyond Dualism', *Cambridge Journal of Economics*, **14**(2), June, pp. 143–57.

Dow, Sheila C. (2007) 'Varieties of Methodological Approach in Economics', *Journal of Economic Surveys*, **21**(3), July, pp. 447–65.

Dow, Sheila C. (2008) 'Future Directions for Heterodox Economics', in Harvey, John T. and Garnett, Robert F. Jr (eds) *Future Directions for Heterodox Economics* (Ann Arbor, MI: University of Michigan Press), pp. 9–26.

Dow, Sheila C. (2011a) 'Cognition, Market Sentiment and Financial Instability', *Cambridge Journal of Economics*, **35**(2), March, pp. 233–49.

Dow, Sheila C. (2011b) 'Heterodox Economics: History and Prospects', *Cambridge Journal of Economics*, **35**(6), November, pp. 1151–65.

Dow, Sheila C. (2013) 'Formalism, Rationality and Evidence: The Case of Behavioural Economics', *Erasmus Journal for Philosophy and Economics*, **6**(3) (Special Issue), pp. 26–43.

Dow, Sheila C., Earl, Peter E., Foster, John, Harcourt, Geoffrey C., Hodgson, Geoffrey M., Metcalfe, J. Stanley, Ormerod, Paul et al. (2009). Letter to the Queen of 10 August 2009. Available in *Homo Oeconomicus*, **27**(3), 2010, pp. 329–37 and at https://www.geoffrey mhodgson.uk/letter-to-the-queen. (Retrieved 22 January 2019.)

Downward, Paul (2000) 'A Realist Appraisal of Post-Keynesian Pricing Theory', *Cambridge Journal of Economics*, **24**(2), March, pp. 211–24.

Downward, Paul (ed.) (2003) *Applied Economics: A Critical Realist Approach* (London, UK and New York, NY, USA: Routledge).

Duesenberry, James S. (1949) *Income, Saving and the Theory of Consumer Behavior* (Cambridge, MA: Harvard University Press).

Dunning, John H. (1989) 'The Study of International Business: A Plea for a More Interdisciplinary Approach', *Journal of International Business Studies*, **20**(3), Fall, pp. 411–36.

Durand, Rodolphe (2006) *Organizational Evolution and Strategic Management* (London: Sage).

Durbin, Elizabeth (1985) *New Jerusalems: The Labour Party and the Economics of Democratic Socialism* (London: Routledge and Kegan Paul).

Dymski, Gary A. and Pollin, Robert (eds) (1994) *New Perspectives in Monetary Macroeconomics: Explorations in the Tradition of Hyman P. Minsky* (Ann Arbor, MI: University of Michigan Press).

Earl, Peter E. (2010) 'Economics fit for the Queen: A Pessimistic Assessment of its Prospects', *Prometheus*, **28**(3), pp. 209–25.

Earl, Peter E. (2018) Personal communication with Geoffrey M. Hodgson, 24 July.

Earl, Peter E. and Peng, Ti-Ching (2012) 'Brands of Economics and the Trojan Horse of Pluralism', *Review of Political Economy*, **24**(3), July, pp. 451–67.

Eaton, B. Curtis (1984) 'Review of *An Evolutionary Theory of Economic Change* by R.R. Nelson and S.G. Winter', *Canadian Journal of Economics*, **17**(4), November, pp. 868–71.

Eatwell, John and Panico, Carlo (1987) 'Sraffa, Piero', in Eatwell, John, Milgate, Murray and Newman, Peter (eds) *The New Palgrave Dictionary of Economics*, vol. 4 (London: Macmillan), pp. 445–52.

Edgeworth, Francis Y. (1881) *Mathematical Psychics: An Essay on the Application of Mathematics to the Moral Sciences* (London: Kegan Paul).

Edgeworth, Francis Y. (1904) 'The Theory of Distribution', *Quarterly Journal of Economics*, **18**, pp. 159–219.

Edgeworth, Richard Lovell and Edgeworth, Maria (1844) *Memoirs of Richard Lovell Edgeworth Esq. Begun by Himself and Concluded by His Daughter, Maria Edgeworth*, 3rd edn (London: Richard Bentley).

Edwards, Richard C., Reich, Michael and Weisskopf, Thomas E. (1972) *The Capitalist System* (New York: Prentice Hall).

Elster, Jon (1982) 'Marxism, Functionalism and Game Theory', *Theory and Society*, **11**(4), pp. 453–82. Reprinted in Roemer, John E. (ed.) (1986) *Analytical Marxism* (Cambridge: Cambridge University Press).

Elster, Jon (1985) *Making Sense of Marx* (Cambridge: Cambridge University Press).

Elster, Jon (1986) *An Introduction to Karl Marx* (Cambridge: Cambridge University Press).

Epstein, Brian (2015) *The Ant Trap: Rebuilding the Foundations of the Social Sciences* (Oxford, UK and New York, NY, USA: Oxford University Press).

Etzioni, Amitai (1988) *The Moral Dimension: Toward a New Economics* (New York: Free Press).

Fayazmanesh, Sasan (1998) 'On Veblen's Coining of the Term "Neoclassical"', in Sasan Fayazmanesh and Marc R. Tool (eds) *Institutionalist Method and Value: Essays in Honour of Paul Dale Bush Volume 1* (Cheltenham, UK and Northampton, MA, USA: Edward Elgar Publishing), pp. 74–97.

Fehr, Ernst and Camerer, Colin F. (2007) 'Social Neuroeconomics: The Neural Circuitry of Social Preferences', *Trends in Cognitive Science*, **11**(1), pp. 419–27.

Fehr, Ernst and Fischbacher, Urs (2002) 'Why Do Social Preferences Matter: The Impact of Non-Selfish Motives on Competition, Cooperation and Incentives', *Economic Journal*, **112**, March, pp. C1–C33.

Fetter, Frank A. (1927) 'Clark's Reformulation of the Capital Concept', in Hollander, Jacob H. (ed.) *Economic Essays Contributed in Honor of John Bates Clark* (New York: Macmillan), pp. 136–56.

Fetter, Frank A. (1930) 'Capital', in Seligman, Edwin R.A. and Johnson, Alvin (eds) *Encyclopaedia of the Social Sciences* (New York: Macmillan), Vol. 3, pp. 187–90. Reprinted in the *Journal of Institutional Economics*, **4**(1), April 2008, pp. 127–37.

Finch, John H. and McMaster, Robert (2002) 'On Categorical Variables and Non-Parametric Statistical Inference in the Pursuit of Causal Explanations', *Cambridge Journal of Economics*, **26**(6), November, pp. 753–72.

Fine, Ben and Milonakis, Dimitris (2009) *From Economics Imperialism to Freakonomics: The Shifting Boundaries between Economics and Other Social Sciences* (London, UK and New York, NY, USA: Routledge).

Fischer, Lilian, Hasell, Joe, Proctor, J. Christopher, Uwakwe, David, Ward-Perkins, Zach and Wilson, Catriona (eds) (2018) *Rethinking Economics: An Introduction to Pluralist Economics* (London, UK and New York, NY, USA: Routledge).

Fisher, Irving (1892) *Mathematical Investigations in the Theory of Value and Prices* (New Haven, CT: Yale University Press).

Fleetwood, Steve (2017) 'The Critical Realist Conception of Open and Closed Systems', *Journal of Economic Methodology*, **24**(1), March, pp. 41–68.

Fontana, Giuseppe and Gerrard, Bill (2006) 'The Future of Post Keynesian Economics', *Banca Nationale del Lavoro Quarterly Review*, **59**(236), pp. 49–80.

Foss, Nicolai Juul (1994), 'Realism and Evolutionary Economics', *Journal of Social and Evolutionary Systems*, **17**(1), 21–40.

Fourcade, Marion (2006) 'The Construction of a Global Profession: The Transnationalization of Economics', *American Journal of Sociology*, **112**(1), pp. 145–94.

Fourcade, Marion, Ollion, Etienne and Algan, Yann (2015) 'The Superiority of Economists', *Journal of Economic Perspectives*, **29**(1), Winter, pp. 89–114.

Fox, Justin (2009) *The Myth of the Rational Market* (New York: HarperCollins).

Friedman, Daniel (1991) 'Evolutionary Games in Economics', *Econometrica*, **59**(3), pp. 637–66.

Friedman, Milton (1953) 'The Methodology of Positive Economics', in Friedman, M., *Essays in Positive Economics* (Chicago, IL: University of Chicago Press), pp. 3–43.

Friedman, Milton (1962) *Price Theory: A Provisional Text* (Chicago, IL: Aldine).

Friedman, Milton (1999) 'Conversation with Milton Friedman', in Snowdon, Brian and Vane, Howard (eds) *Conversations with Leading Economists: Interpreting Modern Macroeconomists* (Cheltenham, UK and Northampton, MA, USA: Edward Elgar Publishing), pp. 122–44.

Fullbrook, Edward (ed.) (2003) *The Crisis in Economics: The Post-Autistic Movement: The First 600 Days* (London, UK and New York, NY, USA: Routledge).

Fullbrook, Edward (ed.) (2009) *Ontology and Economics: Tony Lawson and his Critics* (London, UK and New York, NY, USA: Routledge).

Fuller, Steve (1988) *Social Epistemology* (Bloomington, IN: Indiana University Press).

Fuller, Steve and Collier, James H. (2004) *Philosophy, Rhetoric and the End of Knowledge: A New Beginning for Science and Technology Studies*, 2nd edn (Mahwah, NJ, USA and London, UK: Lawrence Erlbaum).

Furubotn, Eirik G. (1997) 'The Old and the New Institutionalism in Economics', in Koslowski, Peter (ed.) *Methodology of the Social Sciences, Ethics, and Economics in the Newer Historical School: From Max Weber and Rickert to Sombart and Rothacker* (Berlin: Springer), pp. 429–63.

Galbraith, John Kenneth (1958) *The Affluent Society* (London: Hamilton).

Gallegati, Mauro and Kirman, Alain (2012) 'Reconstructing Economics: Agent Based Models and Complexity', *Complexity Economics*, **1**(1), pp. 5–31.

Garegnani, Piero (1970) 'Heterogeneous Capital, the Production Function and the Theory of Distribution', *Review of Economic Studies*, **37**, pp. 407–36.

Geroski, Paul A. (2001) 'Exploring the Niche Overlaps Between Organizational Ecology and Industrial Economics', *Industrial and Corporate Change*, **10**(2), pp. 507–40.

Gintis, Herbert (2005) 'Behavioral Game Theory and Contemporary Economic Theory', *Analyse & Kritik*, **27**, pp. 48–72.

Gintis, Herbert (2009) *The Bounds of Reason: Game Theory and the Unification of the Behavioral Sciences* (Princeton, NJ: Princeton University Press).

Gintis, Herbert and Helbing, Dirk (2015) 'Homo Socialis: An Analytical Core for Sociological Theory', *Review of Behavioral Economics*, **2**(1–2), pp. 1–59.

Glimcher, Paul W. (2003) *Decisions, Uncertainty and the Brain: The Science of Neuroeconomics* (Cambridge, MA: MIT Press).

Glimcher, Paul W., Dorris, Michael C. and Bayer, Hannah M. (2005) 'Physiologic Utility Theory and the Neuroeconomics of Choice', *Games and Economic Behavior*, **52**, pp. 213–56.

Gmür, Markus (2003) 'Co-citation Analysis and the Search for Invisible Colleges: A Methodological Evaluation', *Scientometrics*, **57**(1), pp. 27–57.

Golden, Soma (1976) 'Economist Joan Robinson, 72, is Full of Fight', *New York Times*, 23 March.

Granovetter, Mark (1985) 'Economic Action and Social Structure: The Problem of Embeddedness', *American Journal of Sociology*, **91**(3), November, pp. 481–510.

Green, Francis (1979) 'The Consumption Function: A Study in the Failure of Positive Economics', in Green, Francis and Nore, Petter, *Issues in Political Economy: A Critical Approach* (London: Macmillan), pp. 33–60.

Greene, J.D. and Haidt, Jonathan (2002) 'How (and Where) Does Moral Judgement Work?', *Trends in Cognitive Sciences*, **6**(12), pp. 517–23.

Griffith, Belver C., Small, Henry G., Stonehill, Judith A. and Dey, Sandra (1974) 'The Structure of Scientific Literatures II: Toward a Macro- and Microstructure for Science', *Science Studies*, **4**(4), October, pp. 339–65.

Groenewegen, Peter D. (1985) 'Professor Arndt on Political Economy: A Comment', *Economic Record*, **60**(4), December, pp. 744–51.

Groenewegen, Peter D. (1987) '"Political Economy" and "Economics"', in Eatwell, John, Milgate, Murray and Newman, Peter (eds) *The New Palgrave Dictionary of Economics*, vol. 3, pp. 904–907.

Haas, Peter M. (1992) 'Introduction: Epistemic Communities and International Policy Coordination', *International Organization*, **46**(1), pp. 1–35.

Hahn, Frank H. (1975) 'Revival of Political Economy: The Wrong Issues and the Wrong Arguments', *Economic Record*, **51**, September, pp. 360–64.

Hahn, Frank H. (1982) 'The Neo-Ricardians', *Cambridge Journal of Economics*, **6**(4), December, pp. 353–74.

Hahn, Frank H. (1984) *Equilibrium and Macroeconomics* (Oxford: Basil Blackwell).

Hahn, Frank H. (1991) 'The Next Hundred Years', *Economic Journal*, **101**(1), January, pp. 47–50.

Hahnel, Robin (2005) *Economic Justice and Democracy: From Competition to Cooperation* (London, UK and New York, NY, USA: Routledge).

Hahnel, Robin (2007) 'The Case against Markets', *Journal of Economic Issues*, **41**(3), December, pp. 1139–59.

Hair, Joseph F., Anderson, Ronald E., Tatham, Rolph L. and Black, William C. (1998) *Multivariate Data Analysis* (Englewood Cliffs, NJ: Prentice Hall).

Hamermesh, Daniel S. (2013) 'Six Decades of Top Economics Publishing: Who and How?', *Journal of Economic Literature*, **51**(1), March, pp. 162–72.

Hammerstein, Peter (ed.) (2003) *Genetic and Cultural Evolution of Cooperation* (Cambridge, MA: MIT Press).

Hands, D. Wade (2001) *Reflection without Rules: Economic Methodology and Contemporary Science Theory* (Cambridge, UK and New York, NY, USA: Cambridge University Press).

Hannan, Michael T. and Freeman, John (1989) *Organizational Ecology* (Cambridge, MA: Harvard University Press).

Harcourt, Geoffrey C. (1969) 'Some Cambridge Controversies in the Theory of Capital', *Journal of Economic Literature*, **7**(2), June, pp. 369–405.

Harcourt, Geoffrey C. (1972) *Some Cambridge Controversies in the Theory of Capital* (Cambridge: Cambridge University Press).

Harcourt, Geoffrey C. (2017) 'Robert Charles Oliver (Robin) Matthews (1927–2010)', in Cord, Robert A. (ed.) *The Palgrave Companion to Cambridge Economics* (London, UK and New York, NY, USA: Palgrave Macmillan), pp. 955–77.

Harcourt, Geoffrey C. and Kerr, Prue (2009) *Joan Robinson* (London: Palgrave Macmillan).

Harding, Sandra G. (ed.) (1976) *Can Theories be Refuted? Essays on the Duhem–Quine Thesis* (Dordrecht: Reidel).

Hare, Richard M. (1952) *The Language of Morals* (Oxford: Oxford University Press).

Harvey, David (2005) *A Brief History of Neoliberalism* (Oxford, UK and New York, NY, USA: Oxford University Press).

Hayek, Friedrich A. (ed.) (1935) *Collectivist Economic Planning* (London: George Routledge). Reprinted 1975 by Augustus Kelley.

Hayek, Friedrich A. (1944) *The Road to Serfdom* (London: George Routledge).

Hayek, Friedrich A. (1945) 'The Use of Knowledge in Society', *American Economic Review*, **35**(4), September, pp. 519–30.

Hayek, Friedrich A. (1948) *Individualism and Economic Order* (London, UK: George Routledge and Chicago, IL, USA: University of Chicago Press).

Hayek, Friedrich A. (1988) *The Fatal Conceit: The Errors of Socialism. The Collected Works of Friedrich August Hayek, Vol. I*, ed. William W. Bartley III (London: Routledge).

Heckman, James J. and Moktan, Sidharth (2018) 'Publishing and Promotion in Economics: The Tyranny of the Top Five', INET Working Paper No. 82. Available at https://www.ineteconomics.org/uploads/papers/Heckman_Moktan_2018_tyranny-top-five_v3-final-Sept-30.pdf. (Retrieved 27 January 2019.)

Heinsohn, Gunnar and Steiger, Otto (2013) *Ownership Economics: On the Foundations of Interest, Money, Markets, Business Cycles and Economic Development*, trans. and ed. by Frank Decker (London, UK and New York, NY, USA: Routledge).

Heise, Arne and Thieme, Sebastian (2016) 'The Short Rise and Long Fall of Heterodox Economics in Germany after the 1970s: Explorations in a Scientific Field of Power and Struggle', *Journal of Economic Issues*, **50**(4), December, pp. 1105–30.

Henrich, Joseph, Boyd, Robert, Bowles, Samuel, Camerer, Colin, Fehr, Ernst and Gintis, Herbert (2004) *Foundations of Human Sociality: Economic Experiments and Ethnographic Evidence from Fifteen Small-Scale Societies* (Oxford, UK and New York, NY, USA: Oxford University Press).

Henrich, Joseph, Boyd, Robert, Bowles, Samuel, Camerer, Colin, Fehr, Ernst, Gintis, Herbert and McElreath, Richard (2001) 'In Search of Homo Economicus: Behavioral Experiments in 15 Small-Scale Societies', *American Economic Review (Papers and Proceedings)*, **91**(2), May, pp. 73–84.

Heterodox Academy (2019) 'Heterodox Academy'. Available at https://heterodoxacademy.org/. (Retrieved 29 January 2019.)

Higher Education Student Statistics UK (2018) '*HESA*, Higher Education Student Statistics: UK, 2016/17 – Qualifications Achieved'. Available at https://www.hesa.ac.uk/news/11-01-2018/sfr247-higher-education-student-statistics/qualifications. (Retrieved 14 July 2018.)

Hirsch, Fred (1977) *Social Limits to Growth* (London: Routledge).

Hirschman, Albert O. (1982) 'Rival Interpretations of Market Society: Civilizing, Destructive, or Feeble?', *Journal of Economic Literature*, **20**(4), December, pp. 1463–84.

Hobson, John A. (1900) *The Economics of Distribution* (London, UK and New York, NY, USA: Macmillan).

Hodgson, Geoffrey M. (1981) 'Money and the Sraffa System', *Australian Economic Papers*, **20**, June, pp. 83–95.

Hodgson, Geoffrey M. (1982) *Capitalism, Value and Exploitation: A Radical Theory* (Oxford: Martin Robertson).

Hodgson, Geoffrey M. (1988) *Economics and Institutions: A Manifesto for a Modern Institutional Economics* (Cambridge, UK: Polity Press and Philadelphia, PA, USA: University of Pennsylvania Press).

Hodgson, Geoffrey M. (1989) 'Marxism Without Tears: a Review of John E. Roemer's "Free to Lose"', *Review of Social Economy*, **47**(4), December, pp. 433–6.

Hodgson, Geoffrey M. (1993) *Economics and Evolution: Bringing Life Back Into Economics* (Cambridge, UK: Polity Press and Ann Arbor, MI: University of Michigan Press).

Hodgson, Geoffrey M. (1997) 'The Fate of the Cambridge Capital Controversy', in Arestis, Philip and Sawyer, Malcolm C. (eds) *Capital Controversy, Post Keynesian Economics and the History of Economic Theory: Essays in Honour of Geoff Harcourt* (London, UK and New York, NY, USA: Routledge), pp. 95–110. Reprinted in Hodgson (1999b).

Hodgson, Geoffrey M. (ed.) (1998a) *The Foundations of Evolutionary Economics: 1890–1973*, 2 vols (Cheltenham, UK and Northampton, MA, USA: Edward Elgar Publishing).

Hodgson, Geoffrey M. (1998b) 'Socialism against Markets? A Critique of Two Recent Proposals', *Economy and Society*, **27**(4), November, pp. 450–76.

Hodgson, Geoffrey M. (1999a) *Economics and Utopia: Why the Learning Economy is not the End of History* (London, UK and New York, NY, USA: Routledge).

Hodgson, Geoffrey M. (1999b) *Evolution and Institutions: On Evolutionary Economics and the Evolution of Economics* (Cheltenham, UK and Northampton, MA, USA: Edward Elgar Publishing).

Hodgson, Geoffrey M. (2004a) *The Evolution of Institutional Economics: Agency, Structure and Darwinism in American Institutionalism* (London, UK and New York, NY, USA: Routledge).

Hodgson, Geoffrey M. (2004b) 'Social Darwinism in Anglophone Academic Journals: A Contribution to the History of the Term', *Journal of Historical Sociology*, **17**(4), December, pp. 428–63.

Hodgson, Geoffrey M. (2005) 'The Limits to Participatory Planning: A Reply to Adaman and Devine', *Economy and Society*, **31**(1), February, pp. 141–53.

Hodgson, Geoffrey M. (2006a) 'What are Institutions?', *Journal of Economic Issues*, **40**(1), March, pp. 1–25.

Hodgson, Geoffrey M. (2006b) *Economics in the Shadows of Darwin and Marx: Essays on Institutional and Evolutionary Themes* (Cheltenham, UK and Northampton, MA, USA: Edward Elgar Publishing).

Hodgson, Geoffrey M. (2007) 'Meanings of Methodological Individualism', *Journal of Economic Methodology*, **14**(2), June, pp. 211–26.

Hodgson, Geoffrey M. (2008) 'Prospects for Economic Sociology' (review article), *Philosophy of the Social Sciences*, **38**(1), March, pp. 133–49.

Hodgson, Geoffrey M. (2009) 'The Great Crash of 2008 and the Reform of Economics', *Cambridge Journal of Economics*, **33**(6), November, pp. 1205–21.

Hodgson, Geoffrey M. (2010) 'Choice, Habit and Evolution', *Journal of Evolutionary Economics*, **20**(1), January, pp. 1–18.

Hodgson, Geoffrey M. (2012) 'Introduction', in Hodgson, Geoffrey M. (ed.), *Mathematics and Modern Economics* (Cheltenham, UK and Northampton, MA, USA: Edward Elgar Publishing), pp. xiii–xxxii.

Hodgson, Geoffrey M. (2013a) *From Pleasure Machines to Moral Communities: An Evolutionary Economics without Homo Economicus* (Chicago, IL: University of Chicago Press).

Hodgson, Geoffrey M. (2013b) 'Dr Blaug's Diagnosis: Is Economics Sick?' in Boumans, Marcel and Klaes, Matthias (eds) *Mark Blaug: Rebel with Many Causes* (Cheltenham, UK and Northampton, MA, USA: Edward Elgar Publishing), pp. 78–97.

Hodgson, Geoffrey M. (2013c) 'Understanding Organizational Evolution: Toward a Research Agenda using Generalized Darwinism', *Organization Studies*, **34**(7), July, pp. 973–92.

Hodgson, Geoffrey M. (2013d) 'Come back Marshall, all is Forgiven? Complexity, Evolution, Mathematics and Marshallian Exceptionalism', *European Journal of the History of Economic Thought*, **20**(6), December, pp. 957–81.

Hodgson, Geoffrey M. (2014a) 'The Evolution of Morality and the End of Economic Man', *Journal of Evolutionary Economics*, **24**(1), January, pp. 83–106.

Hodgson, Geoffrey M. (2014b) 'What is Capital? Economists and Sociologists have Changed its Meaning – Should it be Changed Back?', *Cambridge Journal of Economics*, **38**(5), September, pp. 1063–86.

Hodgson, Geoffrey M. (2015a) 'A Trojan Horse for Sociology? Preferences versus Evolution and Morality', *Review of Behavioral Economics*, **2**(1–2), pp. 93–112.

Hodgson, Geoffrey M. (2015b) *Conceptualizing Capitalism: Institutions, Evolution, Future* (Chicago, IL: University of Chicago Press).

Hodgson, Geoffrey M. (2015c) 'Much of the "Economics of Property Rights" Devalues Property and Legal Rights', *Journal of Institutional Economics*, **11**(4), December, pp. 683–709.

Hodgson, Geoffrey M. (2018) *Wrong Turnings: How the Left Got Lost* (Chicago, IL: University of Chicago Press).

Hodgson, Geoffrey M. (2019a) 'Taxonomic Definitions in Social Science, with Firms, Markets and Institutions as Case Studies', *Journal of Institutional Economics*, **15**(2), April, pp. 207–33.

Hodgson, Geoffrey M. (2019b) *Evolutionary Economics: Its Nature and Future*, in series edited by John Foster and Jason Potts: Cambridge Elements in Evolutionary Economics (Cambridge and New York: Cambridge University Press), forthcoming.

Hodgson, Geoffrey M. (2019c) *Is Socialism Feasible? Towards an Alternative Future* (Cheltenham, UK and Northampton, MA, USA: Edward Elgar Publishing).

Hodgson, Geoffrey M. (2019d) 'How Mythical Markets Mislead Analysis: An Institutionalist Critique of Market Universalism', *Socio-Economic Review*, forthcoming.

Hodgson, Geoffrey M. and Huang, Kainan (2012) 'Evolutionary Game Theory and Evolutionary Economics: Are they Different Species?', *Journal of Evolutionary Economics*, **22**, pp. 345–66.

Hodgson, Geoffrey M. and Knudsen, Thorbjørn (2010) *Darwin's Conjecture: The Search for General Principles of Social and Economic Evolution* (Chicago, IL: University of Chicago Press).

Hodgson, Geoffrey M. and Lamberg, Juha-Antti (2018) 'The Past and Future of Evolutionary Economics: Some Reflections Based on New Bibliometric Evidence', *Evolutionary and Institutional Economics Review*, **15**(1), pp. 167–87.

Hodgson, Geoffrey M. and Rothman, Harry (1999) 'The Editors and Authors of Economics Journals: A Case of Institutional Oligopoly?', *Economic Journal*, **109**(2), February, pp. F165–F186.

Hodgson, Geoffrey M. and Stoelhorst, J.W. (2014) 'Introduction to the Special Issue on the Future of Institutional and Evolutionary Economics', *Journal of Institutional Economics*, **10**(4), December, pp. 513–40.

Hodgson, Geoffrey M., Gagliardi, Francesca and Gindis, David (2018) 'From Cambridge Keynesian to Institutional Economist: The Unnoticed Contributions of Robert Neild', *Journal of Institutional Economics*, **14**(4), August, pp. 767–86.

Hoffman, D.L. and Holbrook, M.B. (1993) 'The Intellectual Structure of Consumer Research: A Bibliometric Study of Author Cocitations in the First 15 Years of the Journal of Consumer Research', *Journal of Consumer Research*, **19**(4), pp. 505–17.

Hollander, Samuel (2000) 'Sraffa and the Interpretation of Ricardo: The Marxian Dimension', *History of Political Economy*, **32**(2), Summer, pp. 187–232.

Hollis, Martin and Nell, Edward (1975) *Rational Economic Man: A Philosophical Critique of Neo-Classical Economics* (Cambridge and New York: Cambridge University Press).

Hull, David L. (1988) *Science as a Process: An Evolutionary Account of the Social and Conceptual Development of Science* (Chicago, IL: University of Chicago Press).

Hutchins, Edwin (1995) *Cognition in the Wild* (Cambridge, MA: MIT Press).

Infante, Gerardo, Lecouteau, Guilhem and Sugden, Robert (2016) 'Preference Purification and the Inner Rational Agent: A Critique of the Conventional Wisdom of Behavioural Economics', *Journal of Economic Methodology*, **23**(1), March, pp. 1–25.

Jacobs, Struan (2000) 'Spontaneous Order: Michael Polanyi and Friedrich Hayek', *Critical Review of International Social and Political Philosophy*, **3**(4), pp. 49–67.

Jacobs, Struan and Mullins, Phil (2016) 'Friedrich Hayek and Michael Polanyi in Correspondence', *History of European Ideas*, **42**(1), pp. 107–30.

Jaffé, William (1976) 'Menger, Jevons and Walras De-Homogenized', *Economic Inquiry*, **14**(1), January, pp. 511–24.

James, William (1890) *The Principles of Psychology*, 2 vols, 1st edn (New York, NY, USA: Holt and London, UK: Macmillan).

Jessop, Robert (1997a) 'Twenty Years of the (Parisian) Regulation Approach: The Paradox of Success and Failure at Home and Abroad', *New Political Economy*, **2**(3), pp. 503–526.

Jessop, Robert (1997b) 'Survey Article: The Regulation Approach', *Journal of Political Philosophy*, **5**(3), September, pp. 287–326.

Jessop, Robert (ed.) (2001) *Regulation Theory and the Crisis of Capitalism*, 4 vols (Cheltenham, UK and Northampton, MA, USA: Edward Elgar Publishing).

Jevons, William Stanley (1871) *The Theory of Political Economy* (London: Macmillan).

Jo, Tae-Hee, Chester, Lynne and D'Ippoliti, Carlo (eds) (2017) *The Routledge Handbook of Heterodox Economics: Theorizing, Analyzing, and Transforming Capitalism* (London, UK and New York, NY, USA: Routledge).

Jochimsen, Maren A. (2003) *Careful Economics: Integrating Caring Activities and Economic Science* (Boston, MA: Kluwer).

Johnson, Elizabeth S. and Johnson, Harry G. (1978) *The Shadow of Keynes: Understanding Keynes, Cambridge and Keynesian Economics* (Oxford: Basil Blackwell).

Jones, Evan and Stilwell, Frank (1986) 'Political Economy at the University of Sydney', in Martin, Brian, Baker, C.M. Ann, Manwell, Clyde and Pugh, Cedric (eds) *Intellectual Suppression: Australian Case Histories, Analysis and Responses* (Sydney: Angus & Robertson), pp. 24–38.

Joyce, Richard (2006) *The Evolution of Morality* (Cambridge, MA: MIT Press).

Kadish, Alon and Tribe, Keith (eds) (1993) *The Market for Political Economy: The Advent of Economics in British University Culture, 1850–1905* (London: Routledge).

Kagel, John H., Battalio, Raymond C. and Green, Leonard (1995) *Economic Choice Theory: An Experimental Analysis of Animal Behaviour* (Cambridge, UK and New York, NY, USA: Cambridge University Press).

Kahneman, Daniel (2003) 'Maps of Bounded Rationality: Psychology for Behavioral Economics', *American Economic Review*, **93**(5), December, pp. 1449–75.

Kaldor, Nicholas (1966) *Causes of the Slow Rate of Economic Growth in the United Kingdom: An Inaugural Lecture* (Cambridge: Cambridge University Press). Reprinted in Kaldor (1978).

Kaldor, Nicholas (1972) 'The Irrelevance of Equilibrium Economics', *Economic Journal*, **82**(4), December, pp. 1237–55. Reprinted in Kaldor (1978) and Targetti and Thirlwall (1989).

Kaldor, Nicholas (1975a) 'What is Wrong with Economic Theory?', *Quarterly Journal of Economics*, **89**(3), August, pp. 347–57. Reprinted in Kaldor (1978).

Kaldor, Nicholas (1975b) 'Economic Growth and the Verdoorn Law: A Comment on Mr Rowthorn's Article', *Economic Journal*, **85**(4), December, pp. 891–6.

Kaldor, Nicholas (1978) *Further Essays on Economic Theory: (Collected Economic Essays Vol. 5)* (London: Duckworth).

Kaldor, Nicholas (1985) *Economics without Equilibrium* (Cardiff: University College Cardiff Press).

Kapeller, Jakob and Springholz, Florian (eds) (2016) *Heterodox Economics Directory*, 6th edn. Available at http://heterodoxnews.com/directory/. (Retrieved 22 July 2018.)

Kapp, K. William (1950) *The Social Costs of Private Enterprise*, 1st edn (Cambridge, MA: Harvard University Press).

Kapp, K. William (1976) 'The Nature and Significance of Institutional Economics', *Kyklos*, **29**, Fasc. 2, pp. 209–32.

Kapp, K. William (2016) *The Heterodox Theory of Social Costs*, ed. by Sebastian Berger (London, UK and New York, NY, USA: Routledge).

Kauffman, Stuart A. (1995) *At Home in the Universe: The Search for Laws of Self-Organization and Complexity* (Oxford, UK and New York, NY, USA: Oxford University Press).

Kemp, Tom S. (2005) *The Origin and Evolution of Mammals* (Oxford, UK and New York, NY, USA: Oxford University Press).

Keynes, John Maynard (1922) 'Introduction to the Series', in Robertson, Dennis H. *Money*, Cambridge Economic Handbooks II (London: Nisbet and Cambridge: Cambridge University Press), pp. v–vi.

Keynes, John Maynard (1931) *Essays in Persuasion* (London: Macmillan).

Keynes, John Maynard (1936) *The General Theory of Employment, Interest and Money* (London: Macmillan).

King, John E. (2002) *A History of Post Keynesian Economics since 1936* (Cheltenham, UK and Northampton, MA, USA: Edward Elgar Publishing).

King, John E. (2009) *Nicholas Kaldor* (London: Palgrave Macmillan).

King, John E. and Millmow, Alex (2003) 'Death of a Revolutionary Textbook', *History of Political Economy*, **35**(1), Spring, pp. 104–34.

Kirman, Alan P. (1989) 'The Intrinsic Limits of Modern Economic Theory: The Emperor has No Clothes', *Economic Journal (Conference Papers)*, **99**, pp. 126–39.

Kirman, Alan P. (2009) 'Economic Theory and the Crisis', *Vox*, 14 November. Available at www.voxeu.org/index.php?q=node/4208. (Retrieved 2 June 2018.)

Kitcher, Philip (1993) *The Advancement of Science: Science without Legend, Objectivity without Illusions* (Oxford, UK and New York, NY, USA: Oxford University Press).

Kitcher, Philip (2011) *The Ethical Project* (Cambridge, MA: Harvard University Press).

Knorr-Cetina, Karin D. (1981) *The Manufacture of Knowledge: An Essay on the Constructivist and Contextual Nature of Science* (Oxford: Pergamon).

Koestler, Arthur (1959) *The Sleepwalkers: A History of Man's Changing Vision of the Universe* (London: Hutchinson).

Koestler, Arthur (1964) *The Act of Creation* (London: Hutchinson).

Kornai, János (1971) *Anti-Equilibrium: On Economic Systems Theory and the Tasks of Research* (Amsterdam: North-Holland).

Kornai, János (2006) *By Force of Thought: Irregular Memoirs of an Intellectual Journey* (Cambridge, MA: MIT Press).

Kregel, Jan A. (1973) *The Reconstruction of Political Economy: An Introduction to Post-Keynesian Economics* (London: Macmillan).

Krugman, Paul R. (2012) *End this Depression Now!* (New York, NY, USA and London, UK: Norton).

Kuhn, Thomas S. (1957) *The Copernican Revolution* (Cambridge, MA: Harvard University Press).

Kuhn, Thomas S. (1970) *The Structure of Scientific Revolutions*, 2nd edn (Chicago, IL: University of Chicago Press).

Lakatos, Imré (1970) 'Falsification and the Methodology of Scientific Research Programmes', in Lakatos, Imre and Musgrave, Alan (eds) *Criticism and the Growth of Knowledge* (Cambridge: Cambridge University Press), pp. 91–195.

Lam, Alice (2011) 'What Motivates Scientists to Engage in Research Commercialization: "Gold", "Ribbon" or "Puzzle"', *Research Policy*, **40**(1), December, pp. 1354–68.

Lange, Oskar R. (1936–37) 'On the Economic Theory of Socialism: Parts One and Two', *Review of Economic Studies*, **4**(1), pp. 53–71, and **4**(2), pp. 123–42. Reprinted in Lange, Oskar R. and Taylor, Frederick M. (1938).

Lange, Oskar R. and Taylor, Frederick M. (1938) *On the Economic Theory of Socialism* (Minneapolis, MN: University of Minnesota Press).

Laudan, Larry (1977) *Progress and its Problems: Towards a Theory of Scientific Growth* (London: Routledge and Kegan Paul).

Lave, Jean and Wenger, Etienne (1991) *Situated Learning: Legitimate Peripheral Participation* (Cambridge: Cambridge University Press).

Lavoie, Donald (1985) *Rivalry and Central Planning: The Socialist Calculation Debate Reconsidered* (Cambridge: Cambridge University Press).

Lavoie, Marc (2012) 'Perspectives for Post-Keynesian Economics', *Review of Political Economy*, **24**(2), April, pp. 321–35.

Lawson, Tony (1997) *Economics and Reality* (London, UK and New York, NY, USA: Routledge).

Lawson, Tony (2003) *Reorienting Economics* (London, UK and New York, NY, USA: Routledge).

Lawson, Tony (2004) 'On Heterodox Economics, Themata and the Use of Mathematics in Economics', *Journal of Economic Methodology*, **11**(3), September, pp. 329–40.

Lawson, Tony (2006) 'The Nature of Heterodox Economics', *Cambridge Journal of Economics*, **30**(4), July, pp. 483–505.

Lawson, Tony (2009) 'On the Nature and Roles of Formalism in Economics', in Fullbrook, Edward (ed.) *Ontology and Economics: Tony Lawson and His Critics* (London, UK and New York, NY, USA: Routledge), pp. 189–231.

Lawson, Tony (2013) 'What is this "School" called Neoclassical Economics?', *Cambridge Journal of Economics*, **37**(5), September, pp. 947–98.

Lee, Frederic S. (1998) *Post Keynesian Price Theory* (Cambridge: Cambridge University Press).

Lee, Frederic S. (2002) 'Post Keynesian Economics (1930–2000): An Emerging Heterodox Economic Theory of Capitalism', in Douglas Dowd (ed.) *Understanding Capitalism: A Critical Analysis from Karl Marx to Amartya Sen* (London: Pluto), pp. 108–31.

Lee, Frederic S. (2008) 'Heterodox Economics', in Durlauf, Steven N. and Blume, Lawrence E. (eds) *The New Palgrave Dictionary of Economics*, 2nd edn (London, UK and New York, NY, USA: Palgrave Macmillan). Available at https://hetecon.net/?page=about&side=heterodox_economics. (Retrieved 23 July 2018.)

Lee, Frederic S. (2009) *A History of Heterodox Economics: Challenging the Mainstream in the Twentieth Century* (London, UK and New York, NY, USA: Routledge).

Lee, Frederic S. (2012) 'Heterodox Economics and its Critics', *Review of Political Economy*, **24**(2), April, pp. 337–51.

Lee, Frederic S. (2016) 'Critical Realism, Method of Grounded Theory, and Theory Construction', in Lee, Frederic S. and Cronin, Bruce C. (eds) (2016) *Handbook of Research Methods and Applications in Heterodox Economics* (Cheltenham, UK and Northampton, MA, USA: MA: Edward Elgar Publishing), pp. 35–53.

Lee, Frederic S. and Elsner, Wolfram (eds) (2010) *Evaluating Economic Research in a Contested Discipline: Ranking, Pluralism, and the Future of Heterodox Economics* (Chichester, UK and Hoboken, NJ, USA: Wiley-Blackwell).

Lee, Frederic S. and Harley, Sandra (1997) 'Research Selectivity, Managerialism and the Academic Labor Process: The Future of Non-mainstream Economics in U.K. Universities', *Human Relations*, **50**(11), November, pp. 1427–60.

Lee, Frederic S. and Harley, Sandra (1998) 'Peer Review, the Research Assessment Exercise and the Demise of Non-Mainstream Economics', *Capital and Class*, no. 66, Autumn, pp. 23–52.

Lee, Frederic S. and Keen, Steve (2004) 'The Incoherent Emperor: A Heterodox Critique of Neoclassical Microeconomic Theory', *Review of Social Economy*, **62**(2), June, pp. 169–99.

Lee, Frederic S. and Lavoie, Marc (eds) (2013) *In Defense of Post-Keynesian and Heterodox Economics* (London, UK and New York, NY, USA: Routledge).

Lee, Frederic S. and Samuels, Warren J. (eds) (1992) *The Heterodox Economics of Gardiner C. Means: A Collection* (Armonk, NY: M.E. Sharpe).

Leibenstein, Harvey (1976) *Beyond Economic Man: A New Foundation for Microeconomics* (Cambridge, MA: Harvard University Press).

Lenzer, Gertrud (ed.) (1998) *Auguste Comte and Positivism* (New Brunswick, NJ: Transaction).

Lerner, Abba P. (1934) 'Economic Theory and Socialist Economy', *Review of Economic Studies*, **2**(1), pp. 157–75.

Lerner, Abba P. (1937) 'Statics and Dynamics in Socialist Economics', *Economic Journal*, **47**(186), pp. 263–7.

Lerner, Abba P. (1938) 'Theory and Practice in Socialist Economics', *Review of Economic Studies*, **6**(1), pp. 71–5.

Lerner, Abba P. (1944) *The Economics of Control: Principles of Welfare Economics* (New York: Macmillan).

Lewin, Arie Y. and Volberda, Henk W. (1999) 'Prolegmean on Co-evolution: A Framework for Research on Strategy and New Organizational Forms', *Organization Science*, **10**(5), September–October, pp. 519–34.

Lindblom, Charles E. and Cohen, David K. (1979) *Usable Knowledge: Social Science and Social Problem Solving* (New Haven, CT: Yale University Press).

Locke, Robert (1988) 'Educational Tradition and the Development of Business Studies after 1945 (An Anglo–French–German Comparison)', in Davenport-Hines, R.P.T. and Jones, Geoffrey (eds) *The End of Insularity: Essays in Comparative Business History* (London: Frank Cass), pp. 84–103.

Longino, Helen E. (1990) *Science as Social Knowledge: Values and Objectivity in Scientific Inquiry* (Princeton, NJ: Princeton University Press).

Lorenz, Edward H. (2001) 'Models of Cognition, the Development of Knowledge and Organisational Theory', *Journal of Management and Governance*, **5**, pp. 307–30.

Lucio-Arias, Diana and Leydesdorff, Loet (2008) 'Main-Path Analysis and Path-Dependent Transitions in *HistCite*™-Based Historiograms', *Journal of the American Society for Information Science and Technology*, **59**(12), pp. 1948–62.

Luhmann, Niklas (2005) 'Unverständliche Wissenschaft: Probleme einer Theorieeigenen Sprache', in Luhmann, Niklas, *Soziologische Aufklärung 3: Soziales System, Gesellschaft, Organisation* (Wiesbaden: VS Verlag), pp. 193–205.

Lukes, Steven (1973) *Individualism* (Oxford: Basil Blackwell).

Lukes, Steven (1985) *Marxism and Morality* (Oxford: Oxford University Press).

Mackie, John Leslie (1977) *Ethics: Inventing Right and Wrong* (Harmondsworth: Penguin).

Macroberts, Michael H. and Macroberts, Barbara R. (1989) 'Problems of Citation Analysis: A Critical Review', *Journal of the American Society for Information Science*, **40**(5), pp. 342–9.

Mäki, Uskali (1992) 'On the Method of Isolation in Economics', *Poznan Studies in the Philosophy of the Sciences and the Humanities*, **26**, pp. 319–54.

Mäki, Uskali (1994) 'Isolation, Idealization and Truth in Economics', *Poznan Studies in the Philosophy of the Sciences and the Humanities*, **38**, pp. 147–68.

Mäki, Uskali (1999) 'Science as a Free Market: A Reflexivity Test in an Economics of Economics', *Perspectives on Science*, **7**(4), pp. 486–509.

Mäki, Uskali (2005) 'Economic Epistemology: Hopes and Horrors', *Episteme*, **1**(3), February, pp. 211–12.

Maloney, John (1985) *Marshall, Orthodoxy and the Professionalisation of Economics* (Cambridge: Cambridge University Press).

Mantel, Rolf R. (1974) 'On the Characterization of Aggregate Excess Demand', *Journal of Economic Theory*, **12**(2), pp. 348–53.

March, James G. (1991) 'Exploration and Exploitation in Organizational Learning', *Organization Science*, **2**(1), pp. 71–87.

March, James G. and Simon, Herbert A. (1958) *Organizations* (New York: Wiley).

Marcuzzo, Maria Cristina, Pasinetti, Luigi L. and Roncaglia, Alessandro (eds) (1996) *The Economics of Joan Robinson* (London, UK and New York, NY, USA: Routledge).

Marshall, Alfred (1885) 'The Present Position of Economics', in Arthur C. Pigou (ed.) (1925) *Memorials of Alfred Marshall* (London: Macmillan), pp. 152–74. Reprinted with an introduction by Geoffrey M. Hodgson in the *Journal of Institutional Economics*, **1**(1), June 2005, pp. 121–37.

Marshall, Alfred (1920) *Principles of Economics: An Introductory Volume*, 8th edn (London: Macmillan).

Martin, Ben R. (2012) 'The Evolution of Science Policy and Innovation Studies', *Research Policy*, **41**(7), September, pp. 1219–39.

Martins, Nuno Ornelas (2014) *The Cambridge Revival in Political Economy* (London, UK and New York, NY, USA: Routledge).

Martinsons, Marris G., Everett, James E. and Chan, Kathy (2001) 'Mapping the Scholarly Development of Strategic Management', *Journal of Information Science*, **27**(2), pp. 101–10.

Marx, Karl (1976) *Capital*, vol. 1, trans. from the 4th German edn of 1890 (Harmondsworth: Pelican).

Marx, Karl (1978) *Capital*, vol. 2, trans. from the German edn of 1893 (Harmondsworth: Pelican).

Maynard Smith, John (1982) *Evolutionary Game Theory* (Cambridge: Cambridge University Press).

McCloskey, Deirdre N. (2006) *The Bourgeois Virtues: Ethics for an Age of Commerce* (Chicago, IL: Chicago University Press).

McCloskey, Deirdre N. (2008) 'Mr. Max and the Substantial Errors of Manly Economics', *Econ Journal Watch*, **5**(2), May, pp. 199–203.

McCloskey, Deirdre N. (2010) *Bourgeois Dignity: Why Economics Can't Explain the Modern World* (Chicago, IL: University of Chicago Press).

McCloskey, Deirdre N. (2016) 'Max U vs. Humanomics: A Critique of Neo-Institutionalism', *Journal of Institutional Economics*, **12**(1), March, pp. 1–27.

McMaster, Robert and Novarese, Marco (2016) 'Neuroeconomics: Infeasible and Underdetermined', *Journal of Economic Issues*, **50**(4), December, pp. 963–83.

McQuade, Thomas J. (2007) 'Science and Market as Adaptive Classifying Systems', in Krecké, E., Krecké, C. and Koppl, R.G. (eds) *Cognition and Economics: Advances in Austrian Economics Volume 9* (Oxford: Elsevier), pp. 51–86.

McQuade, Thomas J. and Butos, William N. (2003) 'Order-Dependent Knowledge and the Economics of Science', *Review of Austrian Economics*, **16**(2/3), pp. 133–52.

Mearman, Andrew (2006) 'Critical Realism in Economics and Open-Systems Ontology: A Critique', *Review of Social Economy*, **64**(1), March, pp. 47–75.

Mearman, Andrew (2011) 'Who do Heterodox Economists Think they are?', *American Journal of Economics and Sociology*, **70**(2), April, pp. 480–510.

Mearman, Andrew (2012) '"Heterodox Economics" and the Problems of Classification', *Journal of Economic Methodology*, **19**(4), December, pp. 407–24.

Mearman, Andrew, Guizzo, Danielle and Berger, Sebastian (2018) 'Is UK Economics Teaching Changing? Evaluating the New Subject Benchmark Statement', *Review of Social Economy*, **76**(3), September, pp. 377–96.

Mearman, Andrew, Guizzo, Danielle and Berger, Sebastian (eds) (2019) *What is Heterodox Economics? Conversations with Leading Economists* (London, UK and New York, NY, USA: Routledge) forthcoming.

Meek, Ronald L. (1961) 'Mr Sraffa's Rehabilitation of Classical Economics', published simultaneously in *Science and Society*, **25**, Spring, pp. 139–56 and *Scottish Journal of Political Economy*, **8**, June, pp. 119–36. Revised and reprinted in Meek (1967).

Meek, Ronald L. (1967) *Economics and Ideology and Other Essays: Studies in the Development of Economic Thought* (London: Chapman and Hall).

Ménard, Claude and Shirley, Mary M. (2014) 'The Future of the New Institutional Economics: From Early Intuitions to a New Paradigm?', *Journal of Institutional Economics*, **10**(4), December, pp. 541–65.

Menger, Carl (1871) *Grundsätze der Volkwirtschaftslehre*, 1st edn (Tübingen: J.C.B. Mohr). Published in English in 1981 as *Principles of Economics* (New York: New York University Press).

Menger, Carl (1888) 'Zur Theorie des Kapitals', *Jahrbücher für Nationalökonomie und Statistik*, **17**, pp. 1–49.

Merton, Robert K. (1942) 'Science and Technology in a Democratic Order', *Journal of Legal and Political Sociology*, **1**, pp. 115–26.

Milanovic, Branko (2005) *Worlds Apart: Measuring International and Global Inequality* (Princeton, NJ: Princeton University Press).

Mills, C. Wright (1959) *The Sociological Imagination* (Oxford, UK and New York, NY, USA: Oxford University Press).

Milonakis, Dimitris (2012) 'Neoclassical Economics', in Ben Fine and Alfredo Saad Filho (eds) *The Elgar Companion to Marxist Economics* (Cheltenham, UK and Northampton, MA, USA: Edward Elgar Publishing), pp. 246–51.

Milonakis, Dimitris and Fine, Ben (2009) *From Political Economy to Economics: Method, the Social and the Historical in the Evolution of Economic Theory* (London, UK and New York, NY, USA: Routledge).

Minkler, Lanse P. (2008) *Integrity and Agreement: Economics When Principles Also Matter* (Ann Arbor, MI: University of Michigan Press).

Minsky, Hyman P. (1986) *Stabilizing an Unstable Economy* (New Haven, CT: Yale University Press).

Mirowski, Philip (1989) *More Heat than Light: Economics as Social Physics, Physics as Nature's Economics* (Cambridge: Cambridge University Press).

Mirowski, Philip (1995) 'Philip Kitcher's *Advancement of Science:* A Review Article', *Review of Political Economy*, 7(2), pp. 227–41.

Mirowski, Philip and Plehwe, Dieter (eds) (2009) *The Road from Mont Pèlerin: The Making of the Neoliberal Thought Collective* (Cambridge, MA: Harvard University Press).

Mises, Ludwig von (1920) 'Die Wirtschaftsrechnung im Sozialistischen Gemeinwesen', *Archiv für Sozialwissenschaften und Sozialpolitik*, **47**(1), April, pp. 86–121.

Mises, Ludwig von (1935) 'Economic Calculation in the Socialist Commonwealth', in Hayek, Friedrich A. (ed.) *Collectivist Economic*

Planning (London: George Routledge), pp. 87–130. A translation of Mises (1920).

Mises, Ludwig von (1949) *Human Action: A Treatise on Economics* (London, UK: William Hodge and New Haven, CT: Yale University Press).

Mitchell Innes, Alfred (1914) 'The Credit Theory of Money', *The Banking Law Journal*, **31**, December–January, pp. 151–68.

Mohun, Simon and Veneziani, Roberto (2012) 'Reorienting Economics?', *Philosophy of the Social Sciences*, **42**, 126–45.

Moran, Cahal, Earle, Joe and Ward-Perkins, Zach (2017) *The Econocracy: The Perils of Leaving Economics to the Experts* (Manchester: Manchester University Press).

Morgan, Jamie (ed.) (2016) *What is this 'School' called Neoclassical Economics? Debating the Issues* (London, UK and New York, NY, USA: Routledge).

Mouzelis, Nicos (1995) *Sociological Theory: What Went Wrong? Diagnosis and Remedies* (London, UK and New York, NY, USA: Routledge).

Mueller, Dennis C. (1979) *Pubic Choice* (Cambridge, UK and New York, NY, USA: Cambridge University Press).

Murmann, Johann Peter, Aldrich, Howard E., Levinthal, Daniel and Winter, Sidney G. (2003) 'Evolutionary Thought in Management and Organization Theory at the Beginning of the New Millennium: A Symposium on the State of the Art and Opportunities for Future Research', *Journal of Management Inquiry*, **12**(1), March, pp. 22–40.

Murrell, Peter (1983) 'Did the Theory of Market Socialism Answer the Challenge of Ludwig von Mises? A Reinterpretation of the Socialist Controversy?', *History of Political Economy*, **15**(1), Spring, pp. 92–105.

Myrdal, Gunnar (1953) *The Political Element in the Development of Economic Theory*, trans. from the Swedish edn of 1930 by Paul Streeten (London, UK: Routledge and Kegan Paul and Cambridge, MA, USA: Harvard University Press).

National Centre for Education Statistics (2017) *Digest of Education Statistics*. Available at https://nces.ed.gov/fastfacts/display.asp?id=37. (Retrieved 14 July 2018.)

National Committee of Inquiry into Higher Education (1997) *Higher Education in the Learning Society: The Dearing Report* (London: Her Majesty's Stationery Office).

Neild, Robert R. (1995) *The English, the French and the Oyster* (London: Quiller).

Neild, Robert R. (2002) *Public Corruption: The Dark Side of Social Evolution* (London, UK and New York, NY, USA: Anthem).

Neild, Robert R. (2012) *What Next? A Memoir* (privately published).

Nelson, Julie A. (1995) 'Feminism and Economics', *Journal of Economic Perspectives*, **9**(2), Spring, pp. 131–48.

Nelson, Katherine and Nelson, Richard R. (2003) 'The Cumulative Advance of Human Know-How', *Philosophical Transactions of the Royal Society of London: Mathematical, Physical and Engineering Sciences*, **361**(1809), August, pp. 1635–53.

Nelson, Richard R. (1981) 'Assessing Private Enterprise: An Exegesis of Tangled Doctrine', *Bell Journal of Economics*, **12**(1), pp. 93–111.

Nelson, Richard R. (1995) 'Recent Evolutionary Theorizing About Economic Change', *Journal of Economic Literature*, **33**(1), March, pp. 48–90.

Nelson, Richard R. (2003) 'On the Complexities and Limits of Market Organization', *Review of International Political Economy*, **10**(4), November, pp. 697–710.

Nelson, Richard R. (ed.) (2005) *The Limits of Market Organization* (New York: Russell Sage Foundation).

Nelson, Richard R. and Winter, Sidney G. (1982) *An Evolutionary Theory of Economic Change* (Cambridge, MA: Harvard University Press).

Nelson, Richard R. and Winter, Sidney G. (2002) 'Evolutionary Theorizing in Economics', *Journal of Economic Perspectives*, **16**(2), Spring, pp. 23–46.

Nelson, Richard R., Dosi, Giovanni, Helfat, Constance, Pyka, Andreas, Saviotti, Pier Paolo, Lee, Keun, Dopfer, Kurt et al. (2018) *Modern Evolutionary Economics: An Overview* (Cambridge, UK and New York, NY, USA: Cambridge University Press).

Neumann, John von and Morgenstern, Oskar (1944) *The Theory of Games and Economic Behavior* (Princeton, NJ: Princeton University Press).

Noam, Eli M. (1995) 'Electronics and the Dim Future of the University', *Science*, **270**(5234), pp. 247–9.

Nonaka, Ikujiro, von Krogh, Groeg and Voelpel, Sven (2006) 'Organizational Knowledge Creation Theory: Evolutionary Paths and Future Advances', *Organization Studies*, **27**(8), pp. 1179–208.

Nooteboom, Bart (2000) *Learning and Innovation in Organizations and Economies* (Oxford, UK and New York, NY, USA: Oxford University Press).

North, Douglass C. (1977) 'Markets and Other Allocation Systems in History: The Challenge of Karl Polanyi', *Journal of European Economic History*, **6**(3), Winter, pp. 703–16.

Is there a future for heterodox economics?

North, Douglass C. (1990) *Institutions, Institutional Change and Economic Performance* (Cambridge, UK and New York, NY, USA: Cambridge University Press).
North, Douglass C. (1994) 'Economic Performance through Time', *American Economic Review*, **84**(3), June, pp. 359–67.
Nove, Alec (1980) 'The Soviet Economy: Problems and Prospects', *New Left Review*, no. 119, January–February, pp. 3–19. Reprinted in Nove, Alec (1986) *Socialism, Economics and Development* (London: Allen and Unwin).
Nove, Alec (1983) *The Economics of Feasible Socialism* (London: George Allen and Unwin).
Nove, Alec and Nuti, D. Mario (eds) (1972) *Socialist Economics* (Harmondsworth: Penguin).
Nye, Mary Jo (2011) *Michael Polanyi and His Generation: Origins of the Social Construction of Science* (Chicago, IL: University of Chicago Press).
Ollman, Bertell (2004) 'Marx, Markets and Meat Grinders: Interview with Bertell Ollman'. Available at https://www.nyu.edu/projects/ollman/docs/interview02.php. (Retrieved 24 November 2017.)
Orléan, André (ed.) (1994) *Analyse Économique des Conventions* (Paris: Presses Universitaires de France).
Osareh, Farideh (1996) 'Bibliometrics, Citation Analysis and Co-citation Analysis: A Review of Literature II', *Libri*, **46**(4), pp. 217–25.
Pagano, Ugo (2014) 'The Crisis of Intellectual Monopoly Capitalism', *Cambridge Journal of Economics*, **38**(6), November, pp. 1409–29.
Pareto, Vilfredo (1897) 'The New Theories of Economics', *Journal of Political Economy*, **5**(4), September, pp. 485–502.
Parsons, Keith (ed.) (2003) *The Science Wars: Debating Scientific Knowledge and Technology* (Amherst, NY: Prometheus Books).
Parsons, Talcott (1937) *The Structure of Social Action*, 2 vols (New York: McGraw-Hill).
Pasadeos, Yorg, Phelps, Joe and Kim, Bong-Hyun (1998) 'Disciplinary Impact of Advertising Scholars: Temporal Comparisons of Influential Authors, Works and Research Networks', *Journal of Advertising*, **27**(4), pp. 53–4.
Pasinetti, Luigi L. (1974) *Growth and Income Distribution – Essays in Economic Theory* (Cambridge: Cambridge University Press).
Pasinetti, Luigi L. (1981) *Structural Change and Economic Growth: A Theoretical Essay on the Dynamics of the Wealth of Nations* (Cambridge: Cambridge University Press).
Pasinetti, Luigi L. (2007) *Keynes and the Cambridge Keynesians: A 'Revolution in Economics' to be Accomplished* (Cambridge, UK and New York, NY, USA: Cambridge University Press).

Peirce, Charles Sanders ([1882]1958) *Collected Papers of Charles Sanders Peirce, Volume VII, Science and Philosophy*, ed. by A.W. Burks (Cambridge, MA: Harvard University Press).

Penrose, Edith T. (1959) *The Theory of the Growth of the Firm* (Oxford: Basil Blackwell).

Pessali, Huascar F. (2006) 'The Rhetoric of Oliver Williamson's Transaction Cost Economics', *Journal of Institutional Economics*, **2**(1), April, pp. 45–65.

Peterson, Janice and Lewis, Margaret (eds) (1999) *The Elgar Companion to Feminist Economics*. (Cheltenham, UK and Northampton, MA, USA: Edward Elgar Publishing).

Pieters, Rik and Baumgartner, Hans (2002) 'Who Talks to Whom? Intra- and Interdisciplinary Communication of Economics Journals', *Journal of Economic Literature*, **40**(2), June, pp. 483–509.

Pigou, Arthur C. (1920) *The Economics of Welfare* (London: Macmillan).

Pigou, Arthur C. (1937) *Socialism versus Capitalism* (London: Macmillan).

Piketty, Thomas (2014) *Capital in the Twenty-First Century* (Cambridge, MA: Belknap Press).

Piore, Michael J. (2003) 'Society as a Pre-Condition for Individuality: Critical Comments', *Socio-Economic Review*, **1**(1), January, pp. 119–22.

Platt, Michael L. and Glimcher, Paul W. (1999) 'Neural Correlates of Decision Variables in Parietal Cortex', *Nature*, **400**(6741), pp. 233–8.

Plotkin, Henry C. (1994) *Darwin Machines and the Nature of Knowledge: Concerning Adaptations, Instinct and the Evolution of Intelligence* (Harmondsworth: Penguin).

Polanyi, Karl (1944) *The Great Transformation: The Political and Economic Origins of Our Time* (New York: Rinehart).

Polanyi, Michael (1940) *The Contempt of Freedom: The Russian Experiment and After* (London: Watts).

Polanyi, Michael (1941) 'The Growth of Thought in Society', *Economica*, new series, **8**(32), November, pp. 428–56.

Polanyi, Michael (1944) 'Patent Reform', *Review of Economic Studies*, **11**(2), Summer, pp. 61–76.

Polanyi, Michael (1945) *Full Employment and Free Trade* (Cambridge: Cambridge University Press).

Polanyi, Michael (1948) 'Planning and Spontaneous Order', *The Manchester School*, **16**, September, pp. 237–68. Reprinted in Polanyi (1951).

Polanyi, Michael (1951) *The Logic of Liberty: Reflections and Rejoinders* (London: Routledge and Kegan Paul).

Polanyi, Michael (1958) *Personal Knowledge: Towards a Post-Critical Philosophy* (London: Routledge and Kegan Paul).

Polanyi, Michael (1962) 'The Republic of Science: Its Political and Economic Theory', *Minerva*, **1**, pp. 54–73.

Polanyi, Michael (1967) *The Tacit Dimension* (London: Routledge and Kegan Paul).

Polanyi, Michael (1997) *Society, Economics and Philosophy: Selected Papers* (New Brunswick, NJ: Transaction).

Pollak, Robert A. (2003) 'Gary Becker's Contributions to Family and Household Economics', *Review of Economics of the Household*, **1**(1–2), January, pp 111–41.

Popper, Karl R. (1976) *Unended Quest: An Intellectual Autobiography* (LaSalle, IL: Open Court).

Popper, Karl R. (1978) 'Natural Selection and the Emergence of Mind', *Dialectica*, **32**(3–4), pp. 339–55.

Porpora, Douglas V. (1989) 'Four Concepts of Social Structure', *Journal for the Theory of Social Behaviour*, **19**(2), pp. 195–211.

Porter, Michael E. (1980) *Competitive Strategy: Techniques for Analyzing Industries and Competitors* (New York: Free Press).

Porter, Michael E. (1985) *Competitive Advantage: Creating and Sustaining Superior Performance* (New York: Free Press).

Potts, Jason (2000) *The New Evolutionary Microeconomics: Complexity, Competence and Adaptive Behaviour* (Cheltenham, UK and Northampton, MA, USA: Edward Elgar Publishing).

Poynton, A.J. (2011) *The Man who was Never Shakespeare* (Tunbridge Wells: Parapress).

Pratten, Stephen (2007) 'Realism, Closed Systems and Abstraction', *Journal of Economic Methodology*, **14**(4), December, pp. 473–97.

Pullen, John M. (2010) *The Marginal Productivity Theory of Distribution: A Critical History* (London, UK and New York, NY, USA: Routledge).

Quine, Willard van Orman (1953) *From a Logical Point of View* (Cambridge, MA: Harvard University Press).

Rabin, Matthew (1998) 'Psychology and Economics', *Journal of Economic Literature*, **36**(1), March, pp. 11–46.

Ramos-Rodriguez, Antonio-Rafael and Ruiz-Navarro, José (2004) 'Changes in the Intellectual Structure of Strategic Management Research: A Bibliometric Study of the Strategic Management Journal, 1980–2000', *Strategic Management Journal*, **25**(10), October, pp. 981–1004.

Ratnatunga, Janek and Romano, Claudio (1997) 'A "citation classics" Analysis of Articles in Contemporary Small Enterprise Research', *Journal of Business Venturing*, **12**(3), pp. 197–212.

Repec (2018) 'Top 25% Economics Departments, as of December 2018', *Ideas*. Available at https://ideas.repec.org/top/top.econdept.html. (Retrieved 1 February 2019.)

Richiardi, Matteo and Leombruni, Roberto (2005) 'Why Are Economists Sceptical About Agent-Based Simulations?', *Physica A*, **355**(1), pp. 103–109.

Rizvi, S. Abu Turab (1994a) 'The Microfoundations Project in General Equilibrium Theory', *Cambridge Journal of Economics*, **18**(4), August, pp. 357–77.

Rizvi, S. Abu Turab (1994b) 'Game Theory to the Rescue?', *Contributions to Political Economy*, **13**, pp. 1–28.

Robbins, Lionel (1932) *An Essay on the Nature and Significance of Economic Science*, 1st edn (London: Macmillan).

Robinson, E. Austin G. (1978) 'Keynes and his Cambridge Colleagues', in Patinkin, Don and Leith, J. Clarke (eds) *Keynes, Cambridge and the General Theory* (Toronto: University of Toronto Press).

Robinson, Joan (1933a) 'Shakespeare and Mr Looney', *Cambridge Review*, **54**, 12 May, pp. 389–90.

Robinson, Joan (1933b) *The Economics of Imperfect Competition* (London: Macmillan).

Robinson, Joan (1937) 'The Economic System in a Socialist State', *Cambridge Review*, **58**, pp. 289–90.

Robinson, Joan (1942) *An Essay on Marxian Economics* (London: Macmillan).

Robinson, Joan (1943a) *Private Enterprise or Public Control* (London: Association for Education in Citizenship).

Robinson, Joan (1943b) 'Planning', *Fabian Quarterly*, **36**, January, pp. 4–8.

Robinson, Joan (1943c) 'Planning Full Employment I. The Need for a Constructive Approach', *The Times*, 22 January. Reprinted in Robinson (1951).

Robinson, Joan (1943d) 'Planning Full Employment II. Alternative Solutions to the Dilemma', *The Times*, 23 January. Reprinted in Robinson (1951).

Robinson, Joan (1943e) 'The World We Want', series of broadcasts by BBC, October–November, BBC Written Archives Centre, Reading.

Robinson, Joan (1949) 'The Theory of Planning; A Review of *Soviet Economic Development since 1917*, by Maurice Dobb', *Soviet Studies*, **1**, October, pp. 60–64. Reprinted in Robinson (1951).

Robinson, Joan (1951) *Collected Economic Papers – Volume One* (London: Basil Blackwell).

Robinson, Joan (1953) 'The Production Function and the Theory of Capital', *Review of Economic Studies*, **21**(1), pp. 81–106. Reprinted in Robinson (1960).

Robinson, Joan (1960) *Collected Economic Papers – Volume Two* (Oxford: Basil Blackwell).

Robinson, Joan (1964a) *Economic Philosophy* (Harmondsworth: Penguin).

Robinson, Joan (1964b) 'Solow on the Rate of Return', *Economic Journal*, **74**(2), June, pp. 410–17.

Robinson, Joan (1965) *Collected Economic Papers – Volume Three* (Oxford: Basil Blackwell).

Robinson, Joan (1969a) *The Accumulation of Capital*, 3rd edn (London: Macmillan).

Robinson, Joan (1969b) *The Cultural Revolution in China* (Harmondsworth: Penguin).

Robinson, Joan (1973) *Economic Management in China 1972* (London: Anglo-Chinese Educational Institute).

Robinson, Joan (1974) Personal communication with Geoffrey M. Hodgson, December.

Robinson, Joan (1977a) 'Morality and Economics'. Talk given at the University of Maine, USA, in May 1977. Available at http://economists view.typepad.com/economistsview/2007/07/morality-and-ec.html. (Retrieved 6 July 2018.)

Robinson, Joan (1977b) 'What Are the Questions?', *Journal of Economic Literature*, **15**(4), December, pp. 1318–39.

Robinson, Joan (1979) *Collected Economic Papers – Volume Five* (Oxford: Basil Blackwell).

Robinson, Joan and Eatwell, John (1973) *An Introduction to Modern Economics* (London: McGraw-Hill).

Roemer, John E. (1986a) *Value, Exploitation and Class* (New York: Harwood Academic Publishers).

Roemer, John E. (ed.) (1986b) *Analytical Marxism* (Cambridge: Cambridge University Press).

Roemer, John E. (1988) *Free to Lose: An Introduction to Marxist Economic Philosophy* (Cambridge, MA: Harvard University Press).

Rolin, Kristina (2008) 'Science as Collective Knowledge', *Cognitive Systems Research*, **9**(1–2), March, pp. 115–24.

Romer, Paul M. (1986) 'Increasing Returns and Long-Run Growth', *Journal of Political Economy*, **94**(5), October, pp. 1002–37.

Romer, Paul M. (1990) 'Endogenous Technological Change', *Journal of Political Economy*, **98**(5), pp. 71–102.

Roncaglia, Alessandro (2005) *The Wealth of Ideas: A History of Economic Thought* (Cambridge, UK and New York, NY, USA: Cambridge University Press).

Rowthorn, Robert E. (1975a) 'What Remains of Kaldor's Law?', *Economic Journal*, **85**(1), March, pp. 10–19.

Rowthorn, Robert E. (1975b) 'A Reply to Lord Kaldor's Comment', *Economic Journal*, **85**(4), December, pp. 897–901.

Rowthorn, Robert E. (1979) 'A Note on Verdoorn's Law', *Economic Journal*, **89**(1), March, pp. 131–3.

Rowthorn, Robert E. and Wells, John R. (1987) *De-Industrialization and Foreign Trade* (Cambridge: Cambridge University Press).

Rummel, Rudolph J. (1994) *Death by Government* (New Brunswick, NJ: Transaction).

Runciman, Walter Garry (1983) 'Capitalism without Classes: The Case of Classical Rome', *British Journal of Sociology*, **34**(2), pp. 157–81.

Rutherford, Malcolm H. (1998) 'Veblen's Evolutionary Programme: A Promise Unfulfilled', *Cambridge Journal of Economics*, **22**(4), July, pp. 463–77.

Rutherford, Malcolm H. (2001) 'Institutional Economics: Then and Now', *Journal of Economic Perspectives*, **15**(3), Summer, pp. 173–94.

Salam, Abdus (1990) *Unification of Fundamental Forces* (Cambridge, UK and New York, NY, USA: Cambridge University Press).

Salanti, Andrea and Screpanti, Ernesto (eds) (1997) *Pluralism in Economics: New Perspectives in History and Methodology* (Cheltenham, UK and Lyme, NH, USA: Edward Elgar Publishing).

Samuelson, Paul A. (1937) 'A Note on the Measurement of Utility', *Review of Economic Studies*, **4**(2), February, pp. 155–61.

Samuelson, Paul A. (1948) *Economics*, 1st edn (New York: McGraw-Hill).

Samuelson, Paul A. (1954) 'The Pure Theory of Public Expenditure', *Review of Economics and Statistics*, **36**(4), pp. 387–9.

Samuelson, Paul A. (1962) 'Parable and Realism in Capital Theory: The Surrogate Production Function', *Review of Economic Studies*, **39**, pp. 193–206.

Samuelson, Paul A. (1966) 'A Summing Up', *Quarterly Journal of Economics*, **80**(4), November, pp. 568–83.

Sandel, Michael (2012) *What Money Can't Buy: The Moral Limits of Markets* (London: Allen Lane).

Satz, Debra (2010) *Why Some Things Should not be for Sale: The Moral Limits of Markets* (Oxford, UK and New York, NY, USA: Oxford University Press).

Schefold, Bertram (1989) *Mr Sraffa on Joint Production and other Essays* (London: Unwin and Hyman).

Schildt, Henri A. (2002) *SITKIS: Software for Bibliometric Data Management and Analysis* (Espoo: Helsinki University of Technology).

Schildt, Henri A. (2004) *SITKIS: SITKIS 2.0: Software for Bibliometric Data Management and Analysis* (Espoo: Helsinki University of Technology).

Schildt, Henri A. and Mattsson, Juha T. (2006) 'A Dense Network Sub-Grouping Algorithm for Co-citation Analysis and its Implementation in the Software Tool Sitkis', *Scientometrics*, **67**(1), pp. 143–63.

Schildt, Henri A., Zahra, Shaker A. and Sillanpää, Antti (2006) 'Scholarly Communities in Entrepreneurship Research: A Co-citation Analysis', *Entrepreneurship Theory and Practice*, **30**(3), May, pp. 399–415.

Schultz, Walter J. (2001) *The Moral Conditions of Economic Efficiency* (Cambridge, UK and New York, NY, USA: Cambridge University Press).

Schumpeter, Joseph A. (1934) *The Theory of Economic Development: An Inquiry into Profits, Capital, Credit, Interest, and the Business Cycle*, trans. from the 2nd German edn of 1926 (Cambridge, MA: Harvard University Press).

Schumpeter, Joseph A. (1942) *Capitalism, Socialism and Democracy*, 1st edn (London: George Allen and Unwin).

Schumpeter, Joseph A. (1954) *History of Economic Analysis* (Oxford, UK and New York, NY, USA: Oxford University Press).

Sen, Amartya K. (1970) *Collective Choice and Social Welfare* (San Francisco, CA, USA: Holden Day and Edinburgh: Oliver and Boyd).

Sen, Amartya K. (1973) 'Behaviour and the Concept of Preference', *Economica*, **40**, pp. 241–59. Reprinted in Elster, Jon (ed.) (1986) *Rational Choice* (Oxford: Basil Blackwell).

Sen, Amartya K. (1977) 'Rational Fools: A Critique of the Behavioral Foundations of Economic Theory', *Philosophy and Public Affairs*, **6**(4), pp. 317–44.

Sen, Amartya K. (1979) 'Personal Utilities and Public Judgements: Or What's Wrong With Welfare Economics', *Economic Journal*, **89**(3), September, pp. 537–58.

Sen, Amartya K. (1981) *Poverty and Famines: An Essay on Entitlement and Deprivation* (Oxford: Clarendon Press).

Sen, Amartya K. (1985a) *Commodities and Capabilities* (Amsterdam: North-Holland).

Sen, Amartya K. (1985b) 'Goals, Commitment, and Identity', *Journal of Law and Economic Organization*, **1**(2), Fall, pp. 341–55.

Sen, Amartya K. (1987a) *On Ethics and Economics* (Oxford, UK and New York, NY, USA: Basil Blackwell).

Sen, Amartya K. (1987b) 'Rational Behaviour', in Eatwell, John, Milgate, Murray and Newman, Peter (eds) *The New Palgrave Dictionary of Economics*, vol. 4 (London: Macmillan), pp. 68–76.

Sen, Amartya K. (1999) 'Amartya Sen – Biographical', in Tore Frängsmyr (ed.) *Les Prix Nobel. The Nobel Prizes 1998* (Stockholm: Nobel Foundation).

Sen, Amartya K. (ed.) (2002) *Rationality and Freedom* (Cambridge, MA: Harvard University Press).

Sen, Amartya K. (2004) 'Social Identity', *Revue de Philosophie Economique*, **9**(1), pp. 2–26.

Sened, Itai (1997) *The Political Institution of Private Property* (Cambridge: Cambridge University Press).

Sent, Esther-Mirjam (2004) 'Behavioral Economics: How Psychology Made its (Limited) Way Back into Economics', *History of Political Economy*, **36**(4), pp. 735–60.

Shackle, George L.S. (1955) *Uncertainty in Economics* (London: Cambridge University Press).

Shackle, George L.S. (1967) *The Years of High Theory: Invention and Tradition in Economic Thought 1926–1939* (Cambridge: Cambridge University Press).

Shackle, George L.S. (1972) *Epistemics and Economics: A Critique of Economic Doctrines* (Cambridge: Cambridge University Press).

Shackle, George L.S. (1974) *Keynesian Kaleidics: The Evolution of a General Political Economy* (Edinburgh: Edinburgh University Press).

Shleifer, Andrei and Vishny, Robert W. (1994) 'The Politics of Market Socialism', *Journal of Economic Perspectives*, **8**(2), Spring, pp. 165–76.

Siakantaris, Nikos (2000) 'Experimental Economics Under the Microscope', *Cambridge Journal of Economics*, **24**(3), May, pp. 267–81.

Sillanpää, Antti (2006) 'Firm Strategies in the Competition for Dominance of Networked Business Systems', PhD dissertation (Espoo: Helsinki University of Technology).

Silva, Sandra Tavares and Teixeira, Aurora A.C. (2009) 'On the Divergence of Evolutionary Research Paths in the Past 50 years: A Comprehensive Bibliometric Account', *Journal of Evolutionary Economics*, **19**(5), October, pp. 605–42.

Simon, Herbert A. (1947) *Administrative Behavior: A Study of Decision-Making Processes in Administrative Organization* (New York: Free Press).

Simon, Herbert A. (1955) 'A Behavioral Model of Rational Choice', *Quarterly Journal of Economics*, **69**(1), February, pp. 99–118.

Simon, Herbert A. (1956) 'Rational Choice and the Structure of the Environment', *Psychological Review*, **63**, pp. 129–38.

216   *Is there a future for heterodox economics?*

Simon, Herbert A. (1957) *Models of Man: Social and Rational: Mathematical Essays on Rational Human Behavior in a Social Setting* (New York: Wiley).

Simon, Herbert A. (1959) 'Theories of Decision-Making in Economic and Behavioral Sciences', *American Economic Review*, **49**(2), June, pp. 253–83.

Simon, Herbert A. (1969) *The Sciences of the Artificial* (Cambridge, MA: MIT Press).

Simon, Herbert A. (1979) 'Rational Decision Making in Business Organizations', *American Economic Review*, **69**(4), September, pp. 493–513.

Simpson, Renate (1983) *How the PhD came to Britain: A Century of Struggle for Postgraduate Education* (Guildford: Society for Research into Higher Education).

Simpson, Renate (2009) *The Development of the PhD Degree in Britain, 1917–1959 and Since: An Evolutionary and Statistical History in Higher Education* (New York: Edward Mellon).

Singh, Ajit (1975) 'Take-Overs, "Natural Selection" and the Theory of the Firm', *Economic Journal*, **85**(3), September, pp. 497–515.

Sinha, Ajit (2016) *A Revolution in Economic Theory: The Economics of Piero Sraffa* (London, UK and New York, NY, USA: Palgrave Macmillan).

Small, Henry G. (1973) 'Co-citation in the Scientific Literature: A New Measure of the Relationship between Publications', *Journal of the American Society for Information Science*, **24**(4), pp. 265–9.

Small, Henry G. (2004) 'On the Shoulders of Robert Merton: Towards a Normative Theory of Citation', *Scientometrics*, **60**(1), pp. 71–9.

Small, Henry G. and Greenlee, E. (1980) 'Citation Context Analysis of a Co-citation Cluster: Recombinant-DNA', *Scientometrics*, **2**(4), pp. 277–301.

Smart, J.J.C. and Williams, Bernard (1973) *Utilitarianism: For and Against* (Cambridge: Cambridge University Press).

Smith, Adam (1759) *The Theory of Moral Sentiments; or, An Essay Towards an Analysis of the Principles by which Men Naturally Judge Concerning the Conduct and Character, First of their Neighbours, and Afterwards of Themselves* (London: Millar and Edinburgh: Kincaid and Bell).

Smith, Vernon L. (1982) 'Microeconomic Systems as an Experimental Science', *American Economic Review*, **72**(5), December, pp. 923–55.

Smith, Vernon L. (1992) *Papers in Experimental Economics* (Cambridge: Cambridge University Press).

Smith, Vernon L. (2013) 'Adam Smith: From Propriety and Sentiments to Property and Wealth', *Forum for Social Economics*, **42**(4), pp. 283–97.

Smith, Vernon L. and Wilson, Bart J. (2019) *Humanomics: Moral Sentiments and the Wealth of Nations for the Twenty-First Century* (Cambridge, UK and New York, NY, USA: Cambridge University Press).

Sober, Elliott and Wilson, David Sloan (1998) *Unto Others: The Evolution and Psychology of Unselfish Behavior* (Cambridge, MA: Harvard University Press).

Sobrero, Maurizio and Schrader, Stephan (1998) 'Structuring Inter-Firm Relationships: A Meta-Analytic Approach', *Organization Studies*, **19**(4), pp. 585–615.

Sokal, Alan and Jean Bricmont (1998) *Fashionable Nonsense: Post-modern Intellectuals' Abuse of Science* (New York: Picador).

Spash, Clive L. (2009) 'The New Environmental Pragmatists, Pluralism and Sustainability', *Environmental Values*, **18**(3), pp. 253–6.

Spash, Clive L. (2012) 'New Foundations for Ecological Economics', *Ecological Economics*, **77**(1), pp. 36–47.

Spash, Clive L. and Ryan, Anthony (2012) 'Economic Schools of Thought on the Environment: Investigating Unity and Division', *Cambridge Journal of Economics*, **36**, pp. 1091–121.

Sraffa, Piero (1926) 'The Laws of Returns under Competitive Conditions', *Economic Journal*, **36**(4), December, pp. 535–50.

Sraffa, Piero (1960) *Production of Commodities by Means of Commodities: Prelude to a Critique of Economic Theory* (Cambridge: Cambridge University Press).

Starkey, Ken and Madan, Paula (2001) 'Bridging the Relevance Gap: Aligning Stakeholders in the Future of Management Research', *British Journal of Management*, **12** (Supplement S1), December, pp. S3–S26.

Steedman, Ian (1977) *Marx after Sraffa* (London: NLB).

Steedman, Ian (1980) 'Economic Theory and Intrinsically Non-Autonomous Preferences and Beliefs', *Quaderni Fondazione Feltrinelli*, no. 7/8, pp. 57–73. Reprinted in Steedman, Ian (1989) *From Exploitation to Altruism* (Cambridge: Polity Press).

Steele, David Ramsay (1992) *From Marx to Mises: Post-Capitalist Society and the Challenge of Economic Calculation* (La Salle, IL: Open Court).

Steele, Katie (2014) 'Choice Models', in Cartwright, Nancy and Montuschi, Eleonora (eds), *Philosophy of Social Science: A New Introduction*, ch. 10 (Oxford, UK and New York, NY, USA: Oxford University Press).

Steiger, Otto (ed.) (2008) *Property Economics: Property Rights, Creditor's Money and the Foundations of the Economy* (Marburg: Metropolis).

Stigler, George J. (1967) 'Imperfections in the Capital Market', *Journal of Political Economy*, **75**(3), June, pp. 287–92.

Stiglitz, Joseph E. (2010) *Freefall: America, Free Markets, and the Sinking of the World Economy* (New York, NY, USA and London, UK: Norton).

Stiglitz, Joseph E. (2012) *The Price of Inequality: How Today's Divided Society Endangers Our Future* (New York, NY, USA and London, UK: Norton).

Stoelhorst, J.W. (2008) 'The Explanatory Logic and Ontological Commitments of Generalized Darwinism', *Journal of Economic Methodology*, **15**(4), December, pp. 343–63.

Stoelhorst, J.W. (2014) 'The Future of Evolutionary Economics is in a Vision from the Past: A Comment on the Essays on Evolutionary Economics by Sidney Winter and Ulrich Witt', *Journal of Institutional Economics*, **10**(4), December, pp. 665–82.

Sugden, Robert (1991) 'Rational Choice: A Survey of Contributions from Economics and Philosophy', *Economic Journal*, **101**(4), July, pp. 751–85.

Sugden, Robert (2000) 'Credible Worlds: The Status of Theoretical Models in Economics', *Journal of Economic Methodology*, **7**(1), March, pp. 1–31.

Tahir, Pervez, Harcourt, Geoffrey C. and Kerr, Prue (2002) 'On Joan Robinson on China', in Kerr, Prue (ed.) with the collaboration of Geoffrey C. Harcourt, *Critical Assessments of Leading Economists*, vol. 5 (London, UK and New York, NY, USA: Routledge), pp. 267–80.

Tancredi, Laurence (2005) *Hardwired Behavior: What Neuroscience Reveals about Morality* (Cambridge, UK and New York, NY, USA: Cambridge University Press).

Targetti, Ferdinando (1992) *Nicholas Kaldor: The Economics and Politics of Capitalism as a Dynamic System* (Oxford: Clarendon Press).

Thaler, Richard H. and Sunstein, Cass R. (2008) *Nudge: Improving Decisions About Health, Wealth, and Happiness* (New Haven, CT: Yale University Press).

The Economist (1996) 'Dons and Dollars', *The Economist*, 20 July, pp. 53–4.

Thirlwall, Anthony P. (1987) *Nicholas Kaldor* (Brighton, UK: Harvester and New York, NY, USA: New York University Press).

Thirlwall, Anthony P. (2015) *Essays on Keynesian and Kaldorian Economics* (London: Macmillan).

Tielman, Joris, de Muijnck, Sam, Kavelaars, Maarten and Ostermeijer, Francis (2018) *Thinking like an Economist? A Quantitative Analysis of the Economics Bachelor Curricula in the Netherlands* (Rethinking Economics NL).

Tijssen, Robert J.W. and Van Raan, Anthony F.J. (1994) 'Mapping Changes in Science and Technology: Bibliometric Co-occurrence Analysis of the R&D Literature', *Evaluation Review*, **18**(1), pp. 98–115.

Toulmin, Stephen E. (1972) *Human Understanding: The Collective Use and Evolution of Concepts* (Princeton, NJ: Princeton University Press).

Tribe, Keith (2000) 'The Cambridge Economics Tripos 1903–55 and the Training of Economists', *Manchester School*, **68**(2), March, pp. 222–48.

Tullock, Gordon (1994) *The Economics of Non-Human Societies* (Tuscon, AZ: Pallas Press).

Tyler, Tom R. (1990) *Why People Obey the Law* (New Haven, CT: Yale University Press).

Usdiken, B. and Pasadeos, Y. (1995) 'Organizational Analysis in North-America and Europe: A Comparison of Co-citation Networks', *Organization Studies*, **16**(3), pp. 503–26.

Valdés, Juan Gabriel (1995) *Pinochet's Economists: The Chicago School in Chile* (Cambridge, UK and New York, NY, USA: Cambridge University Press).

Van Raan, Anthony F.J. (2000) 'The Interdisciplinary Nature of Science: Theoretical Framework and Bibliometric-Empirical Approach', in Weingart, Peter and Stehr, Nico (eds) *Practising Interdisciplinarity* (Toronto: University of Toronto Press), pp. 66–77.

Vaughn, Karen I. (1980) 'Economic Calculation Under Socialism: The Austrian Contribution', *Economic Inquiry*, **18**, pp. 535–54.

Veblen, Thorstein B. (1898a) 'Why is Economics Not an Evolutionary Science?', *Quarterly Journal of Economics*, **12**(3), July, pp. 373–97. Reprinted in Veblen (1919) and Camic and Hodgson (2011, pp. 143–57).

Veblen, Thorstein B. (1898b) 'The Instinct of Workmanship and the Irksomeness of Labor', *American Journal of Sociology*, **4**(2), September, pp. 187–201. Reprinted in Camic and Hodgson (2011, pp. 158–68).

Veblen, Thorstein B. (1899) *The Theory of the Leisure Class: An Economic Study in the Evolution of Institutions* (New York: Macmillan).

Veblen, Thorstein B. (1900) 'The Preconceptions of Economic Science: III', *Quarterly Journal of Economics*, **14**(2), February, pp. 240–69. Reprinted in Veblen (1919) and Camic and Hodgson (2011).

Veblen, Thorstein B. (1906) 'The Socialist Economics of Karl Marx and his Followers I: The Theories of Karl Marx', *Quarterly Journal of Economics*, **20**(3), August, pp. 578–95. Reprinted in Veblen (1919) and Camic and Hodgson (2011).

Veblen, Thorstein B. (1908) 'Professor Clark's Economics', *Quarterly Journal of Economics*, **22**(2), February, pp. 147–95. Reprinted in Veblen (1919) and Camic and Hodgson (2011).

Veblen, Thorstein B. (1909) 'The Limitations of Marginal Utility', *Journal of Political Economy*, **17**(9), November, pp. 620–36. Reprinted in Veblen (1919) and Camic and Hodgson (2011).

Veblen, Thorstein B. (1914) *The Instinct of Workmanship, and the State of the Industrial Arts* (New York: Macmillan).

Veblen, Thorstein B. (1919) *The Place of Science in Modern Civilisation and Other Essays* (New York: Huebsch).

Venugopal, Rajesh (2015) 'Neoliberalism as a Concept', *Economy and Society*, **44**(2), pp. 165–87.

Vercoe, Moanna and Zak, Paul J. (2010) 'Inductive Modeling using Causal Studies in Neuroeconomics: Brains on Drugs', *Journal of Economic Methodology*, **17**(2), June, pp. 133–46.

Verspagen, Bart and Werker, Claudia (2003) 'The Invisible College of the Economics of Innovation and Technological Change', *Estudios de Economía Aplicada*, **21**(3), pp. 393–419.

Vromen, Jack J. (2008) 'Neuroeconomics as a Natural Extension of Bioeconomics: The Shifting Scope of Standard Economic Theory', *Journal of Bioeconomics*, **9**(2), pp. 145–67.

Vromen, Jack J. (2010) 'On the Surprising Finding that Expected Utility is Literally Computed in the Brain', *Journal of Economic Methodology*, **17**(1), March, pp. 17–36.

Walras, Léon (1874) *Éléments d'Économie Politique Pure, ou Théorie de la Richesse Sociale* (Lausanne: Rouge).

Waring, Marilyn (1988) *If Women Counted: A New Feminist Economics* (New York: Harper and Row).

Weber, Max (1949) *Max Weber on the Methodology of the Social Sciences* (Glencoe, IL: Free Press).

Weber, Max (1968) *Economy and Society: An Outline of Interpretative Sociology*, 2 vols, trans. from the German edn of 1921–22 (Berkeley, CA: University of California Press).

Weingart, Peter and Stehr, Nico (eds) (2000) *Practising Interdisciplinarity* (Toronto: University of Toronto Press).

Weintraub, E. Roy (2002) *How Economics Became a Mathematical Science* (Durham, NC: Duke University Press).

Weisberg, Michael and Muldoon, Ryan (2009) 'Epistemic Landscapes and the Division of Cognitive Labor', *Philosophy of Science*, **76**(2), April, pp. 225–52.

Wenger, Etienne (1998) *Communities of Practice: Learning, Memory and Identity* (Cambridge: Cambridge University Press).

Whitley, Richard (1986) 'The Structure and Context of Economics as a Scientific Field', *Research in the History of Economic Thought and Methodology*, **4**, pp. 179–209.

Whitley, Richard (2000) *The Intellectual and Social Organization of the Sciences*, 2nd edn (Oxford, UK and New York, NY, USA: Oxford University Press).

Williamson, Oliver E. (1975) *Markets and Hierarchies: Analysis and Anti-Trust Implications: A Study in the Economics of Internal Organization* (New York: Free Press).

Williamson, Oliver E. (1985) *The Economic Institutions of Capitalism: Firms, Markets, Relational Contracting* (London, UK and New York, NY, USA: Free Press and Macmillan).

Wilson, Bart J. (2010) 'Social Preferences aren't Preferences', *Journal of Economic Behavior and Organization*, **73**(1), pp. 77–82.

Wilson, Matthew C. (2005) 'Institutionalism, Critical Realism and the Critique of Mainstream Economics', *Journal of Institutional Economics*, **1**(2), December, pp. 217–31.

Winch, Donald (1969) *Economics and Policy: A Historical Study* (London: Hodder and Stoughton).

Winter, Sidney G., Jr (1964) 'Economic "Natural Selection" and the Theory of the Firm', *Yale Economic Essays*, **4**(1), pp. 225–72.

Winter, Sidney G., Jr (2017) 'Pursuing the Evolutionary Agenda in Economics and Management Research', *Cambridge Journal of Economics*, **41**(3), May, pp. 721–47.

Witt, Ulrich (ed.) (1992) *Explaining Process and Change: Approaches to Evolutionary Economics* (Ann Arbor, MI: University of Michigan Press).

Witt, Ulrich (2003) *The Evolving Economy: Essays on the Evolutionary Approach to Economics* (Cheltenham, UK and Northampton, MA, USA: Edward Elgar Publishing).

Witt, Ulrich (2008) 'What is Specific about Evolutionary Economics?', *Journal of Evolutionary Economics*, **18**, pp. 547–75.

Woolley, Frances R. (1993) 'The Feminist Challenge to Neoclassical Economics', *Cambridge Journal of Economics*, **17**(4), December, pp. 485–500.

Wray, L. Randall (1998) *Understanding Modern Money: The Key to Full Employment and Price Stability* (Cheltenham, UK and Lyme, NH, USA: Edward Elgar Publishing).

Wray, L. Randall (2012) *Modern Money Theory: A Primer on Macroeconomics for Sovereign Monetary Systems* (London, UK and New York, NY, USA: Palgrave Macmillan).

Wray, L. Randall (2016) *Why Minsky Matters: An Introduction to the Work of the Maverick Economist* (Princeton, NJ, USA and Oxford, UK: Princeton University Press).

Wright, Erik Olin (1994) *Interrogating Inequality: Essays on Class Analysis, Socialism and Marxism* (London: Verso).

Young, H. Peyton (1998) *Individual Strategy and Social Structure: An Evolutionary Theory* (Princeton, NJ: Princeton University Press).

Yurko, Allana (2018) *Employers' Report* (Rethinking Economics). Available at http://www.rethinkeconomics.org/wp-content/uploads/2016/09/RE_Research_Report_2018_PROOF.pdf. (Retrieved 15 August 2018.)

Zak, Paul J. (2004) 'Neuroeconomics', *Philosophical Transactions of the Royal Society of London*, **B**, **359**, pp. 1737–48.

Zak, Paul J. (2011a) 'The Physiology of Moral Sentiments', *Journal of Economic Behavior and Organization*, **77**(1), pp. 53–65.

Zak, Paul J. (2011b) 'Moral Markets', *Journal of Economic Behavior and Organization*, **77**(2), pp. 212–33.

Index

abstraction or isolation, 66
Acemoglu, Daron, 172
Ackerman, Robert, 91
Adaman, Fikret, vii
agent-based models, 82, 93, 100
Aglietta, Michel, 16, 60
Aistleitner, Matthias, 144
Akerlof, George A., 84, 101
Albert, Michael, vii
Alchian, Armen A., 117–118
Aldrich, Howard E., 109, 121, 125, 128
Ali, Tanweer, viii
Allen, Peter M., 142
Allen, R.T., 9, 81
altruism, 79, 84, 102
American Economic Association, 37, 43, 50
American Economic Review, 94, 105
American Sociological Association, 165
anthropology, 121, 128, 174
Aoki, Masahiko, 172
appreciative theory, 120
Arestis, Philip, viii, 59
Arndt, H.W., 159
Arrow, Kenneth J., 14, 25–7, 39, 48, 52–5, 63, 85, 159
Arthmar, Rogério, 65
Arthur, W. Brian, 111
Aspromourgos, Tony, 85
Association for Evolutionary Economics, 43, 59
Association for Heterodox Economics, 49, 50
Association for Social Economics, 44, 165
Atkinson, Anthony B., 168
austerity, 1, 51–3, 155–6

Australia, 50, 77, 157
Austrian school economics, 7–9, 11, 26, 35–9, 50, 52, 57–61, 72, 136, 160, 166
Axelrod, Robert M., 118, 121, 128
Ayres, Clarence E., 28

Backhouse, Roger E., 2, 17, 19, 69, 84, 159, 172
Bannister, Robert C., 109
Baumgartner, Hans, 112, 143
Becker, Gary S., 79, 84, 86, 91, 93, 173
behavioural economics, 12, 28, 30, 48, 59–60, 73, 78, 84, 87–9, 92, 96–102, 106–7, 116–18, 142–3, 147–9, 160, 162
  new, 12, 87–9, 97, 102
behavioural finance, 88, 142–3
behavioural theory of the firm, 89
Bentham, Jeremy, 78, 81, 100, 168
Berg, Nathan, 88
Berger, Sebastian, viii, 32
Bertalanffy, Ludwig, 57
Besley, Timothy, 1
Bhaskar, Roy, 58, 64, 71–2, 111
Bhupatiraju, Samyukta, 114
bibliometrics, ix, 13, 94, 112–6, 122, 124, 129, 144
biology, 63, 69, 80, 97, 128, 130, 174
Bladel, John P., 136
Blau, Peter J., 139
Blaug, Mark, 24–6, 31, 34, 38–9, 68, 84, 91, 143, 145, 148
Blinov, Evgeny, 5
Bliss, Christopher, 42, 50–51
Boas, Taylor C., 160
Boehm, Christopher, 104, 128, 170
Boettke, Peter J., 37, 166